Phantoms
of a
Blood-Stained
Period

Yours truly
A. S. Bierce

Phantoms
of a
Blood-Stained
Period

THE COMPLETE CIVIL WAR

WRITINGS OF

Ambrose
Bierce

EDITED BY RUSSELL DUNCAN &

DAVID J. KLOOSTER

UNIVERSITY OF MASSACHUSETTS PRESS

AMHERST & BOSTON

Copyright © 2002 by
University of Massachusetts Press
All rights reserved
Printed in the United States of America
LC 2001005764
ISBN 1-55849-327-1 (library cloth); 328-x (paper)
Designed by Richard Hendel
Set in New Baskerville and Didot types by
Keystone Typesetting, Inc.
Printed and bound by
The Maple-Vail Book Manufacturing Group

Library of Congress Cataloging-in-Publication Data
Bierce, Ambrose, 1842–1914?
Phantoms of a blood-stained period : the complete Civil War
writings of Ambrose Bierce / edited by Russell Duncan
and David J. Klooster
   p. cm.
Includes bibliographical references.
ISBN 1-55849-327-1 (alk. paper) —
ISBN 1-55849-328-x (pbk. : alk. paper)
1. United States — History — Civil War, 1861–1865 —
Fiction. 2. United States — History — Civil War, 1861–
1865 — Personal narratives. 3. United States —
History — Civil War, 1861–1865 — Maps. 4. Authors,
American — 19th century — Correspondence. 5. Bierce,
Ambrose, 1842–1914? — Correspondence. I. Duncan,
Russell. II. Klooster, David J. III. Title.
PS1097 .A6 2002
813'.4 — dc21   2001005764

British Library Cataloguing in Publication
data are available.

For Bonnie, Nathaniel, Maria, Benjamin, Eva, Gabriel, & Anna

Contents

Note: Titles not indented are those of full-length works of fiction and nonfiction from *The Collected Works of Ambrose Bierce*. Indented titles are of excerpted works from various sources, with titles supplied by the editors, or of poems.

Acknowledgments

The editors would like to thank all the scholars who have done much to give Ambrose Bierce his due. Particularly for the current volume, we point to the work of Roy Morris Jr., S. T. Joshi, David E. Schultz, and Michael Schaefer, for their insights into the life and writings of Bierce.

In many ways, Alice Fahs provided the impetus for this project at the 1996 Organization of American Historians meeting in Chicago with her paper, "Veterans and the Published Memory of War: Regimental Histories in the Postwar Literary Marketplace." In his comments on that paper, Duncan invoked Bierce's views and, in the audience, editor Paul Wright got interested in Bierce. Wright, of the University of Massachusetts Press, asked the editors to submit a prospectus. He has remained the book's warmest critic throughout the process. Even as we thank Paul, we feel the need to invoke a Biercean definition from *The Devil's Dictionary*:

> EDITOR, *n.* A person who combines the judicial functions of
> Minos, Rhadamanthus and Æacus, but is placable with an
> obolus; a severely virtuous censor. . . . Master of mysteries and
> lord of law, high-pinnacled upon the throne of thought, his face
> suffused with the dim splendors of the Transfiguration, his legs
> intertwisted and his tongue a-cheek, the editor spills his will
> along the paper and cuts it off in lengths to suit.

Many thanks to Harvey Green and Susan Williams for their detailed suggestions concerning the invention of history as boosterism during Gilded Age America and for the comments on Duncan's paper on Bierce at the 1999 Nordic Association for American Studies conference in Turku, Finland. Colleagues in the Hope College Department of English provided useful feedback to Klooster's work on "Chickamauga" and its related articles. William S. McFeely and Michael Schaefer read the manuscript, offering excellent observations to improve the work.

For a travel grant to allow us to meet and work together we thank

Nick R. Baumgartner, Dean of the College of Arts and Sciences at John Carroll University. We are particularly grateful for the generous financial support of this volume provided by Hope College and Provost Jacob Nyenhuis.

The professional staffs of various libraries and archives contributed significantly to this work. Chuck Zarobila of Grasselli Library at John Carroll University photographed the Bierce maps that appear in this volume. The University of Copenhagen provided one of the twenty-five original copies of the "Author's Edition" of *The Collected Works of Ambrose Bierce* (1909–11) — signed by Bierce and in perfect condition — from which we selected the stories, essays, and articles. Hope College librarian Mark Christel provided timely assistance. The staff of the Elkhart County Historical Museum, especially Director Tina Mellott, were gracious in granting permission to reproduce the portrait of Bierce in his Civil War uniform. We thank the Huntington Library, Art Collections, and Botanical Gardens of San Marino, California, and SuperStock for permission to reproduce the John H. E. Parrington portrait of Bierce. Bierce, who built his newspaper career in part by criticizing Henry Huntington mercilessly for amassing his fortune at public expense, might appreciate the irony that the Huntington Collection now owns Bierce's own portrait. Finally, we thank the photoduplication services of the Library of Congress for providing the photograph used on the cover of this volume.

The staff of the University of Massachusetts Press smoothed the process of publication. Special thanks to them for their expertise and for their patience in working with co-authors separated by an ocean.

And finally, thanks to our families, who have remained courageous as we marched along with Bierce and the phantoms of his horrific memories. We have dedicated the book to our children, and we thank our partners, Clara Juncker and Patricia Bloem, for their support, encouragement, and love.

R. D.
D. J. K.

A Note on Sources

The Collected Works of Ambrose Bierce (12 vols., 1909–11) represents Bierce's final intentions for his works, and therefore is the primary source for this collection. Whenever a work appears in the *Collected Works*, we have used it as the text of choice.

For Bierce's writings not included in the *Collected Works*, we have used various sources. S. T. Joshi and David E. Schultz have done scholars a great service in their collection *Ambrose Bierce, Sole Survivor: Bits of Autobiography* (Knoxville: University of Tennessee Press, 1998), which gathers a large portion of Bierce's journalism and organizes it logically. Bertha Pope's *The Letters of Ambrose Bierce* (San Francisco: Book Club of California, 1922) remains the only significant collection of a portion of Bierce's letters.

The two battlefield maps drawn by Ambrose Bierce that we include were published in William B. Hazen's *A Narrative of Military Service* (Boston: Ticknor and Company, 1885).

Other sources are as noted.

Each selection of Bierce's writing is accompanied by the date of initial publication and the source from which we have drawn the text. Pieces not included in the *Collected Works* also carry a footnote to indicate the complete bibliographical data for the source.

Source Abbreviations

ABPO
> Letter of Ambrose Bierce, collected in Bertha Pope, ed. *The Letters of Ambrose Bierce*. San Francisco: Book Club of California, 1922.

BOATNER
> Mark M. Boatner III, ed. *The Civil War Dictionary*. New York: Vintage Books, 1987.

BOWMAN

John S. Bowman, ed. *The Civil War Almanac.* New York: World Almanac Publications, 1983.

CONFED

Richard N. Current, ed. *Encyclopedia of the Confederacy,* 4 vols. New York: Simon & Schuster, 1993.

CWAB

Ambrose Bierce. *The Collected Works of Ambrose Bierce,* 12 vols. New York: Neale Publishing Company, 1909–11.

DICT

Ernest Jerome Hopkins, ed. *The Enlarged Devil's Dictionary by Ambrose Bierce.* Garden City, N.Y.: Doubleday, 1967.

FAUST

Patricia L. Faust, ed. *Historical Times Illustrated Encyclopedia of the Civil War.* New York: Harper Collins, 1991.

HAZEN

William B. Hazen. *A Narrative of Military Service.* Boston: Ticknor and Company, 1885.

LONG

E. B. Long, ed. *The Civil War Day by Day: An Almanac, 1861–1865.* New York: Da Capo Press, 1971.

LOVEMAN

Samuel Loveman, ed. *Twenty-one Letters of Ambrose Bierce.* Cleveland: George Kirk, 1922.

MORRIS

Roy Morris Jr., *Ambrose Bierce: Alone in Bad Company.* New York: Crown Publishers, 1995.

SIFAKIS

Stewart Sifakis, ed. *Who Was Who in the Civil War.* New York: Facts on File, 1988.

SOLE

S. T. Joshi and David E. Schultz, eds. *Ambrose Bierce, A Sole Survivor: Bits of Autobiography.* Knoxville: University of Tennessee Press, 1998.

Phantoms
of a
Blood-Stained
Period

The Bierce Theater in the Civil War.

Ambrose Bierce on History, Memory, and Literature:
"A Sole Survivor"

Among the arts and sciences, the art of Sole Surviving is one of the most interesting, as (to the artist) it is by far the most important. It is not altogether an art, perhaps, for success in it is largely due to accident. One may study how solely to survive, yet, having an imperfect natural aptitude, may fail of proficiency and be early cut off. To the contrary, one little skilled in its methods, and not even well grounded in its fundamental principles, may, by taking the trouble to have been born with a suitable constitution, attain a considerable eminence in the art. Without undue modesty, I think I may fairly claim some distinction in it myself, although I have not regularly acquired it as one acquires knowledge and skill in writing, painting and playing the flute. O yes, I am a notable Sole Survivor, and some of my work in that way attracts great attention, mostly my own.

You would naturally expect, then, to find in me one who has experienced all manner of disaster at sea and several kinds of calamity incident to a life on dry land. It would seem a just inference from my Sole Survivorship that I am familiar with railroad wrecks, inundations (though these are hardly dry-land phenomena), pestilences, carthquakes, conflagrations, and other forms of what the reporters delight to call "a holocaust." This is not entirely true; I have never been shipwrecked, never assisted as "unfortunate sufferer" at a fire or railway collision, and know of the ravages of epidemics only by hearsay. The most destructive *temblor* of which I have had a personal experience decreased the population of San Francisco by fewer, probably, than ten thousand persons, of whom not more than a dozen were killed; the others moved out of town. It is true that I once followed the perilous trade of solider, but my eminence in Sole Surviving is of a later growth and not specially the product of the sword.

Opening the portfolio of memory, I draw out picture after picture —

"figure-pieces" — groups of forms and faces whereof mine only now remains, somewhat the worse for wear.

Here are three young men lolling at ease on a grassy bank. One, a handsome, dark-eyed chap, with a forehead like that of a Grecian god, raises his body on his elbow, looks straight away to the horizon, where some black trees hold captive certain vestiges of sunset as if they had torn away the plumage of a flight of flamingoes, and says: "Fellows, I mean to be rich. I shall see every country worth seeing. I shall taste every pleasure worth having. When old, I shall become a hermit."

Said another slender youth, fair-haired: "I shall become President and execute a *coup d'etat* making myself an absolute monarch. I shall issue a decree requiring all hermits to be put to death."

The third said nothing. Was he restrained by some prescient sense of the perishable nature of the material upon which he was expected to inscribe the record of his hopes? However it may have been, he flicked his shoe with a hazel switch and kept his own counsel. For twenty years he has been the Sole Survivor of the group.

The scene changes. Six men are on horseback on a hill — a general and his staff.[1] Below, in the gray fog of a winter morning, an army, which has left its intrenchments, is moving upon those of an enemy — creeping silently into position. In an hour the whole wide valley for miles to the left and right will be all aroar with musketry stricken to seeming silence now and again by thunder claps of big guns. In the meantime the risen sun has burned a way through the fog, splendoring a part of the beleaugered city.

"Look at that, General," says an aide; "it looks like an enchantment."

"Go and enchant Colonel Post,"[2] said the general, without taking his field-glass from his eyes, "and tell him to pitch in as soon as he hears Smith's guns."

All laughed. But to-day I laugh alone. I am the Sole Survivor.

It would be easy to fill many pages with instances of Sole Survival, from my own experience. I could mention extinct groups composed

1. Bierce served as the topographical engineer on the staff of General William B. Hazen, 1863–65.

2. Perhaps Colonel Sidney Post, who later replaced Hazen as commander of Bierce's brigade. MORRIS, 91. For similar scenes involving Post and Smith, see pages 264–65 and 279 herein.

wholly (myself excepted) of the opposing sex, all of whom, with the same exception, have long ceased their opposition, their warfare accomplished, their pretty noses blue and chill under the daisies. They were good girls, too, mostly, Heaven rest them! There were Maud and Lizzie and Nanette (ah, Nanette, indeed; she is the deadest of the whole bright band) and Emeline and — but really this is not discreet; one should not survive and tell.

The flame of a camp-fire stands up tall and straight toward the black sky. We feed it constantly with sage brush. A circling wall of darkness closes us in; but turn your back to the fire and walk a little away and you shall see the serrated summit-line of snow-capped mountains, ghastly cold in the moonlight. They are in all directions; everywhere they efface the great gold stars near the horizon, leaving the little green ones of the midheaven trembling viciously, as bleak as steel. At irregular intervals we hear the distant howling of a wolf — now on this side and again on that. We check our talk to listen; we cast quick glances toward our weapons, our saddles, our picketed horses: the wolves may be of the variety known as Sioux, and there are but four of us.

"What would you do, Jim," said Hazen[3], "if we were surrounded by Indians?"

Jim Beckwourth[4] was our guide — a lifelong frontiersman, an old man "beated and chopped with tanned antiquity." He had at one time been a chief of the Crows.

"I'd spit on that fire," said Jim Beckwourth.

The old man has gone, I hope, where there is no fire to be quenched. And Hazen, and the chap with whom I shared my blanket that winter night on the plains — both gone. One might suppose that I would feel something of the natural exultation of a Sole Survivor; but as Byron found that

> our thoughts take wildest flight
> Even at the moment when they should array
> Themselves in pensive order,

3. After the Civil War, Bierce accompanied Hazen and others on a U.S. Army expedition to forts in the western United States, 1866–67.

4. Jim Beckwourth, a former slave, became an adopted Crow chief and served as a guide to Hazen's expedition. MORRIS, 104. Bierce wrote about Beckwourth several times in the British journal *Fun*. SOLE, 337, n.1.

so I find that they sometimes array themselves in pensive order, even at the moment when they ought to be most hilarious.

Of reminiscences there is no end. I have a vast store of them laid up, wherewith to wile away the tedious years of my anecdotage — whenever it shall please Heaven to make me old. . . . .

Introduction
Fighting and Writing the Civil War

Men? There were men enough; all dead apparently, except one... — a
Federal sergeant, variously hurt, who had been a fine giant in his time. He
lay face upward, taking in his breath in convulsive, rattling snorts, and
blowing it out in sputters of froth which crawled creamily down his cheeks,
piling itself alongside his neck and ears. A bullet had clipped a groove in his
skull, above the temple; from this the brain protruded in bosses, dropping off
in flakes and strings. I had not previously known one could get on, even in this
unsatisfactory condition, with so little brain. One of my men whom I knew for
a womanish fellow, asked if he should put his bayonet through him. Inexpres-
sibly shocked by the cold-blooded proposal, I told him I thought not; it was
unusual, and too many were looking.
—from "What I Saw of Shiloh"

CYNIC, *n. A blackguard whose faulty vision sees things as they are, not as*
they ought to be. Hence the custom among the Scythians of plucking out a
cynic's eyes to improve his vision.
—from The Devil's Dictionary

Ambrose Gwinnett Bierce knew more than a few things about soldiering; but when he wrote about the war he knew so well, he was too explicit, too ironic, too truthful, and — some might say — too porno-graphic to be popular among his contemporaries. He wrote during a time of intense national smugness, an era Mark Twain dubbed the "Gilded Age." Gilded, not golden, because the unprecedented ex-pansion of the national wealth glossed over serious internal problems. Railroad, banking, and industrial power brokers such as John D. Rocke-feller, John Pierpont Morgan, and Jay Gould moved virtually un-checked by government regulation even while they were heavily subsidized with government lands and contracts. In one of his many satiric verses, Bierce offered a new "Rational Anthem" for this country:

My country, 'tis of thee,
Sweet land of felony,
    Of thee I sing —

    . . .

I love thy thieving bills
That tap the people's tills;
I love the mob whose will's
    All laws above.[1]

The laissez-faire philosophy of noninterference, together with the Social Darwinist slogan of "survival of the fittest" and the basic American creed of equal opportunity for everyone, resulted in the creation of enormous wealth by a few men. A flood tide of peoples from southern and eastern Europe — called the "New Immigration" by historians — poured in and brought cultural and competitive tensions between these newcomers who wanted a foothold in the labor force and the "Old Immigrants" from western Europe who had arrived earlier. City workers struggled to get and hold on to jobs paying eight to ten cents an hour. As the nineteenth century gave way to the twentieth, the rich consumed conspicuously, the poor survived in city slums and rural hovels, and the rapidly growing middle class began the accumulation of material goods and cultural clout that would make it the envy of the world in the new century.

Dime novels of pulp fiction or the understandably popular works by H. G. Wells about time machines and worlds at war topped the bestseller lists.[2] Among the nonfiction favorites, the Reverend Josiah Strong's book *Our Country* (1885) warned that the future of the "Anglo-Saxon Race" was in jeopardy and preached that "commerce follows the missionary." Strong's gospel fueled American imperialism, convincing politicians to take Hawaii from Hawaiians and the Phillippines, Puerto Rico, and Guam from Spain.[3] Of course, this gospel of American supremacy fit squarely into the Puritan ideology that was part of the

---

1. "A Rational Anthem," CWAB, 5:201.
2. H. G. Wells, *The Time Machine* (1895) and *War of the Worlds* (1898).
3. Josiah Strong, *Our Country* (1885).

national myth: Americans were God's chosen people and the nation was a "city on a hill."

Science and technology were the new secular gods. Darwin's theory of evolution, reworked to see which nations proved fittest in the competition for survival, and the acceptance of racial theories of difference and hierarchy—scientifically proven—again promoted white, "100% American," male power at the expense of browner nations and peoples. Women struggled to gain the vote and to change ideas about female sexuality and physical abilities—and while they would ultimately be successful, their era was not yet. It was a masculine age, Protestant and heterosexual.

Bierce's Early Life and War Experiences

Ambrose Gwinnett Bierce was born in Ohio on June 4, 1842, the tenth of thirteen children, all christened with names beginning with "A." Biographers note that Ambrose was an unhappy and neglected child in a family of religious fanatics adhering to Church of Christ activism. His ancestors had immigrated from Scotland to settle in Puritan Connecticut before resettling in the most evangelical region of the United States in the 1830s, the Western Reserve, Ohio. His father, with the grandiose name Marcus Aurelius, and his mother, Laura Sherwood, continued the westward migration, resettling the brood in Warsaw, Indiana, in 1846, where they took to farming and praying.[4]

Bierce's uncle Lucius was the most colorful of kin. His neighbors called him "General Bierce" after he put together a private army of 180 men to invade Canada in 1837 in support of a small rebellion there. He was certain that Canadians would rise up en masse to throw off Great Britain once and for all, with Canada joining itself to the United States. That venture failed—with a loss of 130 of his men. Lucius helped ensure the failure by supplying his men with broadswords instead of more efficient firepower. Upon returning to Akron, Lucius stored the broadswords until a friend on his way to Kansas Territory—old John Brown—gladly accepted the Christian Crusade–style weaponry. Brown

4. Mary E. Grenander, *Ambrose Bierce* (New York: Twayne Publishers, 1971), 15–16; Roy Morris Jr., *Alone in Bad Company* (New York: Crown, 1995), 9–15.

and his sons used these same swords to chop up pro-slavery settlers at Pottawatomie Creek in 1856.[5] Certainly young Ambrose knew something of all this lunacy. The next year, Bierce learned about saner activism by working as a printer's devil for an anti-slavery newspaper.[6]

Lucius persuaded Bierce's parents to send the boy, in Ambrose's single year of "higher" education, to the Kentucky Military Institute.[7] It was 1859, and in Virginia, Captain John Brown was hanged after his raid on the U.S. Army Arsenal at Harpers Ferry, becoming, in Melville's phrase, "the Meteor of the War," as well as embarking on his career as a martyr "a'mouldering in the grave."[8] By 1860, Bierce had had enough of cadet discipline and was back home in Indiana as the election of Lincoln quickly led to the secession of the Southern states. The firing by Confederates in Charleston upon government troops inside Fort Sumter officially began the war on April 12, 1861.

Ambrose Bierce must have run down to the recruiting station and camped out all night to save his place in line for the honor of being the second man in Elkhart County to join the community's regiment, the Ninth Indiana Volunteers, after Lincoln's call for troops on April 15. Bierce was eighteen years old. Three years, nine months, and six days later, he left the army reluctantly, forced out by a head wound received at Kennesaw Mountain, Georgia.

From the beginning of his service, while many soldiers wished for relief from the boredom of camp life and wanted the chance to test themselves in battle, Bierce had a mouthful of fighting. Just forty-four days after enlisting, he fought in the war's very first "battle," Philippi, where the casualties were so small that Bierce wrote, "we shot off a Confederate leg."[9] Then on July 10, in the little battle at Girard Hill, as the *Indianapolis Journal* reported: "[Private] Boothroyd was wounded in the neck by a rifle ball paralyzing him. Bierce, in open view of the enemy, carried poor Boothroyd and his gun without other assistance,

5. Richard O'Connor, *Ambrose Bierce: A Biography* (Boston: Little, Brown, 1967), 11–12, 20.

6. Grenander, 16; MORRIS, 15.

7. MORRIS, 18.

8. Herman Melville, "The Portent," in *Battle-Pieces and Aspects of the War* (1866; reprint, New York: Da Capo Press, 1995), 11; song by unknown author, "John Brown's Body," circa 1861.

9. "On a Mountain," CWAB, 1:225.

fully twenty rods, balls falling around him like hail."[10] As Hemingway would do in a later war, Bierce had proven his manhood early on—something he would re-prove monthly during the war, receiving an astonishing fifteen commendations for bravery under fire. Promotions followed. Cited for bravery for carrying Private Boothroyd from Girard Hill, Bierce was promoted to sergeant when the regiment swore into three-year service a few days after their ninety-days service expired.

In April 1862, he fought at Shiloh with his Ninth Indiana showing its valor—and happenstance placement—by sustaining the most casualties of any and all regiments in that bloody battle.[11] A handsome hero, Bierce was six feet tall with thick, golden blond hair, blue eyes, and "a sweeping gunfighter's mustache."[12] He was tall among soldiers who generally went 5'6" to 5'9", had a look-you-in-the-eyes stare, a completely erect way of holding himself, and a walk measured by long, strong strides.[13] His bravery at Shiloh and his physicality gained the attention of his commanding officers and no doubt led to his promotion to the officer corps as a second lieutenant on December 1, 1862.

Thirty days later, on New Year's Eve, Bierce was recognized for his bravery during the battle of Stone's River, Tennessee. As his regiment recoiled from the attack of Confederate General Braxton Bragg at "Hell's Half Acre," Bierce rescued a wounded fellow officer, Major Braden, by carrying him under fire from where he had fallen. For that action—and by the fact that officers above him had been killed, wounded, or reassigned—Bierce soon wore the rank of a first lieutenant.[14]

He also did duty as provost marshall overseeing two military executions—one of a soldier who had killed civilians; the other of a cavalry officer who had deserted under fire—before General William B. Hazen appointed him to the headquarters staff in the position as topographical engineer.[15] Perhaps he had learned the skills of surveying

10. *Indianapolis Journal,* quoted in Paul Fatout, *Ambrose Bierce: The Devil's Lexicographer* (Norman: University of Oklahoma Press, 1951), 39–40.

11. Grenander, 18.

12. O'Connor, 75.

13. Adolph Danziger DeCastro, *Portrait of Ambrose Bierce* (New York: Beckman Publishers, 1974), 255.

14. Grenander, 19–20.

15. MORRIS, 53–54.

Ambrose Bierce in Civil War lieutenant's uniform, c. 1863–64. From the collections of the Elkhart County Historical Museum, Bristol, Indiana. Collection on loan from D. W. Strauss. Photography courtesy of Troyer Studios.

and mapmaking at the Kentucky Military Institute. Bierce's Civil War stories pay careful attention to the lay of the land, especially to the placement of troops and guns on the battlefield. Later in life, Bierce acknowledged the lingering influence of his experiences as a mapmaker when he wrote, "To this day I cannot look over a landscape without noting the advantages of the ground for attack or defense; here is an admirable site for an earthwork, there an able place for a field battery."[16] Bierce fought actively at Chickamauga, Missionary Ridge, and Kennesaw Mountain, where he was severely wounded. Up to that time, he had not been wounded, sick, or absent without leave for one single day of the war. After Kennesaw he convalesced while doctors removed the lead ball from his skull, beat the odds by recovering, and rejoined the army in its pursuit of Braxton Bragg's strike into Tennessee following the capitulation of Atlanta.[17]

Excepting only the action immediately around Atlanta, he seems hardly to have missed a major battle in the western theater. During the Franklin-Nashville campaign, Bierce had recurring spells of dizziness and fainting, which finally forced his resignation. The War Department released him from active duty on January 25, 1865.[18]

Bierce's Civil War days were not quite over as he took a job as a Treasury Department agent. Assigned to Alabama, Bierce helped track down contraband property, mostly cotton, abandoned or hidden by Confederates. There was too much corruption swirling around this kind of work for scrupulously honest Bierce to take. When Hazen suddenly invited him to accompany an expedition into Indian country, Bierce quickly accepted, joining his old commander and friend in Omaha, Nebraska, in July 1866. The expedition traveled through the Black Hills, Little Big Horn, and Yellowstone. They met old Civil War comrades in some of the forts along the way, and narrowly missed violent encounters with Chief Red Cloud of the Oglala Sioux, who was angered by yet another broken promise by the U.S. government. Bierce saw Montana, Wyoming, and Utah, and the group camped at Donner's Pass, where the smell of meat roasting over the campfire gave Bierce the chance to remark on the "slightly uncanny" resemblance to the

16. Quoted in MORRIS, 55.
17. MORRIS, 88–90.
18. Ibid., 97.

cannibal meal that had made the place famous.[19] Hazen's group finally disbanded in San Francisco in late autumn of 1866. Hazen had been commissioned a regular colonel in the post–Civil War army, and he returned to the East by ship via Panama to resume his career in the military. Bierce went his own way, remaining in San Francisco to write a new life.[20]

The Victory Culture

When Ambrose Bierce began to write his memoirs of the Civil War, the United States had thrown off a Reconstruction era that sought to raise African Americans to equality with white Americans. Nathaniel Hawthorne — in his final year of life in 1864 — had predicted that once the North won, the White House would be ruled by "one bullet-headed general after another."[21] That prophecy had come true enough when six Civil War officers gained the Oval Office as Ulysses S. Grant begat Rutherford B. Hayes begat James Garfield begat Chester Arthur begat Benjamin Harrison begat William McKinley (Grover Cleveland twice broke this cycle, elected once before and again after Harrison). The victory culture and national reconciliation began at Grant's first inaugural, as the victor of the war embodied the national mood: "Let us have peace."[22] Eight years later, when the Compromise of 1877 put Hayes into the White House on his promise to end Reconstruction and give the South home rule — alone to decide what to do with its "negro problem" — the nation was on the road toward a national confirmation of racial segregation. In 1896, the Supreme Court ruled that "separate but equal" public and private facilities were constitutional.

The national culture in the Gilded Age debated issues of competitive glory and honor. This period is highlighted by the rampant boosterism of local communities and growing urban metropolises. Chambers of Commerce and local auxiliaries sponsored and printed town,

19. Ibid., 106.

20. Ibid., 97–107.

21. Nathaniel Hawthorne, "Chiefly About War Matters," *Atlantic Monthly* (July 1864). Quoted from Hyatt H. Waggoner, *Nathaniel Hawthorne: Selected Tales and Sketches* (New York: Rinehart and Winston, 1970), 599.

22. James M. McPherson, *Ordeal by Fire: The Civil War and Reconstruction* (New York: Knopf, 1982), 546.

county, and state histories to show the progress and "ideal" conditions of this place or that. The completion of the Brooklyn Bridge in 1883, erection of the Statue of Liberty in 1886, elimination of the last major Indian resistance at Wounded Knee in 1890, and quick triumph in the Spanish-American War in 1898 all pointed to the arrival of an American Century.

Concurrently, there was a "colonial revival" in architecture as Americans celebrated the national myth. After all, the nineteenth century had begun with the declarer of independence, Thomas Jefferson, taking office; the century closed with a celebration that the nation had lived up to the founder's vision and sat more-than-evenly in the world of nations. The country's official history demanded an unbroken line of progress from idea to fulfillment. But the Civil War contradicted this narrative. It was a major failure in the national myth if writ large as a destructive fight of American killing American. Because national histories are public histories, which cannot be written as failure, the war became an atonement and resurrection — honorable, patriotic, and glorious — just the way the national memory demanded. Lincoln already knew this in 1861, when he made reference to the sacrifices in blood made by the Revolutionary generation and which continued to the present. In closing his first inaugural address, Lincoln upheld the patriotic progression of national history: "The mystic chords of memory, stretching from every battlefield and patriot grave, to every living heart and hearth-stone, all over this broad land, will yet swell the chorus of the Union when again touched, as surely they will be, by the better angels of our nature."[23]

In the years just after the war, there was a notable literary silence on the conflict except for a few, mostly unread pieces, including Herman Melville's *Battle-Pieces* (1866), John W. DeForest's *Miss Ravenel's Conversion* (1867), and Sidney Lanier's *Tiger-Lilies* (1867). It was as if the conflict was too much for poetry or fiction to handle; in the first poem of his collection, Melville called the war "the anguish none can tell."[24] People seemed more content reading Mark Twain's southwestern humor — it was something they could laugh at, romantic and be-

23. Abraham Lincoln, "First Inaugural Address," in John G. Hunt, ed., *The Essential Abraham Lincoln* (New York: Gramercy Books, 1993).

24. Melville, "The Portent," in *Battle-Pieces*, 11.

nign in many ways because of its locale in the innocence of antebellum youth and a natural world of a western river among an agrarian folk.[25] Twain's work was part of a larger body of regionalist writing, stories and novels that waxed nostalgic about vanishing ways of life and disappearing customs and dialects as the nation raced toward a national culture.

Then, suddenly, in the 1880s, the literary moratorium on the Civil War was over. Bierce began to write his short stories about the war; but he was far from alone. Frederick Douglass reinvented himself again in *Life and Times of Frederick Douglass* (1881) for the few readers who still cared. This third and final of his autobiographical narratives devoted large sections to his Civil War experiences. Walt Whitman composed another song of himself in *Specimen Days* (1882–83), a sort of scrapbook of Civil War memories.[26] The majority of readers were more interested in the "facts" — the history and the memoirs of what had happened in battle. The American public had spent nearly $8 billion on the war, lost some 620,000 sons, and freed four million slaves. They wanted an explanation of what it all had been about. They wanted nonfiction. They wanted feel-good glory, not patriotic gore. William Sherman's *Memoirs of General William T. Sherman* (1875) led the way for an outpouring of "I was there" victorious narratives.[27]

Almost everyone who had been anyone in the war decided to write his recollections or to contribute them to the literary fad of the age: regimental histories. These book-length chronicles told the stories of a particular regiment or other military unit. Compilers collected the traveling adventures, the camp-life customs, and, most importantly, the battlefield bravery of the soldiers and officers of the company. These histories held strong appeal for the aging war veterans in the 1870s and

25. Mark Twain, *The Adventures of Tom Sawyer* (1876) and *The Adventures of Huckleberry Finn* (1884), reflect this style. Only later, after the death of his daughters and wife, did Twain turn to pessimism, darkness, and disgust with humankind. Examples of this type are *The Man Who Corrupted Hadleyburg* (1899) and *The Mysterious Stranger* (1916).

26. Frederick Douglass, *The Life and Times of Frederick Douglass* (1881; reprint, New York: Gramercy Books, 1993); Walt Whitman, *Specimen Days* (1882; reprint, Boston: Godine, 1971).

27. William Tecumseh Sherman, *Memoirs of General William T. Sherman*, 2 vols. (1875; reprint, New York: Da Capo Press, 1988).

1880s, as the ten-, fifteen-, and twenty-year anniversaries of the war rolled around. Of course, when one regimental history came out, the "manhood" of the other regiments was shamed and men had to stand up to the challenge to show that: Hey, we too were at Shiloh — or Bull Run or Gettysburg or Fort Wagner — and without us the battle would have been lost! Regimental histories by the hundreds poured from printing houses to provide a record of the valor, devotion to duty, and manly sacrifice of the troops.

The U.S. government helped stir this enthusiasm by publishing *The War of the Rebellion: A Compilation of the Official Records of Union and Confederate Armies*, 128 volumes (1880–1901). This massive archive aimed to collect all of the orders, battlefield reports, casualty lists, bravery commendations, official letters, and other military documents of the war. It served then and continues to serve today as an essential collection of primary documents about the American Civil War. More accessible to all readers was the four-volume *Battles and Leaders of the Civil War* (1887–88), a reprinting of *Century* magazine's well-received series of articles (1884–87) written by prominent generals. Of course, everyone who could afford it rushed to buy the *Personal Memoirs of U. S. Grant* (1885) completed just before throat cancer overcame the "hero of the war" on July 23, 1885.[28]

During the culture of reunion and reconciliation of the 1890s, regimental histories contributed to the growth of a new interpretation of the Civil War. Both veterans and the culture at large began to construct memorials in a ceremonial and romantic style, and a period of "aggressive heroizing" of patriots fighting in an inspirational war began. Historian Alice Fahs argues that the 1880s and 1890s were a time when Americans worked intently to create heroic images of the officers and soldiers who fought in the war.[29] By emphasizing the bravery, courage, and heroism of the soldiers and the glory of the cause, the collective memory of the people began to exclude the horrors of battle, the

28. Ulysses S. Grant, *Personal Memoirs of U. S. Grant*, 2 vols. (1885–86; reprint, New York: Da Capo Press, 1982).

29. Alice Fahs, "The Feminized Civil War: Gender, Northern Popular Literature, and the Memory of the War, 1860–1900," *Journal of American History* 85 (March 1999): 1461–94.

barbarity of the fighting, the psychological trauma of civil war. It was just that kind of "aggressive heroizing" that would offend Bierce and incite him to write a much different kind of war memorial.

The ever-graying ranks of the Grand Army of the Republic (GAR), the United Confederate Veterans (UCV), and the associated women's organizations built monuments in every town of any size in the North and South — and sometimes West — to the sacrifices of local manhood. Marble and stone monuments, standing in formation where men had once stood, crowded former battlefields as states and regiments felt ashamed if another's sacrifice was remembered in granite when their own remained unmarked.[30] The GAR had been successful in getting Congress to recognize a "Decoration Day" so that the living would "not let Johnny go by," buried and forgotten.[31] Every year many regiments held reunions on the anniversary of the founding muster, biggest battle, or ending muster. Bierce never managed to attend even one of these events, even if he did once write a sergeant in his unit that he hoped to do that very thing one day.[32] Perhaps the closest he came to this kind of ceremonial reunion was his contribution to his old company, the Ninth Indiana Volunteers, of a long letter written as he toured old battle sites in West Virginia. A revised version of this letter was published as "A Bivouac of the Dead," a telling Biercian emphasis on the priority of the dead over the living.

In the 1890s, the surging tide of New Immigrants, the rise in the number of lynchings of African Americans, the martial music of John Philip Sousa, wars against Spaniards and Filipinos and Hawaiians, the development of a more powerful navy, and the implementation of the Dawes Act against Native Americans all pointed to a redefinition of manhood along reactionary lines. Turn-of-the-century America was a time when the history textbooks were rewritten and the Pledge of Alle-

---

30. For a comprehensive analysis of the history of Civil War monuments, see Kirk Savage, *Standing Soldiers, Kneeling Slaves: Race, War, and Monument in Nineteenth-Century America* (Princeton: Princeton University Press, 1997).

31. For the best fictional treatment of the GAR, Decoration Day, and the determination "not to let Johnny go by," see Elizabeth Stuart Helps Ward, "Comrades," in Frank McSherry Jr., Charles G. Waugh, and Martin Greenberg, eds. *Civil War Women* (New York: Simon & Schuster, 1988), 142–57.

32. Fatout, 159.

giance and the American flag appeared in all classrooms. It was an era of country, flag, and men.

Editor Bierce in San Francisco

In one reality the war had ended for Ambrose Bierce; in another it had just begun. In San Francisco and London he worked as a newspaperman and independent writer who satirized or criticized outright the corruption and foibles of the rich and famous. Bierce was insolent. He sharpened his wit and discovered a real ability for satire and sarcasm — an ability stemming from a deep understanding that in the Civil War men had died for causes they did not understand, died to have their manhood recognized according to history's definition at the time: courage, honor, duty. In a "protector" role, men were recognized as men by going into uniform for the purpose of dying or killing other protectors. Because they confronted historical expectations in their own training — and in those in the separate sphere where women lived and acted out their own roles — they killed and died as honest, if highly deluded, foemen.

In San Francisco, Bierce wrote newspaper columns about suicides and deaths, published horror stories, and lived a tumultuous life mostly of his own making. Married in 1871 to socialite Mollie Day, Bierce lived unhappily in the marriage until their estrangement in 1889 over Mollie's alleged love affair with a Dane. Bierce had discovered some love letters and even though Mollie always swore nothing had happened, he was furious over her keeping the physical reminders. Perhaps the omnipresent skull he thereafter kept on his desk reminded him of the Danish Hamlet as well as of the Civil War and man's inability to overcome a pernicious fate. Mollie and Ambrose did have three children together before they separated. One son, Day, died in a shootout with his best friend, when that friend eloped with Day's fiancée. Day managed to kill his friend and wound his girlfriend in the affair. Another son, Leigh, died of pneumonia. His daughter, Helen, was his closest relative, a woman described by Bierce's friend and biographer Adolph DeCastro as "a girl of splendid intellectual power and womanhood."[33]

33. DeCastro, 50.

Bierce gained international fame as a writer and editor for William Randolph Hearst's *San Francisco Examiner*. His attacks on railroad interests of Leland Stanford — whom Bierce called "\$tealing Landford" — and Henry Huntington were vicious and important. He spent much time in Washington, D.C., writing for Hearst about the corruption he found there.[34]

From 1872 until 1875, Bierce lived and wrote in London. He went to England seeking a change of scenery and a chance to move away from the daily work of a journalist for a different kind of literary work. He socialized with a group of young literati, sought the favor of John Camden Hotten, the British publisher of Mark Twain and Artemus Ward, and worked on collecting a series of short stories into his first book, *The Fiend's Delight*.[35]

Bierce returned to San Francisco, his family having preceded him in the return trip by some months, a sign perhaps that the marriage was in crisis. Eventually Bierce resumed his newspaper work, but he increasingly identified himself as a literary writer. Bierce secured a position as columnist for the *Argonaut*, writing a regular column called "Prattle," and in 1881 he began to write for the satirical weekly *The Wasp*. All manner of politicians, business leaders, fellow writers, and socially prominent persons came in for the biting sarcasm of Bierce's pen. He made himself easy to hate during these years, as he served up the stinging critiques of people and policies that earned him the nicknames "Bitter Bierce" and "The Wickedest Man in San Francisco."

His famous *The Devil's Dictionary* assembled and expanded the sarcastic definitions he had been trying out in his newspaper columns. First published in 1906 as *The Cynic's Word Book*, the work was retitled in the 1909–11 *Collected Works* by Bierce's preferred title of *The Devil's Dictionary*, and the book has never been out of print since. Ernest J. Hopkins eventually published an *Enlarged Devil's Dictionary* in which he gathered all of the definitions Bierce had published in newspaper columns over the years. Bierce's dictionary is one of the best indicators of his peculiar manner of seeing the world, especially its domestic, political, and military aspects. Here are a few representative definitions:

34. MORRIS, 174–76.
35. Ibid., 140–44.

BRIDE, *n.* A woman with a fine prospect for happiness behind her.

BRUTE, *n.* See Husband.

CABBAGE, *n.* A familiar kitchen vegetable about as large and wise as a man's head.

CAPITAL, *n.* The seat of misgovernment.

CHRISTIAN, *n.* One who follows the teachings of Christ in so far as they are not inconsistent with a life of sin.

DANCE, *v.* To leap about to the sound of tittering music, preferably with arms about your neighbor's wife or daughter.

FAMOUS, *adj.* Conspicuously miserable.

HERS, *pro.* His.

ONCE, *adv.* Enough.

Among the more poignant definitions in the dictionary is this:

ALONE, *adj.* In bad company.

And for the purpose of examining Bierce's preparation to write fiction based on the Civil War, this definition is important:

HISTORY, *n.* An account mostly false, of events mostly unimportant, which are brought about by rulers mostly knaves and soldiers mostly fools.[36]

Writing the Civil War

Bierce had sharpened his pen and his memory while he wrote for Hearst. When he wrote his Civil War, he confronted the gilded hypocrisy of the times. He marched out of step and away from the formation of those creating and saluting the national myth. While the publishers and monument makers built a pantheon of dignified and honorable "marble" heroes, Bierce told a different story, one lacking patriotic young men fighting bravely and proudly for country.[37] For the celebrators of the "good war" myth, he was bad news in a good news world. His private recollections confronted public memory, and embarrassed it.

Of course, Bierce knew about romantic pageantry, patriotism, and

36. All definitions drawn from DICT.

37. Richard Saunders, *Ambrose Bierce: The Making of a Misanthrope* (San Francisco: Chronicle Books, 1985), 48–49.

youthful innocence. But he also remembered the contours of courage, fear, and death. Biographer Roy Morris said that Bierce discovered quickly that war was more than "fairy-tale fighting in Virginia" by college boys in spotless uniforms.[38] He was the first American to write faithfully about war. Bierce wrote of wild hogs eating the faces and stomachs from still-living casualties, of bloated corpses with open wounds and yellow faces, of mutilated children, of brothers not recognizing the dead faces of their own brothers, of wounded men being burned alive when woods caught fire, of men doing their duty even if it meant killing their closest relatives, of the best soldiers being the first ones to die, of cowards acting manly, of brave men becoming cowards, and always, always, of death. Critic Edmund Wilson correctly concluded — a bit accusingly and more than a little dismissively — that Bierce's "only real character" was Death. If Vietnam veteran and author Tim O'Brien's basic contradiction — "War makes you a man. War makes you dead" — is correct, then Death is a key figure who deserves a major role in war stories.[39] H. L. Mencken recognized the role of Death and praised Bierce as the "the first writer of fiction ever to treat war realistically" and to compare soldiers in battle with the "bewildered animals dying like hogs in Chicago" stockyards.[40] Biographer and critic Carey McWilliams, using one of Bierce's titles, explained Bierce's understanding "that in the midst of life there is always death; that in pursuit of great dreams men stumble over cadavers and fall headlong into pools of blood."[41]

Daniel Aaron added that "Ambrose Bierce not only choked on the blood of the Civil War, he practically drowned in it."[42] Critic Larzer Ziff said that until Bierce, "the murderous side of the war was an oral tradition only."[43] Eric Solomon wrote that Bierce's stories were "replete

38. MORRIS, 38.

39. Edmund Wilson, *Patriotic Gore, Patriotic Gore: Studies in the Literature of the American Civil War* (New York: Oxford University Press, 1962), 622; Tim O'Brien, *The Things They Carried* (Boston: Houghton Mifflin, 1990), 65.

40. Mencken quoted in Saunders, 62.

41. Carey McWilliams, introduction to *The Devil's Dictionary* (New York: Sagamore Press, 1957), xi.

42. Daniel Aaron, *The Unwritten War: American Writers and the Civil War* (Madison: University of Wisconsin Press, 1987), 181.

43. Ziff cited in Michael Schaefer, *Just What War Is: The Civil War Writings of De Forest and Bierce* (Knoxville: University of Tennessee Press, 1997), 149, n.5.

with disgusting ugliness."[44] Edmund Wilson understood that Bierce's exposé of "violent death . . . was never a tragedy, but merely a bitter jest."[45] Biographer Richard Saunders christened Bierce the "true father of black humor."[46] Stuart Woodruff admired him as "the arch prince of Literary Darkness."[47] All of those are accurate evaluations. Joseph Epstein posits that the Civil War killed the idealism in Bierce and replaced it with cynicism.[48] This view, however, doesn't quite square with the stories, even if Bierce admitted, "When I ask myself what has happened to Ambrose Bierce the youth, who fought at Chickamauga, I am bound to answer that he is dead."[49]

More likely was that the heroizing memorials and intense melodrama Bierce saw after the war killed his idealism. The memory of the war as put forth by romantics and accepted by the American public incensed Bierce. When DeCastro asked him to write an accurate history of the war, Bierce told him, "The fools would probably not understand a word of it."

Alone among American writers of the first rank, Bierce fought for nearly four years in the Civil War. When, between 1880 and 1910, he turned his attention to writing about the Civil War, he was the only major American writer who knew first-hand what the war had meant to soldiers on the battlefield, in the camps, on the picket lines, or serving through the night as a sentry. His Civil War writings thus have inestimable value as both a historical record of one man's remembered experience and as a literary account of what happened and why it mattered.

We have already seen how Bierce was out of step with the patriotic ideology of his times. Not surprisingly, his literary methods are also at odds with what other writers were doing. He preferred satire, irony, and sarcasm, at a time when romance and realism dominated. Although many of his stories are startlingly realistic, they are also shot through with sarcasm and ironic attacks on complacency. Further, the stories

44. Soloman cited from Schaefer, 73.

45. Wilson, 623.

46. Saunders, 103.

47. Stuart C. Woodruff, *The Short Stories of Ambrose Bierce: A Study in Polarity* (Pittsburgh, Pa.: University of Pittsburgh Press, 1964), 4.

48. Joseph Epstein, "Our Favorite Cynic: Will Ambrose Bierce Ever Get His Due?" *New Yorker,* March 25, 1996, 86.

49. Bierce quoted in Woodruff, 76.

are always exploring the mythic and supernatural dimensions of war experience. By the time Bierce turned to writing war stories, he had already written a large number of ghost stories and Poe-like investigations of the mysterious, marvelous, and miraculous workings of the human psyche. It is not surprising, then, that the war stories are also engaged in an examination of paranormal experience, supernatural events, and fantastic occurrences. Even Bierce's representation of war experience on battlefield maps eschews the traditional, realistic convention of labeling the opponent's position by the name of the commanding officer. Instead, Bierce labels it starkly, almost surrealistically, as "Enemy."

Morris praises the stories for being "revolutionary," "hallucinatory," "absurd," and very modern.[50] Besides his true depictions of the psychological surrealism of men in battle, Bierce's stories are noteworthy for their understanding of geographical space and for what biographer Richard O'Connor praised as the "limpid clarity of physical setting that gave his Civil War stories such a startling air of realism."[51] Biographers S. T. Joshi and David Schultz cite Bierce's "fine memory" and the accuracy of his stories, which "harmonize in every significant particular with the known facts."[52] Daniel Aaron cited his "almost uncanny visual sense," which Bierce employed "so that the reader can visualize every copse or ravine or stream he mentions."[53] Bierce's keen rendering of geography is easily traced to his wartime service as the topographical engineer on the staff of General William B. Hazen. Bierce filed many reports and drew scores of maps, which show his skill in understanding terrain. (See the battlefield maps drawn by Bierce in Chapter Four.) But his knowledge came also from his experience in the mud, woods, mountains, rivers, and fields as he looked around bushes and climbed hills during his nearly four years with the Army of the Ohio.[54]

Bierce's finest critic, Cathy Davidson, praises the stories as "experimental fictions," works surprisingly sophisticated for their day. In her

50. MORRIS, 180.
51. O'Connor, 5.
52. SOLE, x.
53. Aaron, 184.
54. Ishmael Reed, "On Ambrose Bierce's *Tales of Soldiers and Civilians*," in David Madden and Peggy Bach, eds., *Classics of Civil War Fiction* (Jackson: University Press of Mississippi, 1991), 38.

view, Bierce's fictions are marked by "extreme dislocations of linear plot lines, radical disruptions of chronological time, deliberate departures from expected fictional resolutions, and compulsive expositions of the indeterminacy of language and the fatuity of belief."[55] For Davidson, Bierce's short stories need to be understood not in the context of the other writers of his day but as forerunners of such twentieth-century innovators as Julio Cortazar and Jorge Luis Borges. She argues that Bierce's experiments in language, perception, and fictional form allowed him to explore those indeterminate or "ineffable" zones of human experience, and he turned repeatedly to ghost stories and war stories for the material for these experiments.[56]

It is little wonder that most contemporary readers did not favor Bierce's works. In the consensus-building era, Bierce's stories told the truth about combat in ways that most soldiers during the war had been unable even to write about in their own journals or in letters home to loved ones. These veterans certainly did not want their sacrifices and the nation's atonement smeared by the gore and surrealistic memory of Ambrose Bierce. Many veterans — and politicians — used forms and symbols of the truth, not necessarily the truth itself, for their own glorification and justification. A sanitized story makes us more comfortable than history that bleeds, and so we construct in Fah's term "aggressive heroizing," super-patriotic, sublime, family-metaphor histories. The war was more than memory; it was politically-charged memory making of the highest order. The public quickly accepted the war stories of the generals, who painted panoramic views of battle, grand charges, bugle calls, and gallantry on both sides of the front.

Bierce recognized the temptations of this sort of story-telling. In his memoir "What I Saw at Shiloh," a frightening tale of how after the battle the woods on fire brought a special terror and death to the wounded soldiers, Bierce wrote:

How they come back to me . . . — those years of youth when I was soldiering! Again I *hear* the far off warble of blown bugles. Again I *see* the tall, blue smoke of camp-fires ascending from the dim valleys of Wonderland. There steals upon my *sense* the ghost of an *odor* from

55. Cathy N. Davidson, *The Experimental Fictions of Ambrose Bierce: Structuring the Ineffable* (Lincoln: University of Nebraska Press, 1984), 5.

56. Ibid., 3.

pines that canopy the ambuscade. I *feel* upon my cheek the morning mist. . . . Is it not strange that the phantoms of a blood-stained period have so airy a grace and look with so tender eyes? — that I *recall* with difficulty the danger and death and horrors of the time, and without effort all that was gracious and picturesque.[57]

He knew war from the inside in ways no other writer of his time — and few other writers of any time — could understand. In the passage above, Bierce helps us feel the war through our senses of hearing, seeing, sensing, smelling, feeling, and remembering. He might have written of the "gracious and picturesque" but he didn't. He did the difficult chore of writing about the individuals outside the realm of the "great leader" or battlefield panorama. Bierce concentrated on single incidents, sometimes bounded by a few minutes, to show intimately what an individual soldier feared, saw, believed, and did at the moment of his mortality. As Michael Schaefer pointed out, Bierce knew that the act of soldiering is subjective and "to believe that one can behave objectively in battle" is to miss the irrationality and fall to the illusion of combat.[58] Almost every protagonist dies or kills based upon an illusion — and an ideal — of how he should act. Bierce's stories are honest, trustworthy, and highly personal. Walt Whitman suggested that "the real war would never get into the books."[59] He obviously never read Bierce.

Bierce's process of writing about the war varied a bit from story to story, but the sequence of newspaper articles, short story, memoir, and letter he wrote about the important battle of Chickamauga is instructive. As with many of the Civil War stories, the process of writing the great story "Chickamauga" was likely incited by a late 1880s news item, the Republican victory in the Illinois governor's race in 1888. Writing in his "Prattle" column, Bierce laments the campaign loss of a former Civil War general, John M. Palmer. He was, Bierce says, "the only commander on either side who ever made a mistake: he made a good one at the battle of Chickamauga."[60] As the column develops, Bierce praises

57. Ambrose Bierce, "What I Saw at Shiloh," collected herein (italics added).
58. Schaefer, 102.
59. Walt Whitman quoted from Louis P. Masur, *The Real War Will Never Get in the Books: Selections from Writers during the Civil War* (New York: Oxford University Press, 1993), x.
60. SOLE, 35.

Palmer's unusual modesty in being willing to admit making an error in ordering troop movements during the battle. But with Bierce, praise is always tempered with sarcasm: "There were greater soldiers than General Palmer, but as the author of the only error of the war which was not committed by the other fellow, he had, in my judgment, a just and reasonable claim to the distinction of governing Illinois, which is not much of a State anyhow."[61]

Bierce published the story "Chickamauga" in the *San Francisco Examiner* on January 20, 1889, around the time his marriage to Mollie Day was breaking up and a few months before Bierce's son Day was killed. The story is a particularly disturbing one, as a small boy becomes embroiled in a gruesome battle and then wanders home to find his mother dead, her wounds graphically described. In one wrenching scene, the boy sees a group of wounded soldiers crawling toward a creek to slake their awful thirst, and he climbs on one's back, thinking he is playing horsey, as his father's slaves had once done with him. The soldier throws him off and turns a nightmarishly shattered face to the boy. Family destruction and the initiation of a boy into the horrors of adult violence are central issues in the story, and the parallels to Bierce's own life are obvious.

As Roy Morris analyzes it, the story also bears a number of clear parallels to the historical events of the battle — the movement of troops, the horrible thirst of the wounded soldiers, and the tactical importance of a woman's home (the Widow Glenn's cabin served as the Union headquarters during the battle) are a few of the details that track well with actual events of Chickamauga.[62] Yet the short story is far more than an echo of memory. Bierce's description of the young boy, a deaf mute, wielding his wooden toy sword, playing in the woods, hunting wild game only to be frightened by a rabbit, falling asleep while the battle rages unheard around him, awakening to the horrifying scene of the wounded soldiers creeping toward water and being utterly confused about what he is seeing, finally wandering home to a destroyed farm and a murdered mother — this is writing of a high order, a story that lodges in the reader's memory like the best works of American literature.

61. Ibid., 36.
62. MORRIS, 56–64.

Bierce's memory was drawn back to Chickamauga in 1898, when the Army used the old battlefield as a training ground for soldiers preparing for what became the Spanish-American War. His memoir, "A Little of Chickamauga," was published in the *San Francisco Examiner* on April 24, 1898, and he answered a reader's response to the piece a few weeks later, on May 8, 1898, in a column titled "War Topics." Claiming that his purpose in "A Little of Chickamauga" is "not instruction, but entertainment," Bierce offers a detailed account of his own experiences during the battle. He concentrates on incidents that were "particularly horrible," such as one encounter that resulted in the slaughter of huge numbers of Confederate troops by the Union artillery. It was, he says, "too dreadful to describe," although of course he does, in gruesome detail. Perhaps most interesting in the essay, however, is Bierce's careful critique of the strategies, movements, and motivations of various participating officers, including those of the future president James Garfield.

In the two additional pieces Bierce wrote about Chickamauga, the response to a reader of the newspaper article and an answer to a letter from Col. Archibald Gracie, who asked Bierce for some information to help with a book Gracie was writing about the battle, Bierce's central concern is to tell the truth as he saw it about actions of officers — both the acts of bravery and the mistakes — such as Thomas, Rosecrans, Hazen, and Brannan. In these writings, Bierce affirms his role as witness: he was there, he saw what happened, he knows whose mistakes cost lives and whose bravery saved them. Above all, he knows about the suffering and the horrors of the battle.

This movement from news article to fiction and back to memoir and historical reporting characterizes Bierce's multipurposed writing about the Civil War. These five efforts to the tell the truth about one battle, composed between 1888 and 1911, illustrate the ways Bierce's mind returned again and again to the same ground, in an effort to understand, to come to grips with the suffering, and to find the deeper truths embodied in those horrible days of a single battle.

Bierce's stories are set not in the center of the hottest fire, where most war tales focus, but at the edges. For Bierce, the real action of combat was in the center of the psyche, the mind, the psychological twists and turns of the protagonist, weighing his duty, usually, against

Ambrose Bierce by John H. E. Partington, c. 1893. From the Huntington Library,
Art Collections, and Botanical Gardens, San Marino, California. Huntington Library/
SuperStock.

his fear of dying. No one had ever written this kind of war story, one
eschewing patriotism and glory to focus on terror and death. In
Bierce's war, men died, and that was that. All their thinking and fear
could not stop fate. Bierce combined Darwin with Calvin to see events
unfolding in an orderly, predestined, and evolutionary way within the

realm of an honest universe, which paid little attention to the will of man.[63] Nothing like Bierce had ever been read before.

In the most thorough study of the motivations of men at war, Pulitzer prize–winning historian James M. McPherson convincingly argued that men North and South joined the war and fought "for cause and comrades."[64] Bierce's stories and essays do not support that thesis. Bierce would probably have labeled as "romantic" any conclusion that ideology and friendship are the keys to unlocking the motivations and staying power of a soldier. In fact, the greatness of Bierce was his ability to laugh at life and at all the intensity of the serious ones who displayed manhood upright in the face of rifled weaponry, whose adherence to duty overcame logic, who boasted that one regiment was "better" than all the others, who became politicians on the basis of being the "hero" of this battle or that, who focused self-servingly on profits instead of people, who extended imperialism to others based on a "white man's burden," and who touted the "oh my goodness" overpoliteness of the Victorian drawing room.

McPherson's conclusion that causes put men into war and comrades kept them there does not fit Bierce's story. Fear of being left behind and the embarrassment of being called a coward put men into war, and fear for their lives kept them fighting; it was that plain to Bierce. Embarrassment and fear. Bierce's stories have very little to say about comradeship and, except for one instance, mention nothing whatsoever about cause.[65] They overflow with situations highlighting fear of failing to do one's duty or fear that death was imminent. Bierce's soldiers show little heroism as that is commonly understood, for they are nearly automa-

---

63. Robert A. Wiggins, *Ambrose Bierce* (Minneapolis: University of Minnesota Press, 1964), 45; Woodruff, 20–23, 39, 45, 57; Reed, 40–41.

64. James M. McPherson, *For Cause and Comrades: Why Men Fought in the Civil War* (New York: Oxford University Press, 1997) and *What They Fought For, 1861–1865* (Baton Rouge: Louisiana State University Press, 1994). McPherson does not mention Bierce's writings or his views on the war in his textbook surveys *Ordeal by Fire* or *Battle Cry of Freedom: The Civil War Era* (New York: Oxford University Press, 1988).

65. "At one time in my green and salad days, I was sufficiently zealous for universal and unqualified Freedom to engage in a four years' battle for its promotion. There were other issues involved, but they did not count much for me." Collected herein, 316.

tons in action, but not in mind, when it comes to expectations of duty and manhood.

Unlike McPherson's soldiers, Bierce's don't have intimate friendships with other men. Indeed, the most characteristic action in his stories is the killing of a family member or close acquaintance. Fathers, brothers, wives, children — all are victims of Bierce's isolated soldiers. Execution of one's peers is as much a duty as killing the enemy. The characters in these stories are nearly always alone, isolated, postmodern. Michael Schaefer argues in *Just What War Is* (1997) that not only are soldiers on their own during the swirl of battle, they don't even know what is happening around them.[66] They see no grand scheme and know not where the rest of the army is, except what they can see between the trees, smoke, fog, night, sweat, and men in a zone of "limited sight." Schaefer explains that their tactical knowledge consists only of the knowledge that "the enemy may emerge from any direction at any moment."[67] Bierce's stories conform to that understanding and so he is most interested in delving into "character" — the inner qualities of a man that lead to actions. Most of the time, character is defined as adherence to discipline and duty but not to "my cause" or to protecting "my comrades." Certainly revenge may be taken for the death of a fellow soldier when the blood is up during battle, but Bierce insists that embarrassment or fear are the true motivators.

Bierce writes what might be termed the "situation tragedy," although Bierce himself would see it as a situation comedy. It is just that tragic-comic understanding that is the point of war and makes his stories truth, if not true. Daniel Aaron criticized Bierce's war stories as "not in the least realistic; they are . . . incredible events . . . they abound in coincidences."[68] Responding to very similar criticism from William Dean Howells and others who complained of his impossible situations and unlikely circumstances, Bierce insisted, "Nothing is so improbable as that which is true. It is the unexpected that occurs; but that is not saying enough; it is also the unlikely — one might almost say the impossible."[69] Tim O'Brien sided with Bierce when he taught us, "Almost

66. Schaefer, xiv.
67. Ibid., xiv, 100.
68. Aaron, 184.
69. Ambrose Bierce, "The Short Story," in CWAB, 10:246–47.

everything is true. Almost nothing is true. At its core, perhaps, war is just another name for death."[70] O'Brien explained:

> A true war story is never moral. It does not instruct, nor encourage virtue, nor suggest models of proper human behavior, nor restrain men from doing the things men have always done. If a story seems moral, do not believe it. If at the end of a war story you feel uplifted, or if you feel that some small bit of rectitude has been salvaged from the larger waste, then you have been made the victim of a very old and terrible lie. There is no rectitude whatsoever. There is no virtue. As a first rule of thumb, therefore, you can tell a true war story by its absolute and uncompromising allegiance to obscenity and evil.[71]

Certainly Bierce laced his short stories and short memoirs with obscenity, evil, and immorality. For some readers, Bierce's treatment of the obscenity of war might seem pornographic. Others have criticized him for attacking the hypocrisy or naïveté of his fellow Americans. Critics have labeled him cynical, wicked, bitter, the devil's lexicographer, a misanthrope, and unreal.

Bierce wrote the war as bravely as he had served when he had been a'soldiering in the Union's army. As his memories of the war became the most important part of his memory, he returned time and again to his old battlefields. He had few, if any, real friends as his infamous temper and ill humor ran everyone away. By 1913, at seventy-one years old, he had had enough. After taking a well-publicized last tour of the battlefields, Bierce disappeared into the Mexican Civil War. No one is sure how and where he died, and his body was never found. He should be remembered as the man who got the real war into the books and for his understanding of what war does to a thinking soldier, at least to a thinker like Bierce: "I never hear a rifle-shot without a thrill in my veins. I never catch the peculiar odor of gunpowder without having visions of the dead and dying. I never see a parade of the militia without laughing."[72]

70. O'Brien, 65
71. Ibid., 58.
72. *San Francisco Examiner,* June 12, 1887; quoted in Fatout, 159.

CHAPTER ONE

Patricide in the House Divided, 1861

Americans were thrilled when the South fired upon Fort Sumter on April 12, 1861. For years the country had quarreled about the "Slave Power Conspiracy" — the idea that the Southern states had the political power to force the institution on the North and West as "proven" when the Compromise of 1850 opened up Kansas to "popular sovereignty" and allowed slave catchers to search the North for fugitive slaves. The 1857 Dred Scott decision and the 1859 hanging of John Brown increased the tension, and the South deepened in its belief that the North wanted to revoke the Constitution and overturn the South's agrarian way of life. In November 1860 Northerners elected Abraham Lincoln and the new Republican Party on a promise to limit the expansion of slavery in the middle of the continent. But before Lincoln's inauguration four months later, the Union had seven fewer states, as South Carolina, Mississippi, Louisiana, Texas, Florida, Alabama, and Georgia formed a new country, the Confederate States of America. The shots on Sumter relieved the pent-up pressure as men rushed to arms to prove that they would not be cowed, would not be cowards, in the face of physical challenge. Out went Tennessee, Arkansas, North Carolina, and Virginia. Northern militia companies mustered and marched toward Washington, D.C., in response to Lincoln's fear that the capital might fall to the Virginians. Volunteers enlisted for ninety days — time enough, they thought, to win the war and save the Union.

Older men in political positions or well-known in communities, young men out of college, and regular soldiers in the U.S. army raced to their governors asking for commissions and the authority to raise regiments. These politically appointed officers would show an ineptness on the battlefield, winning or losing by the courage of their men,

luck, superior numbers, or accidents of geography, weather, and tim-
ing. They commanded mostly young men who left their families and
places of work to join in the excitement and adventure of the moment;
they could not know that the war would be a long and desperate struggle. Bierce was in the forefront, eagerly looking for "new things under a
new sun" — a comment on the youthful, wide-eyed adventure of what
he variously called "green and salad days," "Realm of Adventure," "the
Enchanted Forest," and "halcyon days" of "our Heroic Age." Women
rushed to sew flags and join organizations to help "our boys." The New
York Yacht Club offered its sailboats to the U.S. navy and patriotic
speeches asked for duty, honor, bravery, and courage.

In the area that would become West Virginia — after seceding from
Virginia and being recognized as a separate state in 1863 — loyal
Unionists needed protecting, and the vital communication link of
the Baltimore and Ohio Railroad needed securing. General George
McClellan took charge and ordered his new volunteer regiments into
the area. On June 3, Private Ambrose Bierce marched along with
his Ninth Indiana regiment through the valleys around Grafton, was
soaked to the bone by thunderstorms, but engaged in the defeat of a
small Confederate force at Philippi. One month later, McClellan ordered his men into action at Laurel Hill, Rich Mountain, Cheat Mountain, and Carrick's Ford. These small battles were Union victories and
Bierce did his duty in every one; but the victories paled beside the rout
of Northern forces at Bull Run on July 21. The ninety-day enlistment
expired and Bierce's Ninth took trains back to Indiana, enjoyed the
plaudits and kisses of the community, signed on to three years of service, and returned to Cheat Mountain for the rest of 1861.

Mostly confusion prevailed as heavy rains and rough mountains frus-
trated Robert E. Lee's attempts to expel the Federals from his state.
Both armies struggled to distinguish friends from enemies in the non-
standardized uniforms of the day, having blue and gray on both sides.
Soldiers often waited too late to fire as they could not discern which
flag was coming at them; others fired too soon and killed their own
men. The situation in western Virginia exemplified the brother's war
like nowhere else, as families divided in their loyalty to nation, state,
community, or each other. Brothers and fathers joined different sides
and sometimes faced each other along the farm roads, houses, and

mountains they knew so well. Men pondered the question of whether or not they would kill friends and family if the occasion arose.

In these early days when "war was young, and soldiering a new industry," the quality of leadership in the army was uneven. Bierce, who never suffered fools easily, made much of the bungled orders, the mistaken judgments, and the simple stupidity of some of the men commissioned to lead the inexperienced soldiers. Whether in parodies like "Jupiter Doke, Brigadier-General" or serious fictions like "One Kind of Officer," Bierce investigates the qualities that make a man a leader.

The roles of manhood were clear in the middle of the nineteenth century. Men were to do their duty at any and all costs. Honor was at stake and honor demanded courage — courage to do one's duty and courage to face and kill or be killed by the enemy. In the military, duty required obeying orders even if they were disagreeable. Men did their best to make battles into "fields of honor." Civilian boys became veteran soldiers as they grew accustomed to dead bodies, feared for their lives, and worried about losing honor if not recognized as men who could bravely do whatever was asked of them. For many, the difficulty of overcoming imagined enemies matched the difficulty of marching directly toward real enemies.

This section opens with several nonfiction pieces written in the early twentieth century, as Bierce revisits the fields of his first Civil War battles. They serve to remind readers that even the immediacy of the short fiction — the sense that we are on the battlefield with the characters — is in fact a revisiting of the author's experience of twenty and thirty years previous.

From *The Devil's Dictionary*[1]

POLITICS, *n*. A strife of interests masquerading as a contest of
principles. The conduct of public affairs for private advantage.

REBEL, *n*. A proponent of a new misrule who has failed to establish it.

YANKEE, *n*. In Europe, an American. In the Northern States of our
Union, a New Englander. In the Southern States the word is
unknown. (See DAMYANK.)

DRAGOON, *n*. A soldier who combines dash and steadiness in so equal
measure that he makes his advances on foot and his retreats on
horseback.

ENEMY, *n*. In military affairs, a body of men actuated by the basest
motives and pursuing the most iniquitous aim.

FLAG, *n*. A colored rag borne above troops and hoisted on forts and
ships. It appears to serve the same purpose as certain signs that one
sees on vacant lots in London — "Rubbish may be shot here."

RANK, *n*. Relative elevation in the scale of human worth.

1. All quotations herein from DICT.

A THIN BLUE GHOST[2]

I have told her of a certain "enchanted forest" hereabout to which I feel myself sometimes strongly drawn as a fitting place to lay down "my weary body and my head." . . . The element of enchantment in that forest is supplied by my wandering and dreaming in it forty-one years ago when I was a-soldiering and there were new things under a new sun. It is miles away, but from a near-by summit I can overlook the entire region — ridge beyond ridge, parted by purple valleys full of sleep. Unlike me, it has not visibly altered in all these years, except that I miss, here and there, a thin blue ghost of smoke from an enemy's camp. Can you guess my feelings when I view this Dream-land — my Realm of Adventure, inhabited by memories that beckon me from every valley? I shall go; I shall retrace my old routes and lines of march; stand in my old camps; inspect my battlefields to see that all is right and undisturbed. I shall go to the Enchanted Forest.

2. Letter abstract of Ambrose Bierce. Recipient, date, location unknown. ABPO, 204.

[1904; SOLE]

BATTLEFIELDS AND GHOSTS[3]

I passed the greater part of the summer before the last at the little village of Aurora, West Virginia, just west of the Maryland line, and overlooking the Cheat River valley in the Alleghany Mountains. Through
Aurora a part of the Confederate force retreated after the engagement
at Carrick's Ford,[4] a few miles to the southwest, and the older inhabitants still tell many tales of that to them memorable event. From some
of the peaks near Aurora I could see down into several of the blue and
purple valleys, where, with some of the comrades who, I hope, will be
with you when this paper is read, I campaigned in the distant days of
'61 and '62.

That region had ever since been to me, as I suppose it has to them, a
kind of dreamland. I was reluctant to descend into it for fear of dispell-
ing the illusion, but finally I did so, and passed a few of the most
interesting weeks of my life, following the track of the Ninth, visiting its
camps, the forts that it helped to build, those that it assisted to take, or
try to take, the graves of its fallen and those of the misguided gentlemen whom it sent to their long rest, and who, doubtless, sleep not less
soundly than the others.

At Grafton[5] is a beautiful National Cemetery, where lie some twelve
hundred of the Federal dead, removed to that place from their scattered graves in that part of the state. About one-half of them are
marked "unknown." Many of the Ninth, however, were identified, and
I forward herewith some notes concerning them which I copied from
the records of the cemetery.

3. Ambrose Bierce to Alexander Whitehall, September 30, 1904, *Ninth Indiana
Veteran Volunteer Infantry Association: Proceedings of the Eighteenth Annual Reunion*
(N.p., 1904), 13–18. Reprinted as *Battlefields and Ghosts* (Palo Alto, Calif.: Harvest
Press, 1931). SOLE, 3–6.

4. The battle at Carrick's Ford, western Virginia, was fought July 13, 1861.
General George McClellan became an instant media star and was named by
Lincoln to head the Army of the Potomac. FAUST.

5. Grafton, western Virginia, was center of General McClellan's efforts to protect the Baltimore & Ohio Railroad from May 30 to June 3, 1861. From here, the
movement began that became the first battle of the war, Philippi. LONG.

Some of the entries doubtless are incorrect, or at least inaccurate. The very first on the books stood thus:

"Abbott, E. J. (Ind.). Removed July 17, 1867, from Geo. Burns' farm, Travelers' Repose, Pocahontas Co. Head southeast, 150 yards from road."

This entry I took to refer to James A. Abbott of my company (C), who fell at the battle of Greenbrier River[6] — Travelers' Repose being a wayside inn and postoffice on the field of engagement. Afterward I was shown the grave from which the body had been removed. On returning to Washington I went to the War Department and had the record corrected in accordance with my belief, although I was not present at the engagement.

Of the other dead members of Company C the Grafton Cemetery has no record, though doubtless some of them are there among the "unknown."

Philippi[7] where we had our first affair with the enemy, is now a considerable town. It was easy to identify the road by which we entered, in the belief that we had the enemy's camp surrounded. The high hill from which a battery of ours pitched shells into the startled Confederate camp (and I believe flung a few at us by mistake) is still there, as is the way of hills, and looked quite familiar. We afterward camped on it, among the trees in a field. It is still a field, but the trees are mostly gone. By the way, that battery of ours did nothing worse than take off a young Confederate's leg. He was living near there a year ago, a prosperous and respectable gentleman, but still minus the leg; no new one had grown on.

The "three months' men" will remember Belington well enough. I think it was little but a blacksmith's shop at a cross-roads. It is now a pleasant little village. Two or three miles out is where we fought the battle of Laurel Hill.[8] It was not much of a battle — none of them were — but it gave us something to think about during the few days that

6. Battle of Greenbrier River, October 3, 1861.

7. Sometimes called the "Philippi Races" in reference to untrained Virginia troops in flight before McClellan's army, the battle of Philippi, western Virginia, took place on June 3, 1861. The Union troops lost one officer, one man — the former killed, the latter wounded. FAUST.

8. July 10, 1861.

it kept us pegging away at Garnett's men,[9] with or without orders. None of the enemy's earthworks remain except an emplacement for guns on the summit of a hill; the rifle pits cannot now be traced. They were lower down the hill in the woods. With the exception of a strip of trees at the very bottom, held by our skirmishers, the forest is gone. In this strip of trees occurred, just before nightfall one day, the only really sharp little fight that we had. It has been represented as a victory for us, but it was not. A few dozens of us, who had been swapping shots with the enemy's skirmishers, grew tired of the resultless quarrel, and by a common impulse, and I think without orders or officers, ran forward into the woods and attacked the Confederate works. We did well enough, considering the hopeless folly of the movement, but we came out of the woods faster than we went in, a good deal. This was the affair in which Corporal Dyson Boothroyd[10] of Company A fell with a mortal wound. I found the very rock against which he lay.

Our camp is now a race track.

On the reorganization of the regiment for the three years' service it returned to this region and lay for weeks at Huttonsville, near the foot of Cheat Mountain, where many of the men died of disease. Their bodies are at Grafton. Then, after the Greenbrier affair, we went to the summit of the mountain. It will be remembered that we built a row of big log houses, one for each company, all connected for mutual protection and loopholed for rifle firing. These military defenses commanded the road — almost straddled it. I fancy we feared that if the enemy got a chance he would sneak by us at arm's length and conquer all the country in our rear. Certainly there was many a prediction of disaster when we went into an earthwork a considerable distance from the road.

The stone foundations of the houses are still there, as are all the stone and earth elements of the fort. Everything wooden has disappeared. The parapet of the fort is in so good condition that an hour's work by a regiment would make it serviceable. The old cemetery on

9. Robert Seldon Garnett (1819–1861), commanding the Confederate army in western Virginia, was the first general to be killed in Civil War fighting, at Carrick's Ford, July 13, 1861. SIFAKIS.

10. Bierce received his first commendation for bravery in action for carrying the wounded corporal from the field under heavy fire. MORRIS, 28.

the hillside opposite (I think none of our regiment was buried there) shows twenty-five or thirty graves from which all the bodies have been removed. One headstone remains, propped against a rock and rudely carved: "W. Walkerson. Died Aug. 9, 1861."

For many square miles the forests on the slopes of the mountains have been thinned by the lumbermen, with their sawmills. But the old wooden covered bridge across the Cheat River looks hardly a day older, and is still elaborately decorated with the soldiers' names carven with jack-knives. I think the summit used to be a farm, with a farm house. There is now neither field nor dwelling—just a desolate area of rock and scanty grass, where nothing dwells but memories and ghosts.

At Greenbrier River Confederate earthworks are almost good as new. If they were all there at the time of the engagement the wisdom of not assaulting them cannot be doubted. The best thing to do was to call it a "reconnaissance in force," and let it go at that. I found a number of opened graves besides that of Abbott, and a few undisturbed ones which had apparently been overlooked. Back of the fortifications is the burial ground of the Confederates. It is nearly obliterated. The graves are in rows that can hardly be traced in the dense undergrowth. Persons living within a mile did not know of its existence. I made out between eighty and a hundred graves—depressions that had been mounds. Fallen into them were eight or ten rude headstones with inscriptions that I copied. It did not seem quite fair that these poor fellows should lie there under the forest leaves, their graves forgotten even by their own people, while our dead were so well housed under the big flag at Grafton, with monuments and flowers, music and Memorial days.

The last place that I visited was the old Confederate fort at the summit of Buffalo Mountain.[11] Officially, in the postoffice department, the name is "Top of Alleghany," and it *is* the top of the main ridge. Here the regiment had its hardest fight in Western Virginia, and was most gloriously thrashed. When I saw the place (with better opportunities for observation than we had then) I knew why. The works are skilfully constructed and nearly a half mile in length, with emplace-

11. On December 13, 1861, Union troops attacked the Confederate army encampment of Camp Allegheny. Union casualties were 137, Confederate 146. LONG.

ments for several batteries. They are built on a narrow ridge and are hardly more than one hundred and fifty yards wide at any point. At the rear, where our attack was made (after the garrison, having defeated our co-operating force in front, had got "good and ready" for us to "surprise" them) there was but one approach, and that was by a narrow road, through acres of slashed timber, impenetrable to a cat. The trunks of the trees are still there, all pointing away from the fort, all decaying and none of them having even their largest branches. A big head-log across the embrasure commanding the road is so rotten that one can pick it to pieces with the fingers. I fancy the Yankee bullets have all been picked out of it; I found none.

The slashed timber, which prevented us from attacking in line, saved our lives — most of them — when we attacked in column. We took cover in it and potshotted the fellows behind the parapet all day, as I recollect it, and then withdrew and began our long retreat in a frame of mind that would have done credit to an imp of Satan.

The road that penetrated the slashed timber is easily traced; I recognized the spot where Captain Madden fell, at the extreme head of the column. Lord! how close to the works it was — I had thought it farther away.

This fortification is distant from our camp at the summit of Cheat Mountain some twenty miles, with nothing intervening but valleys and low hills. In those winter days of '61 we used to watch the blue smoke of the Confederate camp with intense interest, but that was all we could see of our enemies. But from their position they could see all that we did, if they had glasses of moderate power. They could see our houses, our fort, our parade ground, all our movements; for our position was a little over on their side of the summit. Both camps guarded the old Staunton and Parkersburg turnpike, a fine and famous road in its day, but now fallen into disuse and no longer a "main traveled road." But the whole region is wild and grand, and if any one of the men who in his golden youth soldiered through its sleepy valleys and over its gracious mountains will revisit it in the hazy season when it is all aflame with the autumn foliage I promise him sentiments that he will willingly entertain and emotions that he will care to feel. Among them, I fear, will be a haunting envy of those of his comrades whose fall and burial in that enchanted land he once bewailed.

ONE KIND OF OFFICER

I

OF THE USES OF CIVILITY

"CAPTAIN RANSOME, it is not permitted to you to know *anything*. It is sufficient that you obey my order—which permit me to repeat. If you perceive any movement of troops in your front you are to open fire, and if attacked hold this position as long as you can. Do I make myself understood, sir?"

"Nothing could be plainer. Lieutenant Price,"—this to an officer of his own battery, who had ridden up in time to hear the order—"the general's meaning is clear, is it not?"

"Perfectly."

The lieutenant passed on to his post. For a moment General Cameron[12] and the commander of the battery sat in their saddles, looking at each other in silence. There was no more to say; apparently too much had already been said. Then the superior officer nodded coldly and turned his horse to ride away. The artillerist saluted slowly, gravely, and with extreme formality. One acquainted with the niceties of military etiquette would have said that by his manner he attested a sense of the rebuke that he had incurred. It is one of the important uses of civility to signify resentment.

When the general had joined his staff and escort, awaiting him at a little distance, the whole cavalcade moved off toward the right of the guns and vanished in the fog. Captain Ransome was alone, silent, motionless as an equestrian statue. The gray fog, thickening every moment, closed in about him like a visible doom.

12. Fictional character perhaps based upon or named for Robert Alexander Cameron (1828–1894), who joined the Ninth Indiana as a captain on April 23, 1861, and fought in western Virginia before being promoted quickly to colonel and general and transferred to the Army of the Gulf. SIFAKIS.

II

UNDER WHAT CIRCUMSTANCES MEN DO NOT
WISH TO BE SHOT

The fighting of the day before had been desultory and indecisive. At
the points of collision the smoke of battle had hung in blue sheets
among the branches of the trees till beaten into nothing by the falling
rain. In the softened earth the wheels of cannon and ammunition
wagons cut deep, ragged furrows, and movements of infantry seemed
impeded by the mud that clung to the soldiers' feet as, with soaken
garments and rifles imperfectly protected by capes of overcoats they
went dragging in sinuous lines hither and thither through dripping
forest and flooded field. Mounted officers, their heads protruding
from rubber ponchos that glittered like black armor, picked their way,
singly and in loose groups, among the men, coming and going with
apparent aimlessness and commanding attention from nobody but one
another. Here and there a dead man, his clothing defiled with earth,
his face covered with a blanket or showing yellow and claylike in the
rain, added his dispiriting influence to that of the other dismal features
of the scene and augmented the general discomfort with a particular
dejection. Very repulsive these wrecks looked — not at all heroic, and
nobody was accessible to the infection of their patriotic example. Dead
upon the field of honor, yes; but the field of honor was so very wet! It
makes a difference.

The general engagement that all expected did not occur, none of
the small advantages accruing, now to this side and now to that, in
isolated and accidental collisions being followed up. Half-hearted attacks provoked a sullen resistance which was satisfied with mere repulse. Orders were obeyed with mechanical fidelity; no one did any
more than his duty.

"The army is cowardly to-day," said General Cameron, the commander of a Federal brigade, to his adjutant-general.

"The army is cold," replied the officer addressed, "and — yes, it
doesn't wish to be like that."

He pointed to one of the dead bodies, lying in a thin pool of yellow
water, its face and clothing bespattered with mud from hoof and wheel.

The army's weapons seemed to share its military delinquency. The
rattle of rifles sounded flat and contemptible. It had no meaning

and scarcely roused to attention and expectancy the unengaged parts of the line-of-battle and the waiting reserves. Heard at a little distance, the reports of cannon were feeble in volume and *timbre;* they lacked sting and resonance. The guns seemed to be fired with light charges, unshotted. And so the futile day wore on to its dreary close, and then to a night of discomfort succeeded a day of apprehension.

An army has a personality. Beneath the individual thoughts and emotions of its component parts it thinks and feels as a unit. And in this large, inclusive sense of things lies a wiser wisdom than the mere sum of all that it knows. On that dismal morning this great brute force, groping at the bottom of a white ocean of fog among trees that seemed as sea weeds, had a dumb consciousness that all was not well; that a day's manœuvring had resulted in a faulty disposition of its parts, a blind diffusion of its strength. The men felt insecure and talked among themselves of such tactical errors as with their meager military vocabulary they were able to name. Field and line officers gathered in groups and spoke more learnedly of what they apprehended with no greater clearness. Commanders of brigades and divisions looked anxiously to their connections on the right and on the left, sent staff officers on errands of inquiry and pushed skirmish lines silently and cautiously forward into the dubious region between the known and the unknown. At some points on the line the troops, apparently of their own volition, constructed such defenses as they could without the silent spade and the noisy ax.

One of these points was held by Captain Ransome's battery of six guns. Provided always with intrenching tools, his men had labored with diligence during the night, and now his guns thrust their black muzzles through the embrasures of a really formidable earthwork. It crowned a slight acclivity devoid of undergrowth and providing an unobstructed fire that would sweep the ground for an unknown distance in front. The position could hardly have been better chosen. It had this peculiarity, which Captain Ransome, who was greatly addicted to the use of the compass, had not failed to observe: it faced northward, whereas he knew that the general line of the army must face eastward. In fact, that part of the line was "refused" — that is to say, bent backward, away from the enemy. This implied that Captain Ransome's battery was somewhere near the left flank of the army; for an army in line of battle retires its flanks if the nature of the ground will permit, they being its vulnerable points. Actually, Captain Ransome appeared to hold the extreme left of the line, no troops being visible in that direction beyond his own. Immediately in rear of his guns occurred that conversation between him and his brigade commander, the concluding and more picturesque part of which is reported above.

III

HOW TO PLAY THE CANNON WITHOUT NOTES

Captain Ransome sat motionless and silent on horseback. A few yards away his men were standing at their guns. Somewhere — everywhere within a few miles — were a hundred thousand men, friends and enemies. Yet he was alone. The mist had isolated him as completely as if he had been in the heart of a desert. His world was a few square yards of wet and trampled earth about the feet of his horse. His comrades in that ghostly domain were invisible and inaudible. These were conditions favorable to thought, and he was thinking. Of the nature of his thoughts his clear-cut handsome features yielded no attesting sign. His face was as inscrutable as that of the sphinx. Why should it have made a record which there was none to observe? At the sound of a footstep he merely turned his eyes in the direction whence it came; one of his sergeants, looking a giant in stature in the false perspective of the fog, approached, and when clearly defined and reduced to his true dimensions by propinquity, saluted and stood at attention.

"Well, Morris," said the officer, returning his subordinate's salute.

"Lieutenant Price directed me to tell you, sir, that most of the infantry has been withdrawn. We have not sufficient support."

"Yes, I know."

"I am to say that some of our men have been out over the works a hundred yards and report that our front is not picketed."

"Yes."

"They were so far forward that they heard the enemy."

"Yes."

"They heard the rattle of the wheels of artillery and the commands of officers."

"Yes."

"The enemy is moving toward our works."

Captain Ransome, who had been facing to the rear of his line —

toward the point where the brigade commander and his cavalcade had been swallowed up by the fog — reined his horse about and faced the other way. Then he sat motionless as before.

"Who are the men who made that statement?" he inquired, without looking at the sergeant; his eyes were directed straight into the fog over the head of his horse.

"Corporal Hassman and Gunner Manning."

Captain Ransome was a moment silent. A slight pallor came into his face, a slight compression affected the lines of his lips, but it would have required a closer observer than Sergeant Morris to note the change. There was none in the voice.

"Sergeant, present my compliments to Lieutenant Price and direct him to open fire with all the guns. Grape."

The sergeant saluted and vanished in the fog.

IV

TO INTRODUCE GENERAL MASTERSON

Searching for his division commander, General Cameron and his escort had followed the line of battle for nearly a mile to the right of Ransome's battery, and there learned that the division commander had gone in search of the corps commander. It seemed that everybody was looking for his immediate superior — an ominous circumstance. It meant that nobody was quite at ease. So General Cameron rode on for another half-mile, where by good luck he met General Masterson, the division commander, returning.

"Ah, Cameron," said the higher officer, reining up, and throwing his right leg across the pommel of his saddle in a most unmilitary way — "anything up? Found a good position for your battery, I hope — if one place is better than another in a fog."

"Yes, general," said the other, with the greater dignity appropriate to his less exalted rank, "my battery is very well placed. I wish I could say that it is as well commanded."

"Eh, what's that? Ransome? I think him a fine fellow. In the army we should be proud of him."

It was customary for officers of the regular army to speak of it as "the army." As the greatest cities are most provincial, so the self-complacency of aristocracies is most frankly plebeian.

"He is too fond of his opinion. By the way, in order to occupy the hill that he holds I had to extend my line dangerously. The hill is on my left — that is to say the left flank of the army."

"Oh, no, Hart's brigade is beyond. It was ordered up from Drytown during the night and directed to hook on to you. Better go and — "

The sentence was unfinished: a lively cannonade had broken out on the left, and both officers, followed by their retinues of aides and orderlies making a great jingle and clank, rode rapidly toward the spot. But they were soon impeded, for they were compelled by the fog to keep within sight of the line-of-battle, behind which were swarms of men, all in motion across their way. Everywhere the line was assuming a sharper and harder definition, as the men sprang to arms and the officers, with drawn swords, "dressed" the ranks. Color-bearers unfurled the flags, buglers blew the "assembly," hospital attendants appeared with stretchers. Field officers mounted and sent their impedimenta to the rear in care of negro servants. Back in the ghostly spaces of the forest could be heard the rustle and murmur of the reserves, pulling themselves together.

Nor was all this preparation vain, for scarcely five minutes had passed since Captain Ransome's guns had broken the truce of doubt before the whole region was aroar: the enemy had attacked nearly everywhere.

V

HOW SOUNDS CAN FIGHT SHADOWS

Captain Ransome walked up and down behind his guns, which were firing rapidly but with steadiness. The gunners worked alertly, but without haste or apparent excitement. There was really no reason for excitement; it is not much to point a cannon into a fog and fire it. Anybody can do as much as that.

The men smiled at their noisy work, performing it with a lessening alacrity. They cast curious regards upon their captain, who had now mounted the banquette of the fortification and was looking across the parapet as if observing the effect of his fire. But the only visible effect was the substitution of wide, low-lying sheets of smoke for their bulk of fog. Suddenly out of the obscurity burst a great sound of cheering, which filled the intervals between the reports of the guns with startling distinctness! To the few with leisure and opportunity to observe, the sound was inexpressibly strange — so loud, so near, so menacing, yet nothing seen! The men who had smiled at their work smiled no more, but performed it with a serious and feverish activity.

From his station at the parapet Captain Ransome now saw a great multitude of dim gray figures taking shape in the mist below him and swarming up the slope. But the work of the guns was now fast and furious. They swept the populous declivity with gusts of grape and canister, the whirring of which could be heard through the thunder of the explosions. In this awful tempest of iron the assailants struggled forward foot by foot across their dead, firing into the embrasures, reloading, firing again, and at last falling in their turn, a little in advance of those who had fallen before. Soon the smoke was dense enough to cover all. It settled down upon the attack and, drifting back, involved the defense. The gunners could hardly see to serve their pieces, and when occasional figures of the enemy appeared upon the parapet — having had the good luck to get near enough to it, between two embrasures, to be protected from the guns — they looked so unsubstantial that it seemed hardly worth while for the few infantrymen to go to work upon them with the bayonet and tumble them back into the ditch.

As the commander of a battery in action can find something better to do than cracking individual skulls, Captain Ransome had retired from the parapet to his proper post in rear of his guns, where he stood with folded arms, his bugler beside him. Here, during the hottest of the fight, he was approached by Lieutenant Price, who had just sabred a daring assailant inside the work. A spirited colloquy ensued between the two officers — spirited, at least, on the part of the lieutenant, who gesticulated with energy and shouted again and again into his commander's ear in the attempt to make himself heard above the infernal din of the guns. His gestures, if cooly noted by an actor, would have been pronounced to be those of protestation: one would have said that he was opposed to the proceedings. Did he wish to surrender?

Captain Ransome listened without a change of countenance or attitude, and when the other man had finished his harangue, looked him coldly in the eyes and during a seasonable abatement of the uproar said:

"Lieutenant Price, it is not permitted to you to know *anything*. It is sufficient that you obey my orders."

The lieutenant went to his post, and the parapet being now apparently clear Captain Ransome returned to it to have a look over. As he mounted the banquette a man sprang upon the crest, waving a great brilliant flag. The captain drew a pistol from his belt and shot him dead. The body, pitching forward, hung over the inner edge of the embankment, the arms straight downward, both hands still grasping the flag. The man's few followers turned and fled down the slope. Looking over the parapet, the captain saw no living thing. He observed also that no bullets were coming into the work.

He made a sign to the bugler, who sounded the command to cease firing. At all other points the action had already ended with a repulse of the Confederate attack; with the cessation of this cannonade the silence was absolute.

VI

WHY, BEING AFFRONTED BY A, IT IS NOT BEST TO AFFRONT B

General Masterson rode into the redoubt. The men, gathered in groups, were talking loudly and gesticulating. They pointed at the dead, running from one body to another. They neglected their foul and heated guns and forgot to resume their outer clothing. They ran to the parapet and looked over, some of them leaping down into the ditch. A score were gathered about a flag rigidly held by a dead man.

"Well, my men," said the general cheerily, "you have had a pretty fight of it."

They stared; nobody replied; the presence of the great man seemed to embarrass and alarm.

Getting no response to his pleasant condescension, the easy-mannered officer whistled a bar or two of a popular air, and riding forward to the parapet, looked over at the dead. In an instant he had whirled his horse about and was spurring along in rear of the guns, his eyes everywhere at once. An officer sat on the trail of one of the guns, smoking a cigar. As the general dashed up he rose and tranquilly saluted.

"Captain Ransome!" — the words fell sharp and harsh, like the clash of steel blades — "you have been fighting our own men — our own men, sir; do you hear? Hart's brigade!"

"General, I know that."

"You know it — you know that, and you sit here smoking? Oh, damn it, Hamilton, I'm losing my temper," — this to his provost-marshal. "Sir — Captain Ransome, be good enough to say — to say why you fought our own men."

"That I am unable to say. In my orders that information was withheld."

Apparently the general did not comprehend.

"Who was the aggressor in this affair, you or General Hart?" he asked.

"I was."

"And could you not have known — could you not see, sir, that you were attacking our own men?"

The reply was astounding!

"I knew that, general. It appeared to be none of my business."

Then, breaking the dead silence that followed his answer, he said:

"I must refer you to General Cameron."

"General Cameron is dead, sir — as dead as he can be — as dead as any man in this army. He lies back yonder under a tree. Do you mean to say that he had anything to do with this horrible business?"

Captain Ransome did not reply. Observing the altercation his men had gathered about to watch the outcome. They were greatly excited. The fog, which had been partly dissipated by the firing, had again closed in so darkly about them that they drew more closely together till the judge on horseback and the accused standing calmly before him had but a narrow space free from intrusion. It was the most informal of courts-martial, but all felt that the formal one to follow would but affirm its judgment. It had no jurisdiction, but it had the significance of prophecy.

"Captain Ransome," the general cried impetuously, but with something in his voice that was almost entreaty, "if you can say anything to put a better light upon your incomprehensible conduct I beg you will do so."

Having recovered his temper this generous soldier sought for something to justify his naturally sympathetic attitude toward a brave man in the imminence of a dishonorable death.

"Where is Lieutenant Price?" the captain said.

That officer stood forward, his dark saturnine face looking somewhat forbidding under a bloody handkerchief bound about his brow.

He understood the summons and needed no invitation to speak. He did not look at the captain, but addressed the general:

"During the engagement I discovered the state of affairs, and apprised the commander of the battery. I ventured to urge that the firing cease. I was insulted and ordered to my post."

"Do you know anything of the orders under which I was acting?" asked the captain.

"Of any orders under which the commander of the battery was acting," the lieutenant continued, still addressing the general, "I know nothing."

Captain Ransome felt his world sink away from his feet. In those cruel words he heard the murmur of the centuries breaking upon the shore of eternity. He heard the voice of doom; it said, in cold, mechanical, and measured tones: "Ready, aim, fire!" and he felt the bullets tear his heart to shreds. He heard the sound of the earth upon his coffin and (if the good God was so merciful) the song of a bird above his forgotten grave. Quietly detaching his sabre from its supports, he handed it up to the provost-marshal.

[1893; CWAB, II]

THE MOCKING-BIRD

The time, a pleasant Sunday afternoon in the early autumn of 1861. The place, a forest's heart in the mountain region of southwestern Virginia. Private Grayrock of the Federal Army is discovered seated comfortably at the root of a great pine tree, against which he leans, his legs extended straight along the ground, his rifle lying across his thighs, his hands (clasped in order that they may not fall away to his sides) resting upon the barrel of the weapon. The contact of the back of his head with the tree has pushed his cap downward over his eyes, almost concealing them; one seeing him would say that he slept.

Private Grayrock did not sleep; to have done so would have imperiled the interests of the United States, for he was a long way outside the lines and subject to capture or death at the hands of the enemy. Moreover, he was in a frame of mind unfavorable to repose. The cause of his perturbation of spirit was this: during the previous night he had served on the picket-guard, and had been posted as a sentinel in this very forest. The night was clear, though moonless, but in the gloom of the wood the darkness was deep. Grayrock's post was at a considerable distance from those to right and left, for the pickets had been thrown out a needless distance from the camp, making the line too long for the force detailed to occupy it. The war was young, and military camps entertained the error that while sleeping they were better protected by thin lines a long way out toward the enemy than by thicker ones close in. And surely they needed as long notice as possible of an enemy's approach, for they were at that time addicted to the practice of undressing — than which nothing could be more unsoldierly. On the morning of the memorable 6th of April, at Shiloh, many of Grant's men when spitted on Confederate bayonets were as naked as civilians; but it should be allowed that this was not because of any defect in their picket line. Their error was of another sort: they had no pickets. This is perhaps a vain digression. I should not care to undertake to interest the reader in the fate of an army; what we have here to consider is that of Private Grayrock.

For two hours after he had been left at his lonely post that Saturday night he stood stockstill, leaning against the trunk of a large tree, staring into the darkness in his front and trying to recognize known objects; for he had been posted at the same spot during the day. But all was now different; he saw nothing in detail, but only groups of things, whose shapes, not observed when there was something more of them to observe, were now unfamiliar. They seemed not to have been there before. A landscape that is all trees and undergrowth, moreover, lacks definition, is confused and without accentuated points upon which attention can gain a foothold. Add the gloom of a moonless night, and something more than great natural intelligence and a city education is required to preserve one's knowledge of direction. And that is how it occurred that Private Grayrock, after vigilantly watching the spaces in his front and then imprudently executing a circumspection of his whole dimly visible environment (silently walking around his tree to accomplish it) lost his bearings and seriously impaired his usefulness as a sentinel. Lost at his post — unable to say in which direction to look for an enemy's approach, and in which lay the sleeping camp for whose security he was accountable with his life — conscious, too, of many another awkward feature of the situation and of considerations affecting his own safety, Private Grayrock was profoundly disquieted. Nor was he given time to recover his tranquillity, for almost at the moment that he realized his awkward predicament he heard a stir of leaves and a snap of fallen twigs, and turning with a stilled heart in the direction whence it came, saw in the gloom the indistinct outlines of a human figure.

"Halt!" shouted Private Grayrock, peremptorily as in duty bound, backing up the command with the sharp metallic snap of his cocking rifle — "who goes there?"

There was no answer; at least there was an instant's hesitation, and the answer, if it came, was lost in the report of the sentinel's rifle. In the silence of the night and the forest the sound was deafening, and hardly had it died away when it was repeated by the pieces of the pickets to, right and left, a sympathetic fusillade. For two hours every unconverted civilian of them had been evolving enemies from his imagination, and peopling the woods in his front with them, and Grayrock's shot had started the whole encroaching host into visible existence. Having fired, all retreated, breathless, to the reserves — all but Grayrock, who did not know in what direction to retreat. When, no enemy appearing, the roused camp two miles away had undressed and got itself into bed again, and the picket line was cautiously re-established, he was discovered bravely holding his ground, and was complimented by the officer of the guard as the one soldier of that devoted band who could rightly be considered the moral equivalent of that uncommon unit of value, "a whoop in hell."

In the mean time, however, Grayrock had made a close but unavailing search for the mortal part of the intruder at whom he had fired, and whom he had a marksman's intuitive sense of having hit; for he was one of those born experts who shoot without aim by an instinctive sense of direction, and are nearly as dangerous by night as by day. During a full half of his twenty-four years he had been a terror to the targets of all the shooting-galleries in three cities. Unable now to produce his dead game he had the discretion to hold his tongue, and was glad to observe in his officer and comrades the natural assumption that not having run away he had seen nothing hostile. His "honorable mention" had been earned by not running away anyhow.

Nevertheless, Private Grayrock was far from satisfied with the night's adventure, and when the next day he made some fair enough pretext to apply for a pass to go outside the lines, and the general commanding promptly granted it in recognition of his bravery the night before, he passed out at the point where that had been displayed. Telling the sentinel then on duty there that he had lost something,—which was true enough—he renewed the search for the person whom he supposed himself to have shot, and whom if only wounded he hoped to trail by the blood. He was no more successful by daylight than he had been in the darkness, and after covering a wide area and boldly penetrating a long distance into "the Confederacy" he gave up the search, somewhat fatigued, seated himself at the root of the great pine tree, where we have seen him, and indulged his disappointment.

It is not to be inferred that Grayrock's was the chagrin of a cruel nature balked of its bloody deed. In the clear large eyes, finely wrought lips, and broad forehead of that young man one could read quite another story, and in point of fact his character was a singularly felicitous compound of boldness and sensibility, courage and conscience.

"I find myself disappointed," he said to himself, sitting there at the bottom of the golden haze submerging the forest like a subtler sea— "disappointed in failing to discover a fellow-man dead by my hand! Do I then really wish that I had taken life in the performance of a duty as well performed without? What more could I wish? If any danger threatened, my shot averted it; that is what I was there to do. No, I am glad indeed if no human life was needlessly extinguished by me. But I am in a false position. I have suffered myself to be complimented by my officers and envied by my comrades. The camp is ringing with praise of my courage. That is not just; I know myself courageous, but this praise is for specific acts which I did not perform, or performed — otherwise. It is believed that I remained at my post bravely, without firing, whereas it was I who began the fusillade, and I did not retreat in the general alarm because bewildered. What, then, shall I do? Explain that I saw an enemy and fired? They have all said that of themselves, yet none believes it. Shall I tell a truth which, discrediting my courage, will have the effect of a lie? Ugh! it is an ugly business altogether. I wish to God I could find my man!"

And so wishing, Private Grayrock, overcome at last by the languor of the afternoon and lulled by the stilly sounds of insects droning and prosing in certain fragrant shrubs, so far forgot the interests of the United States as to fall asleep and expose himself to capture. And sleeping he dreamed.

He thought himself a boy, living in a far, fair land by the border of a great river upon which the tall steamboats moved grandly up and down beneath their towering evolutions of black smoke, which announced them long before they had rounded the bends and marked their movements when miles out of sight. With him always, at his side as he watched them, was one to whom he gave his heart and soul in love — a twin brother. Together they strolled along the banks of the stream; together explored the fields lying farther away from it, and gathered pungent mints and sticks of fragrant sassafras in the hills overlooking all — beyond which lay the Realm of Conjecture, and from which, looking southward across the great river, they caught glimpses of the Enchanted Land. Hand in hand and heart in heart they two, the only children of a widowed mother, walked in paths of light through valleys of peace, seeing new things under a new sun. And through all the golden days floated one unceasing sound — the rich, thrilling melody of a mocking-bird in a cage by the cottage door. It pervaded and possessed all the spiritual intervals of the dream, like a musical benediction. The joyous bird was always in song; its infinitely various notes seemed to flow from its throat, effortless, in bubbles and rills at each heartbeat, like the waters of a pulsing spring. That fresh, clear melody

seemed, indeed, the spirit of the scene, the meaning and interpretation to sense of the mysteries of life and love.

But there came a time when the days of the dream grew dark with
sorrow in a rain of tears. The good mother was dead, the meadowside
home by the great river was broken up, and the brothers were parted
between two of their kinsmen. William (the dreamer) went to live in a
populous city in the Realm of Conjecture, and John, crossing the river
into the Enchanted Land, was taken to a distant region whose people in
their lives and ways were said to be strange and wicked. To him, in
the distribution of the dead mother's estate, had fallen all that they
deemed of value—the mocking-bird. They could be divided, but it
could not, so it was carried away into the strange country, and the world
of William knew it no more forever. Yet still through the aftertime of his
loneliness its song filled all the dream, and seemed always sounding in
his ear and in his heart.

The kinsmen who had adopted the boys were enemies, holding no
communication. For a time letters full of boyish bravado and boastful narratives of the new and larger experience—grotesque descrip-
tions of their widening lives and the new worlds they had conquered—
passed between them; but these gradually became less frequent, and
with William's removal to another and greater city ceased altogether.
But ever through it all ran the song of the mocking-bird, and when the
dreamer opened his eyes and stared through the vistas of the pine
forest the cessation of its music first apprised him that he was awake.

The sun was low and red in the west; the level rays projected from the
trunk of each giant pine a wall of shadow traversing the golden haze to
eastward until light and shade were blended in undistinguishable blue.

Private Grayrock rose to his feet, looked cautiously about him, shouldered his rifle and set off toward camp. He had gone perhaps a half-
mile, and was passing a thicket of laurel, when a bird rose from the
midst of it and perching on the branch of a tree above, poured from its
joyous breast so inexhaustible floods of song as but one of all God's
creatures can utter in His praise. There was little in that—it was only to
open the bill and breathe; yet the man stopped as it struck—stopped
and let fall his rifle, looked upward at the bird, covered his eyes with his
hands and wept like a child! For the moment he was, indeed, a child, in
spirit and in memory, dwelling again by the great river, over-against the
Enchanted Land! Then with an effort of the will he pulled himself

together, picked up his weapon and audibly damning himself for an idiot strode on. Passing an opening that reached into the heart of the little thicket he looked in, and there, supine upon the earth, its arms all abroad, its gray uniform stained with a single spot of blood upon the breast, its white face turned sharply upward and backward, lay the image of himself—the body of John Grayrock, dead of a gunshot wound, and still warm! He had found his man.

As the unfortunate soldier knelt beside that masterwork of civil war the shrilling bird upon the bough overhead stilled her song and, flushed with sunset's crimson glory, glided silently away through the solemn spaces of the wood. At roll-call that evening in the Federal camp the name William Grayrock brought no response, nor ever again thereafter.

[1891; CWAB, II]

A HORSEMAN IN THE SKY

I

One sunny afternoon in the autumn of the year 1861 a soldier lay in a clump of laurel by the side of a road in western Virginia. He lay at full length upon his stomach, his feet resting upon the toes, his head upon the left forearm. His extended right hand loosely grasped his rifle. But for the somewhat methodical disposition of his limbs and a slight rhythmic movement of the cartridge-box at the back of his belt he might have been thought to be dead. He was asleep at his post of duty. But if detected he would be dead shortly afterward, death being the just and legal penalty of his crime.

The clump of laurel in which the criminal lay was in the angle of a road which after ascending southward a steep acclivity to that point turned sharply to the west, running along the summit for perhaps one hundred yards. There it turned southward again and went zigzagging downward through the forest. At the salient of that second angle was a large flat rock, jutting out northward, overlooking the deep valley from which the road ascended. The rock capped a high cliff; a stone dropped from its outer edge would have fallen sheer downward one thousand feet to the tops of the pines. The angle where the soldier lay was on another spur of the same cliff. Had he been awake he would have commanded a view, not only of the short arm of the road and the jutting rock, but of the entire profile of the cliff below it. It might well have made him giddy to look.

The country was wooded everywhere except at the bottom of the valley to the northward, where there was a small natural meadow, through which flowed a stream scarcely visible from the valley's rim. This open ground looked hardly larger than an ordinary door-yard, but was really several acres in extent. Its green was more vivid than that of the inclosing forest. Away beyond it rose a line of giant cliffs similar to those upon which we are supposed to stand in our survey of the savage scene, and through which the road had somehow made its climb to the summit. The configuration of the valley, indeed, was such that from this point of observation it seemed entirely shut in, and one could but have wondered how the road which found a way out of it had found a way into it, and whence came and whither went the waters of the stream that parted the meadow more than a thousand feet below.

No country is so wild and difficult but men will make it a theatre of war; concealed in the forest at the bottom of that military rat-trap, in which half a hundred men in possession of the exits might have starved an army to submission, lay five regiments of Federal infantry. They had marched all the previous day and night and were resting. At nightfall they would take to the road again, climb to the place where their unfaithful sentinel now slept, and descending the other slope of the ridge fall upon a camp of the enemy at about midnight. Their hope was to surprise it, for the road led to the rear of it. In case of failure, their position would be perilous in the extreme; and fail they surely would should accident or vigilance apprise the enemy of the movement.

II

The sleeping sentinel in the clump of laurel was a young Virginian named Carter Druse. He was the son of wealthy parents, an only child, and had known such ease and cultivation and high living as wealth and taste were able to command in the mountain country of western Virginia. His home was but a few miles from where he now lay. One morning he had risen from the breakfast-table and said, quietly but gravely: "Father, a Union regiment has arrived at Grafton. I am going to join it."

The father lifted his leonine head, looked at the son a moment in silence, and replied: "Well, go, sir, and whatever may occur do what you conceive to be your duty. Virginia, to which you are a traitor, must get on without you. Should we both live to the end of the war, we will speak further of the matter. Your mother, as the physician has informed you, is in a most critical condition; at the best she cannot be with us longer than a few weeks, but that time is precious. It would be better not to disturb her."

So Carter Druse, bowing reverently to his father, who returned the salute with a stately courtesy that masked a breaking heart, left the home of his childhood to go soldiering. By conscience and courage, by deeds of devotion and daring, he soon commended himself to his fellows and his officers; and it was to these qualities and to some knowledge of the country that he owed his selection for his present perilous duty at the extreme outpost. Nevertheless, fatigue had been stronger than resolution and he had fallen asleep. What good or bad angel came in a dream to rouse him from his state of crime, who shall say? Without a movement, without a sound, in the profound silence and the languor of the late afternoon, some invisible messenger of fate touched with unsealing finger the eyes of his consciousness — whispered into the ear of his spirit the mysterious awakening word which no human lips ever have spoken, no human memory ever has recalled. He quietly raised his forehead from his arm and looked between the masking stems of the laurels, instinctively closing his right hand about the stock of his rifle.

His first feeling was a keen artistic delight. On a colossal pedestal, the cliff, — motionless at the extreme edge of the capping rock and sharply outlined against the sky, — was an equestrian statue of impressive dignity. The figure of the man sat the figure of the horse, straight and soldierly, but with the repose of a Grecian god carved in the marble which limits the suggestion of activity. The gray costume harmonized with its aërial background; the metal of accoutrement and caparison was softened and subdued by the shadow; the animal's skin had no points of high light. A carbine strikingly foreshortened lay across the pommel of the saddle, kept in place by the right hand grasping it at the "grip"; the left hand, holding the bridle rein, was invisible. In silhouette against the sky the profile of the horse was cut with the sharpness of a cameo; it looked across the heights of air to the confronting cliffs beyond. The face of the rider, turned slightly away, showed only an outline of temple and beard; he was looking downward to the bottom of the valley. Magnified by its lift against the sky and by the soldier's testifying sense of the formidableness of a near enemy the group appeared of heroic, almost colossal, size.

For an instant Druse had a strange, half-defined feeling that he had slept to the end of the war and was looking upon a noble work of art reared upon that eminence to commemorate the deeds of an heroic past of which he had been an inglorious part. The feeling was dispelled by a slight movement of the group: the horse, without moving its feet, had drawn its body slightly backward from the verge; the man remained immobile as before. Broad awake and keenly alive to the significance of the situation, Druse now brought the butt of his rifle against his cheek by cautiously pushing the barrel forward through the bushes, cocked the piece, and glancing through the sights covered a vital spot of the horseman's breast. A touch upon the trigger and all would have been well with Carter Druse. At that instant the horseman turned his head and looked in the direction of his concealed foeman seemed to look into his very face, into his eyes, into his brave, compassionate heart.

Is it then so terrible to kill an enemy in war — an enemy who has surprised a secret vital to the safety of one's self and comrades — an enemy more formidable for his knowledge than all his army for its numbers? Carter Druse grew pale; he shook in every limb, turned faint, and saw the statuesque group before him as black figures, rising, falling, moving unsteadily in arcs of circles in a fiery sky. His hand fell away from his weapon, his head slowly dropped until his face rested on the leaves in which he lay. This courageous gentleman and hardy soldier was near swooning from intensity of emotion.

It was not for long; in another moment his face was raised from earth, his hands resumed their places on the rifle, his forefinger sought the trigger; mind, heart, and eyes were clear, conscience and reason sound. He could not hope to capture that enemy; to alarm him would but send him dashing to his camp with his fatal news. The duty of the soldier was plain: the man must be shot dead from ambush — without warning, without a moment's spiritual preparation, with never so much as an unspoken prayer, he must be sent to his account. But no — there is a hope; he may have discovered nothing — perhaps he is but admiring the sublimity of the landscape. If permitted, he may turn and ride carelessly away in the direction whence he came. Surely it will be possible to judge at the instant of his withdrawing whether he knows. It may well be that his fixity of attention — Druse turned his head and looked through the deeps of air downward, as from the surface to the bottom of a translucent sea. He saw creeping across the green meadow a sinuous line of figures of men and horses — some foolish commander was permitting the soldiers of his escort to water their beasts in the open, in plain view from a dozen summits!

Druse withdrew his eyes from the valley and fixed them again upon the group of man and horse in the sky, and again it was through the sights of his rifle. But this time his aim was at the horse. In his memory, as if they were a divine mandate, rang the words of his father at their parting: "Whatever may occur, do what you conceive to be your duty." He was calm now. His teeth were firmly but not rigidly closed; his nerves were as tranquil as a sleeping babe's — not a tremor affected any muscle of his body; his breathing, until suspended in the act of taking aim, was regular and slow. Duty had conquered; the spirit had said to the body: "Peace, be still." He fired.

III

An officer of the Federal force, who in a spirit of adventure or in quest of knowledge had left the hidden *bivouac* in the valley, and with aimless feet had made his way to the lower edge of a small open space near the foot of the cliff, was considering what he had to gain by pushing his exploration further. At a distance of a quarter-mile before him, but apparently at a stone's throw, rose from its fringe of pines the gigantic face of rock, towering to so great a height above him that it made him giddy to look up to where its edge cut a sharp, rugged line against the sky. It presented a clean, vertical profile against a background of blue sky to a point half the way down, and of distant hills, hardly less blue, thence to the tops of the trees at its base. Lifting his eyes to the dizzy altitude of its summit the officer saw an astonishing sight — a man on horseback riding down into the valley through the air!

Straight upright sat the rider, in military fashion, with a firm seat in the saddle, a strong clutch upon the rein to hold his charger from too impetuous a plunge. From his bare head his long hair streamed upward, waving like a plume. His hands were concealed in the cloud of the horse's lifted mane. The animal's body was as level as if every hoof encountered the resistant earth. Its motions were those of a wild gallop, but even as the officer looked they ceased, with all the legs thrown sharply forward as in the act of alighting from a leap. But this was a flight!

Filled with amazement and terror by this apparition of a horseman in the sky — half believing himself the chosen scribe of some new Apocalypse, the officer was overcome by the intensity of his emotions; his legs failed him and he fell. Almost at the same instant he heard a crashing sound in the trees — a sound that died without an echo — and all was still.

The officer rose to his feet, trembling. The familiar sensation of an abraded shin recalled his dazed faculties. Pulling himself together he ran rapidly obliquely away from the cliff to a point distant from its foot;

thereabout he expected to find his man; and thereabout he naturally failed. In the fleeting instant of his vision his imagination had been so wrought upon by the apparent grace and ease and intention of the marvelous performance that it did not occur to him that the line of march of aërial cavalry is directly downward, and that he could find the objects of his search at the very foot of the cliff. A half-hour later he returned to camp.

This officer was a wise man; he knew better than to tell an incredible truth. He said nothing of what he had seen. But when the commander asked him if in his scout he had learned anything of advantage to the expedition he answered:

"Yes, sir; there is no road leading down into this valley from the southward."

The commander, knowing better, smiled.

IV

After firing his shot, Private Carter Druse reloaded his rifle and resumed his watch. Ten minutes had hardly passed when a Federal sergeant crept cautiously to him on hands and knees. Druse neither turned his head nor looked at him, but lay without motion or sign of recognition.

"Did you fire?" the sergeant whispered.

"Yes."

"At what?"

"A horse. It was standing on yonder rock — pretty far out. You see it is no longer there. It went over the cliff."

The man's face was white, but he showed no other sign of emotion. Having answered, he turned away his eyes and said no more. The sergeant did not understand.

"See here, Druse," he said, after a moment's silence, "it's no use making a mystery. I order you to report. Was there anybody on the horse?"

"Yes."

"Well?"

"My father."

The sergeant rose to his feet and walked away. "Good God!" he said.

[1892; SOLE]

DEFENDING REALISM I[13]

Having in the beginning of this screed made certain strolling comments on the Author as I know him, I am minded fairwise to say something of the Critic; for the two go together, like hare and hound, author
a little ahead. The immemorial quarrel between them is comparable to
nothing but the permanent misunderstanding between the driver of a
stage-coach and the off wheeler. The driver has really nothing against
that animal; its only sin is accessibility to the lash. And the driver is
himself not at all bad; he is severely addicted to the whip-habit, and
the awful imprecations accompanying his blows are produced by some
kind of reflex action, without his connivance. The book reviewer, too, is
commonly a very good fellow and would not willingly hurt a fly; and if
he pile his immediate circumference with tumuli of dead the fault is
attributable rather to opportunity than to a bad heart. Who is proof
against opportunity? — it tempts us and we fall as fall the early pious in
the bud and promise of their bloom. But as there are honest publishers, there are wicked critics — critics whose hearts are nests of naughti-
nesses, and who but open their minds to let out and in the evil beasts
infesting them. Such a one I know, and I have it in purpose to expose
the wretch to public reprobation and deprive him even of his own
esteem as an undetected rogue.

The fellow reviews books in the New York *Sun*.[14] That journal is said
to be regarded as "high authority" in matters literary, mainly because
of this chap's works. I'm told that his name is Hazeltine, but of that I'm
not sure. A few months ago I had the hardihood to utter upon an
unoffending world a book of tales, which the critics generally received
with surprising favor. But this *Sun*-dog! — he got hold of it (it was not
sent him) and chewed it into small wads. As he was not invited to the

13. "Concerning Wit and Humor," *San Francisco Examiner*, June 26, 1892.
SOLE, 251–52.

14. One of William Randolph Hearst's main rivals for the eastern market, the
Sun called Bierce "a scoffer and a scorner [who] writes his tales of horror with a
sort of fiendish delight." Quoted from MORRIS, 219.

feast I won't have things left in that condition without exerting the flexors and extensors of my red right leg — no, indeed. He says:

The opening tale, 'A Horseman' in the sky is the worst in the book so far as illusion is concerned. We will venture to say that no such erroneous impression could have been produced in the Federal army, or in any portion of it, as the author here alleges. We are certain that the horseman in the sky was never mistaken for a repetition of the Apocalyptical vision, but was only regarded as a Confederate General and his horse descending a precipice in obedience to the laws of gravitation, as the facts warranted.

Now, the author alleged nothing of the kind — yes, something of the kind, but mark the difference in degree. The only "Federal army" or "portion of it" that saw the horseman in the sky was a single man, who saw him for one instant and for that instant half believed it an Apocalyptic vision. The exact words of the yarn are:

Filled with amazement and terror by this apparition of a horseman in the sky — half-believing himself the chosen scribe of some new Apocalypse, the officer was overcome by the intensity of his emotions.

A moment afterward he was searching for the "vision's" body, among the trees. If the critic's comments on that insignificant passage do not rise to the dignity of virtual lying of a pretty lofty sort there are no pigs.

[1891; CWAB, III]

A TOUGH TUSSLE

One night in the autumn of 1861 a man sat alone in the heart of a forest in western Virginia. The region was one of the wildest on the continent — the Cheat Mountain country. There was no lack of people close at hand, however; within a mile of where the man sat was the now silent camp of a whole Federal brigade. Somewhere about — it might be still nearer — was a force of the enemy, the numbers unknown. It was this uncertainty as to its numbers and position that accounted for the man's presence in that lonely spot; he was a young officer of a Federal infantry regiment and his business there was to guard his sleeping comrades in the camp against a surprise. He was in command of a detachment of men constituting a picket-guard. These men he had stationed just at nightfall in an irregular line, determined by the nature of the ground, several hundred yards in front of where he now sat. The line ran through the forest, among the rocks and laurel thickets, the men fifteen or twenty paces apart, all in concealment and under injunction of strict silence and unremitting vigilance. In four hours, if nothing occurred, they would be relieved by a fresh detachment from the reserve now resting in care of its captain some distance away to the left and rear. Before stationing his men the young officer of whom we are writing had pointed out to his two sergeants the spot at which he would be found if it should be necessary to consult him, or if his presence at the front line should be required.

It was a quiet enough spot — the fork of an old wood-road, on the two branches of which, prolonging themselves deviously forward in the dim moonlight, the sergeants were themselves stationed, a few paces in rear of the line. If driven sharply back by a sudden onset of the enemy — and pickets are not expected to make a stand after firing — the men would come into the converging roads and naturally following them to their point of intersection could be rallied and "formed." In his small way the author of these dispositions was something of a strategist; if Napoleon had planned as intelligently at Waterloo[15] he would have won that memorable battle and been overthrown later.

15. A Prussian-English alliance defeated Napoleon at Waterloo, Belgium, on June 18–22, 1815.

Second-Lieutenant Brainerd Byring was a brave and efficient officer, young and comparatively inexperienced as he was in the business of killing his fellow-men, He had enlisted in the very first days of the war as a private, with no military knowledge whatever, had been made first-sergeant of his company on account of his education and engaging manner, and had been lucky enough to lose his captain by a Confederate bullet; in the resulting promotions he had gained a commission. He had been in several engagements, such as they were — at Philippi, Rich Mountain, Carrick's Ford and Greenbrier — and had borne himself with such gallantry as not to attract the attention of his superior officers. The exhilaration of battle was agreeable to him, but the sight of the dead, with their clay faces, blank eyes and stiff bodies, which when not unnaturally shrunken were unnaturally swollen, had always intolerably affected him. He felt toward them a kind of reasonless antipathy that was something more than the physical and spiritual repugnance common to us all. Doubtless this feeling was due to his unusually acute sensibilities — his keen sense of the beautiful, which these hideous things outraged. Whatever may have been the cause, he could not look upon a dead body without a loathing which had in it an element of resentment. What others have respected as the dignity of death had to him no existence — was altogether unthinkable. Death was a thing to be hated. It was not picturesque, it had no tender and solemn side — a dismal thing, hideous in all its manifestations and suggestions. Lieutenant Byring was a braver man than anybody knew, for nobody knew his horror of that which he was ever ready to incur.

Having posted his men, instructed his sergeants and retired to his station, he seated himself on a log, and with senses all alert began his vigil. For greater ease he loosened his sword-belt and taking his heavy revolver from his holster laid it on the log beside him. He felt very comfortable, though he hardly gave the fact a thought, so intently did he listen for any sound from the front which might have a menacing significance — a shout, a shot, or the footfall of one of his sergeants coming to apprise him of something worth knowing. From the vast, invisible ocean of moonlight overhead fell, here and there, a slender, broken stream that seemed to plash against the intercepting branches and trickle to earth, forming small white pools among the clumps of laurel. But these leaks were few and served only to accentuate the blackness of his environment, which his imagination found it easy to people with all manner of unfamiliar shapes, menacing, uncanny, or merely grotesque.

He to whom the portentous conspiracy of night and solitude and silence in the heart of a great forest is not an unknown experience needs not to be told what another world it all is — how even the most commonplace and familiar objects take on another character. The trees group themselves differently; they draw closer together, as if in fear. The very silence has another quality than the silence of the day. And it is full of half-heard whispers — whispers that startle — ghosts of sounds long dead. There are living sounds, too, such as are never heard under other conditions: notes of strange night-birds, the cries of small animals in sudden encounters with stealthy foes or in their dreams, a rustling in the dead leaves — it may be the leap of a wood-rat, it may be the footfall of a panther. What caused the breaking of that twig? — what the low, alarmed twittering in that bushful of birds? There are sounds without a name, forms without substance, translations in space of objects which have not been seen to move, movements wherein nothing is observed to change its place. Ah, children of the sunlight and the gaslight, how little you know of the world in which you live!

Surrounded at a little distance by armed and watchful friends, Byring felt utterly alone. Yielding himself to the solemn and mysterious spirit of the time and place, he had forgotten the nature of his connection with the visible and audible aspects and phases of the night. The forest was boundless; men and the habitations of men did not exist. The universe was one primeval mystery of darkness, without form and void, himself the sole, dumb questioner of its eternal secret. Absorbed in thoughts born of this mood, he suffered the time to slip away unnoted. Meantime the infrequent patches of white light lying amongst the tree-trunks had undergone changes of size, form and place. In one of them near by, just at the roadside, his eye fell upon an object that he had not previously observed. It was almost before his face as he sat; he could have sworn that it had not before been there. It was partly covered in shadow, but he could see that it was a human figure. Instinctively he adjusted the clasp of his sword-belt and laid hold of his pistol — again he was in a world of war, by occupation an assassin.

The figure did not move. Rising, pistol in hand, he approached. The figure lay upon its back, its upper part in shadow, but standing above it and looking down upon the face, he saw that it was a dead body. He shuddered and turned from it with a feeling of sickness and disgust, resumed his seat upon the log, and forgetting military prudence struck a match and lit a cigar. In the sudden blackness that followed the extinction of the flame he felt a sense of relief; he could no longer see the object of his aversion. Nevertheless, he kept his eyes set in that direction until it appeared again with growing distinctness. It seemed to have moved a trifle nearer.

"Damn the thing!" he muttered. "What does it want?"

It did not appear to be in need of anything but a soul.

Byring turned away his eyes and began humming a tune, but he broke off in the middle of a bar and looked at the dead body. Its presence annoyed him, though he could hardly have had a quieter neighbor. He was conscious, too, of a vague, indefinable feeling that was new to him. It was not fear, but rather a sense of the supernatural — in which he did not at all believe.

"I have inherited it," he said to himself. "I suppose it will require a thousand ages — perhaps ten thousand — for humanity to outgrow this feeling. Where and when did it originate? Away back, probably, in what is called the cradle of the human race — the plains of Central Asia. What we inherit as a superstition our barbarous ancestors must have held as a reasonable conviction. Doubtless they believed themselves justified by facts whose nature we cannot even conjecture in thinking a dead body a malign thing endowed with some strange power of mischief, with perhaps a will and a purpose to exert it. Possibly they had some awful form of religion of which that was one of the chief doctrines, sedulously taught by their priesthood, as ours teach the immortality of the soul. As the Aryans moved slowly on, to and through the Caucasus passes, and spread over Europe, new conditions of life must have resulted in the formulation of new religions.[16] The old belief in the malevolence of the dead body was lost from the creeds and even perished from tradition, but it left its heritage of terror, which is trans-

16. For exposition of the thesis that the Anglo-Saxon race migrated from India westward into Germany, Scandinavia, England, and America, and that the white race always follows the sun westward with empire, see Reginald Horsman, *Race and Manifest Destiny: The Origins of American Racial Anglo-Saxonism* (Cambridge, Mass.: Harvard University Press, 1981).

mitted from generation to generation — is as much a part of us as are
our blood and bones."

In following out his thought he had forgotten that which suggested
it; but now his eye fell again upon the corpse. The shadow had now
altogether uncovered it. He saw the sharp profile, the chin in the air,
the whole face, ghastly white in the moonlight. The clothing was gray,
the uniform of a Confederate soldier. The coat and waistcoat, unbut-
toned, had fallen away on each side, exposing the white shirt. The chest
seemed unnaturally prominent, but the abdomen had sunk in, leaving
a sharp projection at the line of the lower ribs. The arms were extended, the left knee was thrust upward. The whole posture impressed
Byring as having been studied with a view to the horrible.

"Bah!" he exclaimed; "he was an actor — he knows how to be dead."

He drew away his eyes, directing them resolutely along one of the
roads leading to the front, and resumed his philosophizing where he
had left off.

"It may be that our Central Asian ancestors had not the custom of
burial. In that case it is easy to understand their fear of the dead, who
really were a menace and an evil. They bred pestilences. Children were
taught to avoid the places where they lay, and to run away if by inadver-
tence they came near a corpse. I think, indeed, I'd better go away from
this chap."

He half rose to do so, then remembered that he had told his men in
front and the officer in the rear who was to relieve him that he could at
any time be found at that spot. It was a matter of pride, too. If he
abandoned his post he feared they would think he feared the corpse.
He was no coward and he was unwilling to incur anybody's ridicule. So
he again seated himself, and to prove his courage looked boldly at the
body. The right arm — the one farthest from him — was now in shadow.
He could barely see the hand which, he had before observed, lay at the
root of a clump of laurel. There had been no change, a fact which gave
him a certain comfort, he could not have said why. He did not at once
remove his eyes; that which we do not wish to see has a strange fascination, sometimes irresistible. Of the woman who covers her eyes with her
hands and looks between the fingers let it be said that the wits have
dealt with her not altogether justly.

Byring suddenly became conscious of a pain in his right hand. He
withdrew his eyes from his enemy and looked at it. He was grasping the

hilt of his drawn sword so tightly that it hurt him. He observed, too, that he was leaning forward in a strained attitude — crouching like a gladiator ready to spring at the throat of an antagonist. His teeth were clenched and he was breathing hard. This matter was soon set right, and as his muscles relaxed and he drew a long breath he felt keenly enough the ludicrousness of the incident. It affected him to laughter. Heavens! what sound was that? what mindless devil was uttering an unholy glee in mockery of human merriment? He sprang to his feet and looked about him, not recognizing his own laugh.

He could no longer conceal from himself the horrible fact of his cowardice; he was thoroughly frightened! He would have run from the spot, but his legs refused their office; they gave way beneath him and he sat again upon the log, violently trembling. His face was wet, his whole body bathed in a chill perspiration. He could not even cry out. Distinctly he heard behind him a stealthy tread, as of some wild animal, and dared not look over his shoulder. Had the soulless living joined forces with the soulless dead? — was it an animal? Ah, if he could but be assured of that! But by no effort of will could he now unfix his gaze from the face of the dead man.

I repeat that Lieutenant Byring was a brave and intelligent man. But what would you have? Shall a man cope, single-handed, with so monstrous an alliance as that of night and solitude and silence and the dead, — while an incalculable host of his own ancestors shriek into the ear of his spirit their coward counsel, sing their doleful death-songs in his heart, and disarm his very blood of all its iron? The odds are too great — courage was not made for so rough use as that.

One sole conviction now had the man in possession: that the body had moved. It lay nearer to the edge of its plot of light — there could be no doubt of it. It had also moved its arms, for, look, they are both in the shadow! A breath of cold air struck Byring full in the face; the boughs of trees above him stirred and moaned. A strongly defined shadow passed across the face of the dead, left it luminous, passed back upon it and left it half obscured. The horrible thing was visibly moving! At that moment a single shot rang out upon the picket-line — a lonelier and louder, though more distant, shot than ever had been heard by mortal ear! It broke the spell of that enchanted man, it slew the silence and the solitude, dispersed the hindering host from Central Asia and released his modern manhood. With a cry like that of some great bird pouncing upon its prey he sprang forward, hot-hearted for action!

Shot after shot now came from the front. There were shoutings and confusion, hoof-beats and desultory cheers. Away to the rear, in the sleeping camp, were a singing of bugles and grumble of drums. Pushing through the thickets on either side the roads came the Federal pickets, in full retreat, firing backward at random as they ran. A straggling group that had followed back one of the roads, as instructed, suddenly sprang away into the bushes as half a hundred horsemen thundered by them, striking wildly with their sabres as they passed. At headlong speed these mounted madmen shot past the spot where Byring had sat, and vanished round an angle of the road, shouting and firing their pistols. A moment later there was a roar of musketry, followed by dropping shots — they had encountered the reserve-guard in line; and back they came in dire confusion, with here and there an empty saddle and many a maddened horse, bullet-stung, snorting and plunging with pain. It was all over — "an affair of out-posts."

The line was reestablished with fresh men, the roll called, the stragglers were re-formed. The Federal commander with a part of his staff, imperfectly clad, appeared upon the scene, asked a few questions, looked exceedingly wise and retired. After standing at arms for an hour the brigade in camp "swore a prayer or two" and went to bed.

Early the next morning a fatigue-party, commanded by a captain and accompanied by a surgeon, searched the ground for dead and wounded. At the fork of the road, a little to one side, they found two bodies lying close together — that of a Federal officer and that of a Confederate private. The officer had died of a sword-thrust through the heart, but not, apparently, until he had inflicted upon his enemy no fewer than five dreadful wounds. The dead officer lay on his face in a pool of blood, the weapon still in his breast. They turned him on his back and the surgeon removed it.

"Gad!" said the captain — "It is Byring!" — adding, with a glance at the other, "They had a tough tussle."

The surgeon was examining the sword. It was that of a line officer of Federal infantry — exactly like the one worn by the captain. It was, in fact, Byring's own. The only other weapon discovered was an undischarged revolver in the dead officer's belt.

The surgeon laid down the sword and approached the other body. It was frightfully gashed and stabbed, but there was no blood. He took hold of the left foot and tried to straighten the leg. In the effort the body was displaced. The dead do not wish to be moved — it protested with a faint, sickening odor. Where it had lain were a few maggots, manifesting an imbecile activity.

The surgeon looked at the captain. The captain looked at the surgeon.

[1909; CWAB, I]

ON A MOUNTAIN

They say that the lumberman has looked upon the Cheat Mountain country and seen that it is good, and I hear that some wealthy gentlemen have been there and made a game preserve. There must be lumber and, I suppose, sport, but some things one could wish were ordered otherwise. Looking back upon it through the haze of near half a century, I see that region as a veritable realm of enchantment; the Alleghanies as the Delectable Mountains. I note again their dim, blue billows, ridge after ridge interminable, beyond purple valleys full of sleep, "in which it seemed always afternoon." Miles and miles away, where the lift of earth meets the stoop of sky, I discern an imperfection in the tint, a faint graying of the blue above the main range — the smoke of an enemy's camp.

It was in the autumn of that "most immemorial year," the 1861st of our Lord, and of our Heroic Age the first, that a small brigade of raw troops — troops were all raw in those days — had been pushed in across the Ohio border and after various vicissitudes of fortune and mismanagement found itself, greatly to its own surprise, at Cheat Mountain Pass, holding a road that ran from Nowhere to the southeast. Some of us had served through the summer in the "three-months' regiments," which responded to the President's first call for troops.[17] We were regarded by the others with profound respect as "old soldiers." (Our ages, if equalized, would, I fancy, have given about twenty years to each man.) We gave ourselves, this aristocracy of service, no end of military airs; some of us even going to the extreme of keeping our jackets buttoned and our hair combed. We had been in action, too; had shot off a Confederate leg at Philippi, "the first battle of the war," and had lost as many as a dozen men at Laurel Hill and Carrick's Ford, whither the enemy had fled in trying, Heaven knows why, to get away from us. We now "brought to the task" of subduing the Rebellion a patriotism which never for a moment doubted that a rebel was a fiend accursed of

17. On April 15, 1861, Lincoln called for 100,000 men to put down the rebellion and save the capital.

God and the angels — one for whose extirpation by force and arms each youth of us considered himself specially "raised up."

It was a strange country. Nine in ten of us had never seen a mountain, nor a hill as high as a church spire, until we had crossed the Ohio River. In power upon the emotions nothing, I think, is comparable to a first sight of mountains. To a member of a plains-tribe, born and reared on the flats of Ohio or Indiana, a mountain region was a perpetual miracle. Space seemed to have taken on a new dimension; areas to have not only length and breadth, but thickness.

Modern literature is full of evidence that our great grandfathers looked upon mountains with aversion and horror. The poets of even the seventeenth century never tire of damning them in good, set terms. If they had had the unhappiness to read the opening lines of "The Pleasures of Hope," they would assuredly have thought Master Campbell[18] had gone funny and should be shut up lest he do himself an injury.

The flatlanders who invaded the Cheat Mountain country had been suckled in another creed, and to them western Virginia — there was, as yet, no West Virginia — was an enchanted land. How we reveled in its savage beauties! With what pure delight we inhaled its fragrances of spruce and pine! How we stared with something like awe at its clumps of laurel! — real laurel, as we understood the matter, whose foliage had been once accounted excellent for the heads of illustrious Romans and such — mayhap to reduce the swelling. We carved its roots into finger-rings and pipes. We gathered spruce-gum and sent it to our sweethearts in letters. We ascended every hill within our picket-lines and called it a "peak."

And, by the way, during those halcyon days (the halcyon was there, too, chattering above every creek, as he is all over the world) we fought another battle. It has not got into history, but it had a real objective existence, although by a felicitous afterthought called by us who were defeated a "reconnaissance in force." Its short and simple annals are that we marched a long way and lay down before a fortified camp of the enemy at the farther edge of a valley. Our commander had the forethought to see that we lay well out of range of the small-arms of the

18. Scottish poet Thomas Campbell (1777–1844) wrote "The Pleasures of Hope" (1799).

period. A disadvantage of this arrangement was that the enemy was out of reach of us as well, for our rifles were no better than his. Unfortunatcly—one might almost say unfairly—he had a few pieces of artillery very well protected, and with those he mauled us to the eminent satisfaction of his mind and heart. So we parted from him in anger and returned to our own place, leaving our dead—not many.

Among them was a chap belonging to my company, namcd Abbott; it is not odd that I recollect it, for there was something unusual in the manner of Abbott's taking off. He was lying flat upon his stomach and was killed by being struck in the side by a nearly spent cannon-shot that came rolling in among us. The shot remained in him until removed. It was a solid round-shot, evidently cast in some private foundry, whose proprietor, setting the laws of thrift above those of ballistics, had put his "imprint" upon it: it bore, in slightly sunken letters, the name "Abbott." That is what I was told—I was not present.

It was after this, when the nights had acquired a trick of biting and the morning sun appeared to shiver with cold, that we moved up to the summit of Cheat Mountain to guard the pass through which nobody wanted to go. Here we slew the forest and built us giant habitations (astride the road from Nowhere to the southeast) commodious to lodge an army and fitly loopholed for discomfiture of the adversary. The long logs that it was our pride to cut and carry! The accuracy with which we laid them one upon another, hewn to the line and bullet-proof. The Cyclopean doors that we hung, with sliding bolts fit to be "the mast of some great ammiral!" And when we had "made the pile complctc" some marplot of the Regular Army came that way and chatted a few moments with our commander, and we madc an earthwork away off on one side of the road (leaving the other side to take care of itself) and camped outside it in tents! But the Regular Army fellow had not the heart to suggest the demolition of our Towers of Babel, and the foundations remain to this day to attest the genius of the American volunteer soldiery.

We were the original game-preservers of the Cheat Mountain region, for although we hunted in season and out of season over as wide an area as we dared to cover we took less game, probably, than would have been taken by a certain single hunter of disloyal views whom we scared away. There were bear galore and deer in quantity, and many a winter day, in snow up to his knees, did the writer of this pass in tracking bruin to his den, where, I am bound to say, I commonly left him. I agreed with my lamented friend, the late Robert Weeks, poet:

> Pursuit may be, it seems to me,
> Perfect without possession.[19]

There can be no doubt that the wealthy sportsmen who have made a preserve of the Cheat Mountain region will find plenty of game if it has not died since 1861. We left it there.

Yet hunting and idling were not the whole of life's programme up there on that wild ridge with its shaggy pelt of spruce and firs, and in the riparian lowlands that it parted. We had a bit of war now and again. There was an occasional "affair of outposts"; sometimes a hazardous scout into the enemy's country, ordered, I fear, more to keep up the appearance of doing something than with a hope of accomplishing a military result. But one day it was bruited about that a movement in force was to be made on the enemy's position miles away, at the summit of the main ridge of the Alleghanies — the camp whose faint blue smoke we had watched for weary days. The movement was made, as was the fashion in those 'prentice days of warfare, in two columns, which were to pounce upon the foeman from opposite sides at the same moment. Led over unknown roads by untrusty guides, encountering obstacles not foreseen — miles apart and without communication, the two columns invariably failed to execute the movement with requisite secrecy and precision. The enemy, in enjoyment of that inestimable military advantage known in civilian speech as being "surrounded," always beat the attacking columns one at a time or, turning red-handed from the wreck of the first, frightened the other away.

All one bright wintry day we marched down from our eyrie; all one bright wintry night we climbed the great wooded ridge opposite. How romantic it all was; the sunset valleys full of visible sleep; the glades suffused and interpenetrated with moonlight; the long valley of the Greenbrier stretching away to we knew not what silent cities; the river itself unseen under its "astral body" of mist! Then there was the "spice of danger."

Once we heard shots in front; then there was a long wait. As we

19. Robert Kelley Weeks (1840–1876).

trudged on we passed something — some things — lying by the wayside. During another wait we examined them, curiously lifting the blankets from their yellow-clay faces. How repulsive they looked with their blood-smears, their blank, staring eyes, their teeth uncovered by contraction of the lips! The frost had begun already to whiten their deranged clothing. We were as patriotic as ever, but we did not wish to be that way. For an hour afterward the injunction of silence in the ranks was needless.

. . . . .

Repassing the spot the next day, a beaten, dispirited and exhausted force, feeble from fatigue and savage from defeat, some of us had life enough left, such as it was, to observe that these bodies had altered their position. They appeared also to have thrown off some of their clothing, which lay near by, in disorder. Their expression, too, had an added blankness — they had no faces.

As soon as the head of our straggling column had reached the spot a desultory firing had begun. One might have thought the living paid honors to the dead. No; the firing was a military execution; the condemned, a herd of galloping swine. They had eaten our fallen, but — touching magnanimity! — we did not eat theirs.

The shooting of several kinds was very good in the Cheat Mountain country, even in 1861.

[1893; CWAB, VIII]

JUPITER DOKE, BRIGADIER-GENERAL

From the Secretary of War to the Hon. Jupiter Doke, Hardpan Crossroads, Posey County, Illinois.

Washington, November 3, 1861.

Having faith in your patriotism and ability, the President has been pleased to appoint you a brigadier-general of volunteers. Do you accept?

From the Hon. Jupiter Doke to the Secretary of War.

Hardpan, Illinois, November 9, 1861.

It is the proudest moment of my life. The office is one which should be neither sought nor declined. In times that try men's souls the patriot knows no North, no South, no East, no West. His motto should be: "My country, my whole country and nothing but my country." I accept the great trust confided in me by a free and intelligent people, and with a firm reliance on the principles of constitutional liberty, and invoking the guidance of an all-wise Providence, Ruler of Nations, shall labor so to discharge it as to leave no blot upon my political escutcheon. Say to his Excellency, the successor of the immortal Washington in the Seat of Power, that the patronage of my office will be bestowed with an eye single to securing the greatest good to the greatest number, the stability of republican institutions and the triumph of the party in all elections; and to this I pledge my life, my fortune and my sacred honor. I shall at once prepare an appropriate response to the speech of the chairman of the committee deputed to inform me of my appointment, and I trust the sentiments therein expressed will strike a sympathetic chord in the public heart, as well as command the Executive approval.

From the Secretary of War to Major-General Blount Wardorg, Commanding the Military Department of Eastern Kentucky.

Washington, November 14, 1861.

I have assigned to your department Brigadier-General Jupiter Doke, who will soon proceed to Distilleryville, on the Little Buttermilk River, and take command of the Illinois Brigade at that point, reporting to you by letter for orders. Is the route from Covington by way of Bluegrass, Opossum Corners and Horsecave still infested with bushwackers, as reported in your last dispatch? I have a plan for cleaning them out.

From Major-General Blount Wardorg to the Secretary of War.
Louisville, Kentucky,
November 20, 1861.

The name and services of Brigadier-General Doke are unfamiliar to me, but I shall be pleased to have the advantage of his skill. The route from Covington to Distilleryville *via* Opossum Comers and Horsecave I have been compelled to abandon to the enemy, whose guerilla warfare made it impossible to keep it open without detaching too many troops from the front. The brigade at Distilleryville is supplied by steamboats up the Little Buttermilk.

From the Secretary of War to Brigadier-General Jupiter Doke,
Hardpan, Illinois.
Washington, November 26, 1861.

I deeply regret that your commission had been forwarded by mail before the receipt of your letter of acceptance; so we must dispense with the formality of official notification to you by a committee. The President is highly gratified by the noble and patriotic sentiments of your letter, and directs that you proceed at once to your command at Distilleryville, Kentucky, and there report by letter to Major-General Wardorg at Louisville, for orders. It is important that the strictest secrecy be observed regarding your movements until you have passed Covington, as it is desired to hold the enemy in front of Distilleryville until you are within three days of him. Then if your approach is known it will operate as a demonstration against his right and cause him to strengthen it with his left now at Memphis, Tennessee, which it is desirable to capture first. Go by way of Bluegrass, Opossum Corners and Horsecave. All officers are expected to be in full uniform when *en route* to the front.

From Brigadier-General Jupiter Doke to the Secretary of War.
Covington, Kentucky, December 7, 1861.

I arrived yesterday at this point, and have given my proxy to Joel Briller, Esq., my wife's cousin, and a staunch Republican, who will worthily represent Posey County in field and forum. He points with pride to a stainless record in the halls of legislation, which have often echoed to his soul-stirring eloquence on questions which lie at the very foundation of popular government. He has been called the Patrick Henry of Hardpan, where he has done yeoman's service in the cause of civil and religious liberty. Mr. Briller left for Distilleryville last evening, and the standard bearer of the Democratic host confronting that stronghold of freedom will find him a lion in his path. I have been asked to remain here and deliver some addresses to the people in a local contest involving issues of paramount importance. That duty being performed, I shall in person enter the arena of armed debate and move in the direction of the heaviest firing, burning my ships behind me. I forward by this mail to his Excellency the President a request for the appointment of my son, Jabez Leonidas Doke, as postmaster at Hardpan. I would take it, sir, as a great favor if you would give the application a strong oral indorsement, as the appointment is in the line of reform. Be kind enough to inform me what are the emoluments of the office I hold in the military arm, and if they are by salary or fees. My mileage account will be transmitted monthly.

From Brigadier-General Jupiter Doke to Major General Blount Wardorg.
Distilleryville, Kentucky,
January 12, 1862.

I arrived on the tented field yesterday by steamboat, the recent storms having inundated the landscape, covering, I understand, the greater part of a congressional district. I am pained to find that Joel Briller, Esq., a prominent citizen of Posey County, Illinois, and a far-seeing statesman who held my proxy, and who a month ago should have been thundering at the gates of Disunion, has not been heard from, and has doubtless been sacrificed upon the altar of his country. In him the American people lose a bulwark of freedom. I would respectfully move that you designate a committee to draw up resolutions of respect to his memory, and that the office holders and men under your command wear the usual badge of mourning for thirty days. I shall at once place myself at the head of affairs here, and am now ready to entertain any suggestions which you may make, looking to the better enforcement of the laws in this commonwealth. The militant Democrats on the other side of the river appear to be contemplating extreme measures. They have two large cannons facing this way, and yesterday morning, I am told, some of them came down to the water's edge and remained in session for some time, making infamous allegations.

From the Diary of Brigadier-General Jupiter Doke, at Distilleryville, Kentucky.

January 12, 1862. — On my arrival yesterday at the Henry Clay Hotel (named in honor of the late far-seeing statesman) I was waited on by a delegation consisting of the three colonels intrusted with the command of the regiments of my brigade. It was an occasion that will be memorable in the political annals of America. Forwarded copies of the speeches to the Posey *Maverick,* to be spread upon the record of the ages. The gentlemen composing the delegation unanimously reaffirmed their devotion to the principles of national unity and the Republican party. Was gratified to recognize in them men of political prominence and untarnished escutcheons. At the subsequent banquet, sentiments of lofty patriotism were expressed. Wrote to Mr. Wardorg at Louisville for instructions.

January 13, 1862. — Leased a prominent residence (the former incumbent being absent in arms against his country) for the term of one year, and wrote at once for Mrs. Brigadier-General Doke and the vital issues — excepting Jabez Leonidas. In the camp of treason opposite here there are supposed to be three thousand misguided men laying the ax at the root of the tree of liberty. They have a clear majority, many of our men having returned without leave to their constituents. We could probably not poll more than two thousand votes. Have advised my heads of regiments to make a canvass of those remaining, all bolters to be read out of the phalanx.

January 14, 1862. — Wrote to the President, asking for the contract to supply this command with firearms and regalia through my brother-in-law, prominently identified with the manufacturing interests of the country. Club of cannon soldiers arrived at Jayhawk, three miles back from here, on their way to join us in battle array. Marched my whole brigade to Jayhawk to escort them into town, but their chairman, mistaking us for the opposing party, opened fire on the head of the procession and by the extraordinary noise of the cannon balls (I had no conception of it!) so frightened my horse that I was unseated without a contest. The meeting adjourned in disorder and returning to camp I found that a deputation of the enemy had crossed the river in our absence and made a division of the loaves and fishes. Wrote to the President, applying for the Gubernatorial Chair of the Territory of Idaho.

From Editorial Article in the Posey, Illinois, "Maverick," January 20, 1862.
Brigadier-General Doke's thrilling account, in another column, of the Battle of Distilleryville will make the heart of every loyal Illinoisian leap with exultation. The brilliant exploit marks an era in military history, and as General Doke says, "lays broad and deep the foundations of American prowess in arms." As none of the troops engaged, except the gallant author-chieftain (a host in himself) hails from Posey County, he justly considered that a list of the fallen would only occupy our valuable space to the exclusion of more important matter, but his account of the strategic ruse by which he apparently abandoned his camp and so inveigled a perfidious enemy into it for the purpose of murdering the sick, the unfortunate *countertempus* at Jayhawk, the subsequent dash upon a trapped enemy flushed with a supposed success, driving their terrified legions across an impassable river which precluded pursuit — all these "moving accidents by flood and field" are related with a pen of fire and have all the terrible interest of romance.

Verily, truth is stranger than fiction and the pen is mightier than the sword. When by the graphic power of the art preservative of all arts we are brought face to face with such glorious events as these, the *Maverick's* enterprise in securing for its thousands of readers the services of so distinguished a contributor as the Great Captain who made the history as well as wrote, it seems a matter of almost secondary importance. For President in 1864 (subject to the decision of the Republican National Convention) Brigadier-General Jupiter Doke, of Illinois!

From Major-General Blount Wardorg to Brigadier-General Jupiter Doke.
Louisville, January 22, 1862.
Your letter apprising me of your arrival at Distilleryville was delayed in transmission, having only just been received (open) through the courtesy of the Confederate department commander under a flag of truce. He begs me to assure you that he would consider it an act of cruelty to trouble you, and I think it would be. Maintain, however, a threatening attitude, but at the least pressure retire. Your position is simply an outpost which it is not intended to hold.

From Major-General Blount Wardorg to the Secretary of War.
Louisville, January 23, 1862.

I have certain information that the enemy has concentrated twenty thousand troops of all arms on the Little Buttermilk. According to your assignment, General Doke is in command of the small brigade of raw troops opposing them. It is no part of my plan to contest the enemy's advance at that point, but I cannot hold myself responsible for any reverses to the brigade mentioned, under its present commander. I think him a fool.

From the Secretary of War to Major-General Blount Wardorg.
Washington, February 1, 1862.

The President has great faith in General Doke. If your estimate of him is correct, however, he would seem to be singularly well placed where he now is, as your plans appear to contemplate a considerable sacrifice for whatever advantages you expect to gain.

From Brigadier-General Jupiter Doke to Major-General Blount Wardorg.
Distilleryville, February 1, 1862.

To-morrow I shall remove my headquarters to Jayhawk in order to point the way whenever my brigade retires from Distilleryville, as foreshadowed by your letter of the 22d ult. I have appointed a Committee on Retreat, the minutes of whose first meeting I transmit to you. You will perceive that the committee having been duly organized by the election of a chairman and secretary, a resolution (prepared by myself) was adopted, to the effect that in case treason again raises her hideous head on this side of the river every man of the brigade is to mount a mule, the procession to move promptly in the direction of Louisville and the loyal North. In preparation for such an emergency I have for some time been collecting mules from the resident Democracy, and have on hand 2300 in a field at Jayhawk. Eternal vigilance is the price of liberty!

From Major-General Gibeon J. Buxter, C. S. A.,
to the Confederate Secretary of War.
Bung Station, Kentucky,
February 4, 1862.

On the night of the 2d inst., our entire force, consisting of 25,000 men and thirty-two field pieces, under command of Major-General

Simmons B. Flood, crossed by a ford to the north side of Little Buttermilk River at a point three miles above Distilleryville and moved obliquely down and away from the stream, to strike the Covington turnpike at Jayhawk; the object being, as you know, to capture Covington, destroy Cincinnati and occupy the Ohio Valley. For some months there had been in our front only a small brigade of undisciplined troops, apparently without a commander, who were useful to us, for by not disturbing them we could create an impression of our weakness. But the movement on Jayhawk having isolated them, I was about to detach an Alabama regiment to bring them in, my division being the leading one, when an earth-shaking rumble was felt and heard, and suddenly the head-of-column was struck by one of the terrible tornadoes for which this region is famous, and utterly annihilated. The tornado, I believe, passed along the entire length of the road back to the ford, dispersing or destroying our entire army; but of this I cannot be sure, for I was lifted from the earth insensible and blown back to the south side of the river. Continuous firing all night on the north side and the reports of such of our men as have recrossed at the ford convince me that the Yankee brigade has exterminated the disabled survivors. Our loss has been uncommonly heavy. Of my own division of 15,000 infantry, the casualties — killed, wounded, captured, and missing — are 14,994. Of General Dolliver Billow's division, 11,200 strong, I can find but two officers and a nigger cook. Of the artillery, 800 men, none has reported on this side of the river. General Flood is dead. I have assumed command of the expeditionary force, but owing to the heavy losses have deemed it advisable to contract my line of supplies as rapidly as possible. I shall push southward to-morrow morning early. The purposes of the campaign have been as yet but partly accomplished.

From Major-General Dolliver Billows, C. S. A.,
to the Confederate Secretary of War.
Buhac, Kentucky, February 5, 1862.
. . . But during the 2d they had, unknown to us, been reinforced by fifty thousand cavalry, and being apprised of our movement by a spy, this vast body was drawn up in the darkness at Jayhawk, and as the head of our column reached that point at about 11 P.M., fell upon it with astonishing fury, destroying the division of General Buxter in an instant. General Baumschank's brigade of artillery, which was in the rear,

may have escaped—I did not wait to see, but withdrew my division to the river at a point several miles above the ford, and at daylight ferried it across on two fence rails lashed together with a suspender. Its losses, from an effective strength of 11,200, are 11,199. General Buxter is dead. I am changing my base to Mobile, Alabama.

From Brigadier-General Schneddeker Baumschank, C. S. A., to the Confederate Secretary of War.
Iodine, Kentucky, February 6, 1862.
. . . Yoost den somdings occur, I know nod vot it vos—somdings mackneefcent, but it vas nod vor—und I finds meinselluf, afder leedle viles, in dis blace, midout a hors und mit no men und goons. Sheneral Peelows is deadt. You will blease be so goot as to resign me—I vights no more in a dam gontry vere I gets vipped und knows nod how it vos done.

Resolutions of Congress, February 15, 1862.
Resolved, That the thanks of Congress are due, and hereby tendered to Brigadier-General Jupiter Doke and the gallant men under his command for their unparalleled feat of attacking—themselves only 2000 strong—an army of 25,000 men and utterly overthrowing it, killing 5327, making prisoners of 19,003, of whom more than half were wounded, taking 32 guns, 20,000 stand of small arms and, in short, the enemy's entire equipment.
Resolved, That for this unexampled victory the President be requested to designate a day of thanksgiving and public celebration of religious rites in the various churches.
Resolved, That he be requested, in further commemoration of the great event, and in reward of the gallant spirits whose deeds have added such imperishable lustre to the American arms, to appoint, with the advice and consent of the Senate, the following officer:
One major-general.

Statement of Mr. Hannibal Alcazar Peyton, of Jayhawk, Kentucky.
Dat wus a almighty dark night, sho', and dese yere ole eyes aint wuf shuks, but I's got a year like a sque'l, an' wen I cotch de mummer o' v'ices I knowed dat gang b'long on de far side o' de ribber. So I jes' runs in de house an' wakes Marse Doke an' tells him: "Skin outer dis fo' yo'

life!" An' de Lo'd bress my soul! ef dat man didn' go right fru de winder in his shir' tail an' break for to cross de mule patch! An' dem twenty-free hunerd mules dey jes' t'ink it is de debble hese'f wid de brandin' iron, an' dey bu'st outen dat patch like a yarthquake, an' pile inter de upper ford road, an' flash down it five deep, an' it full o' Confed'rates from en' to en'! . . .

[1899; CWAB, VI]

TWO FANTASTIC FABLES

EQUIPPED FOR SERVICE

During the Civil War a Patriot was passing through the State of Maryland with a pass from the President to join Grant's Army and see the fighting. Stopping a day at Annapolis, he visited the shop of a well-known optician and ordered seven powerful telescopes, one for every day of the week. In recognition of this munificent patronage of the State's languishing industries, the Governor comissioned him a colonel.

THE MYSTERIOUS WORD

The Chief of a battalion of war correspondents read a manuscript account of a battle.

"My son," he said to its Author, "your story is distinctly unavailable. You say we lost only two men instead of a hundred; that the enemy's loss is unknown, instead of ten thousand, and that we were defeated and ran away. That is no way to write."

"But consider," expostulated the conscientious scribe, "my story may be tame with regard to the number of our casualities, disappointing as to the damage done the enemy and shocking in its denoument, but it has the advantage of being the truth."

"I don't quite understand," said the Chief, scratching his head.

"Why, the advantage," the other exclaimed — "the merit — the distinction — the profitable excellence — the" —

"Oh," said the Chief, "I know very well the signification of 'advantage;' but what the devil do you mean by 'truth'?"

[1883; SOLE]

THE PROFESSIONAL OFFICER[20]

Some gutter-blooded barbarian, whose acquaintance with military affairs probably consists in drawing a pension for injuries received during the late war in scampering across the Canadian border to escape the draft, is writing in the *Chronicle* in advocacy of closing that "nursery of favorites," the military academy at West Point. This dreg would also have the army officered by promotion from the ranks, and in various other ways give the private soldier "as fair a show" (by which the *residuum* means chance) "as the pampered officer." The hero of Cold Harbor,[21] iconoclast of the Column Vendôme and formidable ally of the "gates of Hell" is also flinging his heels in the direction of West Point. It is probably useless to point out to the dreg, as it has been already explained to the other person, that the life of an army officer commonly is, and always is likely to be, one of exceptional labor, self-denial and responsibility, that his services are more niggardly requited than those of the brainless hired man who does commercial desk-work; that military competency cannot be acquired in the ranks, a promoted private being almost invariably an inefficient officer; that all the successful commanders of armies in the civil war were graduates of the military academy at West Point, their abilities asserting themselves despite the most disheartening administrative discrimination and an ugly popular prejudice which the soiled and stagnant understandings of these scribbling twin relics do but dimly and imperfectly reflect.

20. "Prattle," *Wasp*, December 22, 1883. SOLE, 191–92.

21. Ulysses S. Grant became known as "butcher" Grant after his frontal assaults at Cold Harbor, Virginia, June 3, 1864.

CHAPTER TWO

What War Really Is, 1862

The boastful posturing, rush to recruiting stations, and very limited fighting of 1861 gave way quickly in 1862 to a harsher reality. Bierce spent some long days in winter camp waiting for the weather to warm the roads and dry the mud. Ironically, the Easter resurrection and rebirth that is springtime brought with it death and destruction for American men at war.

Daffodil blooms and peach blossoms opened the season of killing as the Union Army of the Ohio occupied Nashville. Ulysses Grant's Army of the Tennessee fought its way along the Cumberland and Tennessee rivers, taking forts Henry and Donelson as it moved south into Mississippi. By early April, McClellan's Army of the Potomac inched slowly up the peninsula, driving "On to Richmond." It would fight Lee's army at two of the war's biggest battles, Antietam and Fredericksburg, before the year ran out.

On April 6, at Shiloh Church, Confederates burst upon Grant's unprepared forces, plunging into the sleeping command of William Tecumseh Sherman who overstated the obvious, "My God, we are attacked!" Grant rushed to the scene and the men rallied at the banks of the Tennessee River and in a line stretching to good ground along Owl Creek. From Nashville, Don Carlos Buell's Army of the Ohio arrived during the night, saved Grant, and the next day their combined forces counterattacked, pushing the Confederates from the field. Union casualties totaled 13,047 dead, dying, wounded, and missing, out of nearly 62,000 men engaged; Confederates lost 11,694 of 44,000. More Americans had been killed in two days at Shiloh than had died during the Revolution, War of 1812, and Mexican War combined.

The Southern army took a defensive position at Corinth before with-

drawing without giving battle on May 29. The Northern army was operating in an enemy's country where almost everyone was a potential spy
and assassin. Armies not in battle dealt with deserters and other offend-
ers, marched and countermarched, and suffered from the heat and
insects of a Southern summer. The casualties at Shiloh had been so
large that Lincoln censured Grant by replacing him with Henry Halleck. In August, Buell was ordered northward into Tennessee and Kentucky to confront the army of Braxton Bragg. When Buell failed at
Perryville owing to an acoustical shadow, which prevented him from
hearing and supporting the battle, Lincoln came to believe Grant's
story that Buell had been late at Shiloh and so ended Buell's military
career and reinstated Grant. Buell's replacement, William Rosecrans
intended to prove himself at once and on the day after Christmas
marched his army toward Murfreesboro, Tennessee, where it fought a
bloody battle at Stone's River, December 31–January 2.

The casualties at Stone's River were ghastly and matched Shiloh's:
Federals 12,906, Confederates 11,739, total 24,645. Bierce fought
with his regiment in the center of the whirlwind — "Hell's Half Acre"
as it came to be called — with the Ninth Indiana losing 113 men dead
and wounded. Brigade commander — and original organizer and colonel of the Ninth — William B. Hazen was so moved by his men's gallantry that, in 1863, he erected the first monument placed on any
battlefield of the war, putting up a large limestone pillar with the en-
graving: "Hazen's Brigade. To the memory of its soldiers who fell at
Stone River, December 31st, 1862. Their faces toward Heaven, their
feet to the foe."

In Hazen, Bierce found a commanding officer who earned his loyalty and trust, even as Hazen found Bierce to be brave, talented, and
versatile. The debate about the performance of other officers, however,
continued, and in later years Bierce frequently returned to that debate,
offering his own opinions and observations about who had done what,
and to what effect. Often in the 1880s and 1890s the death of one of
these officers provided Bierce another opportunity to reconsider the
quality of their leadership in the Civil War.

If Bierce had any illusions about war, what he saw of Shiloh and
Stone's River, as well as seeing a competent general smeared and replaced, surely disabused him of them. The technology of war — especially the rifles and artillery — impressed him with its ability to murder

randomly with great efficiency. There was little of pomp and circumstance in 1862. Between the large numbers of mutilated men, masses
of deserters being court martialed for having run away during the
swirl of battle, partisan rangers picking off unlucky men, and captured
spies being executed, Bierce came to see what war really is. Of course,
death, casualties, and bravery have another effect on those remaining:
Sergeant Bierce was promoted to second lieutenant.

From *The Devil's Dictionary*

YOUTH, *n*. The Period of Possibility. . . .

YESTERDAY, *n*. The infancy of youth, the youth of manhood, the entire past of age.

DESERTION, *n*. An aversion to fighting, as exhibited by abandoning an army or a wife.

BATTLE, *n*. A method of untying with the teeth a political knot that would not yield to the tongue.

POLITICIAN, *n*. An eel in the fundamental mud upon which the superstructure of organized society is reared. When he wriggles he mistakes the agitation of his tail for the trembling of the edifice. As compared with the statesman, he suffers the disadvantage of being alive.

RATIONAL, *adj*. Devoid of all delusions save those of observation, experience and reflection.

BAYONET, *n*. An instrument for pricking the bubble of a nation's conceit.

CORPSE, *n*. A person who manifests the highest possible degree of indifference that is consistent with a civil regard for the solicitude of others.

WHAT I SAW OF SHILOH

I

This is a simple story of a battle; such a tale as may be told by a soldier who is no writer to a reader who is no soldier.

The morning of Sunday, the sixth day of April, 1862, was bright and warm. Reveille had been sounded rather late, for the troops, wearied with long marching, were to have a day of rest. The men were idling about the embers of their bivouac fires; some preparing breakfast, others looking carelessly to the condition of their arms and accoutrements, against the inevitable inspection; still others were chatting with indolent dogmatism on that never-failing theme, the end and object of the campaign. Sentinels paced up and down the confused front with a lounging freedom of mien and stride that would not have been tolerated at another time. A few of them limped unsoldierly in deference to blistered feet. At a little distance in rear of the stacked arms were a few tents out of which frowsyheaded officers occasionally peered, languidly calling to their servants to fetch a basin of water, dust a coat or polish a scabbard. Trim young mounted orderlies, bearing dispatches obviously unimportant, urged their lazy nags by devious ways amongst the men, enduring with unconcern their good-humored raillery, the penalty of superior station. Little negroes of not very clearly defined status and function lolled on their stomachs, kicking their long, bare heels[1] in the sunshine, or slumbered peacefully, unaware of the practical waggery prepared by white hands for their undoing.

Presently the flag hanging limp and lifeless at headquarters was seen to lift itself spiritedly from the staff. At the same instant was heard a dull, distant sound like the heavy breathing of some great animal below the horizon. The flag had lifted its head to listen. There was a momentary lull in the hum of the human swarm; then, as the flag drooped the hush

---

1. Long heels: The United States Army assisted in the scientific racism of the day by doing anthropometric measurements of black soldiers. One of its findings illustrated that African American soldiers have longer heels than white soldiers, a finding not notable itself except to racists who could claim that difference meant inferiority.

passed away. But there were some hundreds more men on their feet than before; some thousands of hearts beating with a quicker pulse.

Again the flag made a warning sign, and again the breeze bore to our ears the long, deep sighing of iron lungs. The division, as if it had received the sharp word of command, sprang to its feet, and stood in groups at "attention." Even the little blacks got up. I have since seen similar effects produced by earthquakes; I am not sure but the ground was trembling then. The mess-cooks, wise in their generation, lifted the steaming camp-kettles off the fire and stood by to cast out. The mounted orderlies had somehow disappeared. Officers came ducking from beneath their tents and gathered in groups. Headquarters had become a swarming hive.

The sound of the great guns now came in regular throbbings — the strong, full pulse of the fever of battle. The flag flapped excitedly, shaking out its blazonry of stars and stripes with a sort of fierce delight. Toward the knot of officers in its shadow dashed from somewhere — he seemed to have burst out of the ground in a cloud of dust — a mounted aide-de-camp, and on the instant rose the sharp, clear notes of a bugle, caught up and repeated, and passed on by other bugles, until the level reaches of brown fields, the line of woods trending away to far hills, and the unseen valleys beyond were "telling of the sound," the farther, fainter strains half drowned in ringing cheers as the men ran to range themselves behind the stacks of arms. For this call was not the wearisome "general" before which the tents go down; it was the exhilarating "assembly," which goes to the heart as wine and stirs the blood like the kisses of a beautiful woman. Who that has heard it calling to him above the grumble of great guns can forget the wild intoxication of its music?

II

The Confederate forces in Kentucky and Tennessee had suffered a series of reverses, culminating in the loss of Nashville.[2] The blow was severe: immense quantities of war material had fallen to the victor, together with all the important strategic points. General Johnston[3] with-

2. Nashville was occupied by federal forces under General Carlos Buell on February 25, 1862. LONG.

3. Albert Sidney Johnston (1803–1862), the second-highest ranking officer in

drew Beauregard's[4] army to Corinth, in northern Mississippi, where he hoped so to recruit and equip it as to enable it to assume the offensive and retake the lost territory.

The town of Corinth was a wretched place — the capital of a swamp. It is a two days' march west of the Tennessee River, which here and for a hundred and fifty miles farther, to where it falls into the Ohio at Paducah, runs nearly north. It is navigable to this point — that is to say, to Pittsburg Landing, where Corinth got to it by a road worn through a thickly wooded country seamed with ravines and bayous, rising nobody knows where and running into the river under sylvan arches heavily draped with Spanish moss. In some places they were obstructed by fallen trees. The Corinth road was at certain seasons a branch of the Tennessee River. Its mouth was Pittsburg Landing. Here in 1862 were some fields and a house or two; now there are a national cemetery and other improvements.

It was at Pittsburg Landing that Grant established his army, with a river in his rear and two toy steamboats as a means of communication with the east side, whither General Buell with thirty thousand men was moving from Nashville to join him. The question has been asked, Why did General Grant occupy the enemy's side of the river in the face of a superior force before the arrival of Buell? Buell had a long way to come; perhaps Grant was weary of waiting.[5] Certainly Johnston was, for in the gray of the morning of April 6th, when Buell's leading division was *en bivouac* near the little town of Savannah, eight or ten miles below, the Confederate forces, having moved out of Corinth two days before, fell upon Grant's advance brigades and destroyed them. Grant was at Sa-

---

the Confederacy, commanded the western theater, and was the mastermind of the attack on Grant at Shiloh, where he was killed. Bierce mistakenly puts Johnston under Beauregard when it was the other way around. SIFAKIS.

4. Pierre Gustave Toutant Beauregard (1811–1893) commanded the South Carolina troops who had fired upon Fort Sumter to start the Civil War. He took command after the death of Albert Sidney Johnston. SIFAKIS.

5. Major-General Ulysses S. Grant's tactics at Shiloh have been debated for seven score years since the battle. Much of the debate has to do with finger pointing between Grant and Buell. Grant has often been portrayed as drunk and Buell as slow or disloyal. For Grant's side of the story, see his *Personal Memoirs of U. S. Grant* (New York: Webster, 1885), 171–87, and "The Battle of Shiloh," *Battles and Leaders of the Civil War,* edited by Robert Underwood Johnson and Clarence Clough Buel (New York: Century, 1887–88), 1:465–86.

vannah, but hastened to the Landing in time to find his camps in the hands of the enemy and the remnants of his beaten army cooped up with an impassable river at their backs for moral support. I have related how the news of this affair came to us at Savannah. It came on the wind — a messenger that does not bear copious details.

III

On the side of the Tennessee River, over against Pittsburg Landing, are some low bare hills, partly inclosed by a forest. In the dusk of the evening of April 6 this open space, as seen from the other side of the stream — whence, indeed, it was anxiously watched by thousands of eyes, to many of which it grew dark long before the sun went down — would have appeared to have been ruled in long, dark lines, with new lines being constantly drawn across. These lines were the regiments of Buell's leading division, which having moved up from Savannah through a country presenting nothing but interminable swamps and pathless "bottom lands," with rank overgrowths of jungle, was arriving at the scene of action breathless, footsore and faint with hunger. It had been a terrible race; some regiments had lost a third of their number from fatigue, the men dropping from the ranks as if shot, and left to recover or die at their leisure. Nor was the scene to which they had been invited likely to inspire the moral confidence that medicines physical fatigue. True, the air was full of thunder and the earth was trembling beneath their feet; and if there is truth in the theory of the conversion of force, these men were storing up energy from every shock that burst its waves upon their bodies. Perhaps this theory may better than another explain the tremendous endurance of men in battle. But the eyes reported only matter for despair.

Before us ran the turbulent river, vexed with plunging shells and obscured in spots by blue sheets of low-lying smoke. The two little steamers were doing their duty well. They came over to us empty and went back crowded, sitting very low in the water, apparently on the point of capsizing. The farther edge of the water could not be seen; the boats came out of the obscurity, took on their passengers and vanished in the darkness. But on the heights above, the battle was burning brightly enough; a thousand lights kindled and expired in every second of time. There were broad flushings in the sky, against which the branches of the trees showed black. Sudden flames burst out here and there, singly and in dozens. Fleeting streaks of fire crossed over to us by way of welcome. These expired in blinding flashes and fierce little rolls of smoke, attended with the peculiar metallic ring of bursting shells, and followed by the musical humming of the fragments as they struck into the ground on every side, making us wince, but doing little harm. The air was full of noises. To the right and the left the musketry rattled smartly and petulantly; directly in front it sighed and growled. To the experienced ear this meant that the death-line was an arc of which the river was the chord. There were deep, shaking explosions and smart shocks; the whisper of stray bullets and the hurtle of conical shells; the rush of round shot. There were faint, desultory cheers, such as announce a momentary or partial triumph. Occasionally, against the glare behind the trees, could be seen moving black figures, singularly distinct but apparently no longer than a thumb. They seemed to me ludicrously like the figures of demons in old allegorical prints of hell. To destroy these and all their belongings the enemy needed but another hour of daylight; the steamers in that case would have been doing him fine service by bringing more fish to his net. Those of us who had the good fortune to arrive late could then have eaten our teeth in impotent rage. Nay, to make his victory sure it did not need that the sun should pause in the heavens; one of the many random shots falling into the river would have done the business had chance directed it into the engine-room of a steamer. You can perhaps fancy the anxiety with which we watched them leaping down.

But we had two other allies besides the night. Just where the enemy had pushed his right flank to the river was the mouth of a wide bayou, and here two gunboats had taken station. They too were of the toy sort, plated perhaps with railway metals, perhaps with boiler-iron. They staggered under a heavy gun or two each. The bayou made an opening in the high bank of the river. The bank was a parapet, behind which the gunboats crouched, firing up the bayou as through an embrasure. The enemy was at this disadvantage: he could not get at the gunboats, and he could advance only by exposing his flank to their ponderous missiles, one of which would have broken a half-mile of his bones and made nothing of it. Very annoying this must have been — these twenty gunners beating back an army because a sluggish creek had been pleased to fall into a river at one point rather than another. Such is the part that accident may play in the game of war.

As a spectacle this was rather fine. We could just discern the black bodies of these boats, looking very much like turtles. But when they let off their big guns there was a conflagration. The river shuddered in its banks, and hurried on, bloody, wounded, terrified! Objects a mile away sprang toward our eyes as a snake strikes at the face of its victim. The report stung us to the brain, but we blessed it audibly. Then we could hear the great shell tearing away through the air until the sound died out in the distance; then, a surprisingly long time afterward, a dull, distant explosion and a sudden silence of small-arms told their own tale.

IV

There was, I remember, no elephant on the boat that passed us across that evening, nor, I think, any hippopotamus. These would have been out of place. We had, however, a woman. Whether the baby was somewhere on board I did not learn. She was a fine creature, this woman; somebody's wife. Her mission, as she understood it, was to inspire the failing heart with courage; and when she selected mine I felt less flattered by her preference than astonished by her penetration. How did she learn? She stood on the upper deck with the red blaze of battle bathing her beautiful face, the twinkle of a thousand rifles mirrored in her eyes; and displaying a small ivory-handled pistol, she told me in a sentence punctuated by the thunder of great guns that if it came to the worst she would do her duty like a man! I am proud to remember that I took off my hat to this little fool.

V

Along the sheltered strip of beach between the river bank and the water was a confused mass of humanity—several thousands of men. They were mostly unarmed; many were wounded; some dead. All the camp-following tribes were there; all the cowards; a few officers. Not one of them knew where his regiment was, nor if he had a regiment. Many had not. These men were defeated, beaten, cowed. They were deaf to duty and dead to shame. A more demented crew never drifted to the rear of broken battalions. They would have stood in their tracks and been shot down to a man by a provost-marshal's guard, but they could not have been urged up that bank. An army's bravest men are its cowards. The death which they would not meet at the hands of the enemy they will meet at the hands of their officers, with never a flinching.

Whenever a steamboat would land, this abominable mob had to be kept off her with bayonets; when she pulled away, they sprang on her and were pushed by scores into the water, where they were suffered to drown one another in their own way. The men disembarking insulted them, shoved them, struck them. In return they expressed their unholy delight in the certainty of our destruction by the enemy.

By the time my regiment had reached the plateau night had put an end to the struggle. A sputter of rifles would break out now and then, followed perhaps by a spiritless hurrah. Occasionally a shell from a far-away battery would come pitching down somewhere near, with a whir crescendo, or flit above our heads with a whisper like that made by the wings of a night bird, to smother itself in the river. But there was no more fighting. The gunboats, however, blazed away at set intervals all night long, just to make the enemy uncomfortable and break him of his rest.

For us there was no rest. Foot by foot we moved through the dusky fields, we knew not whither. There were men all about us, but no camp-fires; to have made a blaze would have been madness. The men were of strange regiments; they mentioned the names of unknown generals. They gathered in groups by the wayside, asking eagerly our numbers. They recounted the depressing incidents of the day. A thoughtful officer shut their mouths with a sharp word as he passed; a wise one coming after encouraged them to repeat their doleful tale all along the line.

Hidden in hollows and behind clumps of rank brambles were large tents, dimly lighted with candles, but looking comfortable. The kind of comfort they supplied was indicated by pairs of men entering and reappearing, bearing litters; by low moans from within and by long rows of dead with covered faces outside. These tents were constantly receiving the wounded, yet were never full; they were continually ejecting the dead, yet were never empty. It was as if the helpless had been carried in and murdered, that they might not hamper those whose business it was to fall to-morrow.

The night was now black-dark; as is usual after a battle, it had begun to rain. Still we moved; we were being put into position by somebody. Inch by inch we crept along, treading on one another's heels by way of keeping together. Commands were passed along the line in whispers; more commonly none were given. When the men had pressed so closely together that they could advance no farther they stood stock-still, sheltering the locks of their rifles with their ponchos. In this position many fell asleep. When those in front suddenly stepped away those in the rear, roused by the tramping, hastened after with such zeal that the line was soon choked again. Evidently the head of the division was being piloted at a snail's pace by some one who did not feel sure of his ground. Very often we struck our feet against the dead; more frequently against those who still had spirit enough to resent it with a moan. These were lifted carefully to one side and abandoned. Some had sense enough to ask in their weak way for water. Absurd! Their clothes were soaken, their hair dank; their white faces, dimly discernible, were clammy and cold. Besides, none of us had any water. There was plenty coming, though, for before midnight a thunderstorm broke upon us with great violence. The rain, which had for hours been a dull drizzle, fell with a copiousness that stifled us; we moved in running water up to our ankles. Happily, we were in a forest of great trees heavily "decorated" with Spanish moss, or with an enemy standing to his guns the disclosures of the lightning might have been inconvenient. As it was, the incessant blaze enabled us to consult our watches and encouraged us by displaying our numbers; our black, sinuous line, creeping like a giant serpent beneath the trees, was apparently interminable. I am almost ashamed to say how sweet I found the companionship of those coarse men.

So the long night wore away, and as the glimmer of morning crept in through the forest we found ourselves in a more open country. But where? Not a sign of battle was here. The trees were neither splintered nor scarred, the underbrush was unmown, the ground had no footprints but our own. It was as if we had broken into glades sacred to eternal silence. I should not have been surprised to see sleek leopards come fawning about our feet, and milk-white deer confront us with human eyes.

A few inaudible commands from an invisible leader had placed us in order of battle. But where was the enemy? Where, too, were the riddled regiments that we had come to save? Had our other divisions arrived during the night and passed the river to assist us? or were we to oppose our paltry five thousand breasts to an army flushed with victory? What protected our right? Who lay upon our left? Was there really anything in our front?

There came, borne to us on the raw morning air, the long, weird note of a bugle. It was directly before us. It rose with a low, clear, deliberate warble, and seemed to float in the gray sky like the note of a lark. The bugle calls of the Federal and the Confederate armies were the same: it was the "assembly"! As it died away I observed that the atmosphere had suffered a change; despite the equilibrium established by the storm, it was electric. Wings were growing on blistered feet. Bruised muscles and jolted bones, shoulders pounded by the cruel knapsack, eyelids leaden from lack of sleep — all were pervaded by the subtle fluid, all were unconscious of their clay. The men thrust forward their heads, expanded their eyes and clenched their teeth. They breathed hard, as if throttled by tugging at the leash. If you had laid your hand in the beard or hair of one of these men it would have crackled and shot sparks.

VI

I suppose the country lying between Corinth and Pittsburg Landing could boast a few inhabitants other than alligators. What manner of people they were it is impossible to say, inasmuch as the fighting dispersed, or possibly exterminated them; perhaps in merely classing them as non-saurian I shall describe them with sufficient particularity and at the same time avert from myself the natural suspicion attaching to a writer who points out to persons who do not know him the peculiarities of persons whom he does not know. One thing, however, I hope I may without offense affirm of these swamp-dwellers — they were pious. To what deity their veneration was given — whether, like the Egyptians, they worshiped the crocodile, or, like other Americans, adored themselves, I do not presume to guess. But whoever, or whatever, may have been the divinity whose ends they shaped, unto Him, or It, they had builded a temple. This humble edifice, centrally situated in the heart of a solitude, and conveniently accessible to the supersylvan crow, had been christened Shiloh Chapel, whence the name of the battle. The fact

of a Christian church — assuming it to have been a Christian church —
giving name to a wholesale cutting of Christian throats by Christian
hands need not be dwelt on here; the frequency of its recurrence in the
history of our species has somewhat abated the moral interest that
would otherwise attach to it.

VII

Owing to the darkness, the storm and the absence of a road, it had
been impossible to move the artillery from the open ground about the
Landing. The privation was much greater in a moral than in a material
sense. The infantry soldier feels a confidence in this cumbrous arm
quite unwarranted by its actual achievements in thinning out the opposition. There is something that inspires confidence in the way a gun
dashes up to the front, shoving fifty or a hundred men to one side as if it
said, "Permit *me*!" Then it squares its shoulders, calmly dislocates a
joint in its back, sends away its twenty-four legs and settles down with a
quiet rattle which says as plainly as possible, "I've come to stay." There is
a superb scorn in its grimly defiant attitude, with its nose in the air; it
appears not so much to threaten the enemy as deride him.

Our batteries were probably toiling after us somewhere; we could
only hope the enemy might delay his attack until they should arrive.
"He may delay his defense if he like," said a sententious young officer
to whom I had imparted this natural wish. He had read the signs aright;
the words were hardly spoken when a group of staff officers about the
brigade commander shot away in divergent lines as if scattered by a
whirlwind, and galloping each to the commander of a regiment gave
the word. There was a momentary confusion of tongues, a thin line of
skirmishers detached itself from the compact front and pushed forward, followed by its diminutive reserves of half a company each — one
of which platoons it was my fortune to command. When the straggling
line of skirmishers had swept four or five hundred yards ahead, "See,"
said one of my comrades, "she moves!" She did indeed, and in fine
style, her front as straight as a string, her reserve regiments in columns
doubled on the center, following in true subordination; no braying of
brass to apprise the enemy, no fifing and drumming to amuse him; no
ostentation of gaudy flags; no nonsense. This was a matter of business.

In a few moments we had passed out of the singular oasis that had so marvelously escaped the desolation of battle, and now the evidences of the previous day's struggle were present in profusion. The ground was tolerably level here, the forest less dense, mostly clear of undergrowth, and occasionally opening out into small natural meadows. Here and there were small pools — mere discs of rainwater with a tinge of blood. Riven and torn with cannonshot, the trunks of the trees protruded bunches of splinters like hands, the fingers above the wound interlacing with those below. Large branches had been lopped, and hung their green heads to the ground, or swung critically in their netting of vines, as in a hammock. Many had been cut clean off and their masses of foliage seriously impeded the progress of the troops. The bark of these trees, from the root upward to a height of ten or twenty feet, was so thickly pierced with bullets and grape that one could not have laid a hand on it without covering several punctures. None had escaped. How the human body survives a storm like this must be explained by the fact that it is exposed to it but a few moments at a time, whereas these grand old trees had had no one to take their places, from the rising to the going down of the sun. Angular bits of iron, concavo-convex, sticking in the sides of muddy depressions, showed where shells had exploded in their furrows. Knapsacks, canteens, haversacks distended with soaken and swollen biscuits, gaping to disgorge, blankets beaten into the soil by the rain, rifles with bent barrels or splintered stocks, waist-belts, hats and the omnipresent sardine-box — all the wretched débris of the battle still littered the spongy earth as far as one could see, in every direction. Dead horses were everywhere; a few disabled caissons, or limbers, reclining on one elbow, as it were; ammunition wagons standing disconsolate behind four or six sprawling mules. Men? There were men enough; all dead, apparently, except one, who lay near where I had halted my platoon to await the slower movement of the line — a Federal sergeant, variously hurt, who had been a fine giant in his time. He lay face upward, taking in his breath in convulsive, rattling snorts, and blowing it out in sputters of froth which crawled creamily down his cheeks, piling itself alongside his neck and ears. A bullet had clipped a groove in his skull, above the temple; from this the brain protruded in bosses, dropping off in flakes and strings. I had not previously known one could get on, even in this unsatisfactory fashion, with so little brain. One of my men, whom I knew for a womanish fellow, asked if he should put his bayonet through him. Inexpressibly shocked by the cold-blooded proposal, I told him I thought not; it was unusual, and too many were looking.

VIII

It was plain that the enemy had retreated to Corinth. The arrival of our fresh troops and their successful passage of the river had disheartened him. Three or four of his gray cavalry videttes moving amongst the trees on the crest of a hill in our front, and galloping out of sight at the crack of our skirmishers' rifles, confirmed us in the belief; an army face to face with its enemy does not employ cavalry to watch its front. True, they might be a general and his staff. Crowning this rise we found a level field, a quarter of a mile in width; beyond it a gentle acclivity, covered with an undergrowth of young oaks, impervious to sight. We pushed on into the open, but the division halted at the edge. Having orders to conform to its movements, we halted too; but that did not suit; we received an intimation to proceed. I had performed this sort of service before, and in the exercise of my discretion deployed my platoon, pushing it forward at a run, with trailed arms, to strengthen the skirmish line, which I overtook some thirty or forty yards from the wood. Then—I can't describe it—the forest seemed all at once to flame up and disappear with a crash like that of a great wave upon the beach—a crash that expired in hot hissings, and the sickening "spat" of lead against flesh. A dozen of my brave fellows tumbled over like ten-pins. Some struggled to their feet, only to go down again, and yet again. Those who stood fired into the smoking brush and doggedly retired. We had expected to find, at most, a line of skirmishers similar to our own; it was with a view to overcoming them by a sudden *coup* at the moment of collision that I had thrown forward my little reserve. What we had found was a line of battle, coolly holding its fire till it could count our teeth. There was no more to be done but get back across the open ground, every superficial yard of which was throwing up its little jet of mud provoked by an impinging bullet. We got back, most of us, and I shall never forget the ludicrous incident of a young officer who had taken part in the affair walking up to his colonel, who had been a calm and apparently impartial spectator, and gravely reporting: "The enemy is in force just beyond this field, sir."

IX

In subordination to the design of this narrative, as defined by its title, the incidents related necessarily group themselves about my own personality as a center; and, as this center, during the few terrible hours of the engagement, maintained a variably constant relation to the open field already mentioned, it is important that the reader should bear in mind the topographical and tactical features of the local situation. The hither side of the field was occupied by the front of my brigade — a length of two regiments in line, with proper intervals for field batteries. During the entire fight the enemy held the slight wooded acclivity beyond. The debatable ground to the right and left of the open was broken and thickly wooded for miles, in some places quite inaccessible to artillery and at very few points offering opportunities for its successful employment. As a consequence of this the two sides of the field were soon studded thickly with confronting guns, which flamed away at one another with amazing zeal and rather startling effect. Of course, an infantry attack delivered from either side was not to be thought of when the covered flanks offered inducements so unquestionably superior; and I believe the riddled bodies of my poor skirmishers were the only ones left on this "neutral ground" that day. But there was a very pretty line of dead continually growing in our rear, and doubtless the enemy had at his back a similar encouragement.

The configuration of the ground offered us no protection. By lying flat on our faces between the guns we were screened from view by a straggling row of brambles, which marked the course of an obsolete fence; but the enemy's grape was sharper than his eyes, and it was poor consolation to know that his gunners could not see what they were doing, so long as they did it. The shock of our own pieces nearly deafened us, but in the brief intervals we could hear the battle roaring and stammering in the dark reaches of the forest to the right and left, where our other divisions were dashing themselves again and again into the smoking jungle. What would we not have given to join them in their brave, hopeless task! But to lie inglorious beneath showers of shrapnel darting divergent from the unassailable sky — meekly to be blown out of life by level gusts of grape — to clench our teeth and shrink helpless before big shot pushing noisily through the consenting air — this was horrible! "Lie down, there!" a captain would shout, and then get up himself to see that his order was obeyed. "Captain, take cover, sir!" the lieutenant-colonel would shriek, pacing up and down in the most exposed position that he could find.

O those cursed guns! — not the enemy's, but our own. Had it not been for them, we might have died like men. They must be supported, forsooth, the feeble, boasting bullies! It was impossible to conceive that these pieces were doing the enemy as excellent a mischief as his were doing us; they seemed to raise their "cloud by day" solely to direct aright the streaming procession of Confederate missiles. They no longer inspired confidence, but begot apprehension; and it was with grim satisfaction that I saw the carriage of one and another smashed into matchwood by a whooping shot and bundled out of the line.

X

The dense forests wholly or partly in which were fought so many battles of the Civil War, lay upon the earth in each autumn a thick deposit of dead leaves and stems, the decay of which forms a soil of surprising depth and richness. In dry weather the upper stratum is as inflammable as tinder. A fire once kindled in it will spread with a slow, persistent advance as far as local conditions permit, leaving a bed of light ashes beneath which the less combustible accretions of previous years will smolder until extinguished by rains. In many of the engagements of the war the fallen leaves took fire and roasted the fallen men. At Shiloh, during the first day's fighting, wide tracts of woodland were burned over in this way and scores of wounded who might have recovered perished in slow torture. I remember a deep ravine a little to the left and rear of the field I have described, in which, by some mad freak of heroic incompetence, a part of an Illinois regiment had been surrounded, and refusing to surrender was destroyed, as it very well deserved. My regiment having at last been relieved at the guns and moved over to the heights above this ravine for no obvious purpose, I obtained leave to go down into the valley of death and gratify a reprehensible curiosity.

Forbidding enough it was in every way. The fire had swept every superficial foot of it, and at every step I sank into ashes to the ankle. It had contained a thick undergrowth of young saplings, every one of which had been severed by a bullet, the foliage of the prostrate tops being afterward burnt and the stumps charred. Death had put his sickle into this thicket and fire had gleaned the field. Along a line which was not that of extreme depression, but was at every point significantly equidistant from the heights on either hand, lay the bodies, half buried in ashes; some in the unlovely looseness of attitude denoting sudden death by the bullet, but by far the greater number in postures of agony that told of the tormenting flame. Their clothing was half burnt away — their hair and beard entirely; the rain had come too late to save their nails. Some were swollen to double girth; others shriveled to manikins. According to degree of exposure, their faces were bloated and black or yellow and shrunken. The contraction of muscles which had given them claws for hands had cursed each countenance with a hideous grin. Faugh! I cannot catalogue the charms of these gallant gentlemen who had got what they enlisted for.

XI

It was now three o'clock in the afternoon, and raining. For fifteen hours we had been wet to the skin. Chilled, sleepy, hungry and disappointed — profoundly disgusted with the inglorious part to which they had been condemned — the men of my regiment did everything doggedly. The spirit had gone quite out of them. Blue sheets of powder smoke, drifting amongst the trees, settling against the hillsides and beaten into nothingness by the falling rain, filled the air with their peculiar pungent odor, but it no longer stimulated. For miles on either hand could be heard the hoarse murmur of the battle, breaking out near by with frightful distinctness, or sinking to a murmur in the distance; and the one sound aroused no more attention than the other.

We had been placed again in rear of those guns, but even they and their iron antagonists seemed to have tired of their feud, pounding away at one another with amiable infrequency. The right of the regiment extended a little beyond the field. On the prolongation of the line in that direction were some regiments of another division, with one in reserve. A third of a mile back lay the remnant of somebody's brigade looking to its wounds. The line of forest bounding this end of the field stretched as straight as a wall from the right of my regiment to Heaven knows what regiment of the enemy. There suddenly appeared, marching down along this wall, not more than two hundred yards in our front, a dozen files of gray-clad men with rifles on the right shoulder. At an interval of fifty yards they were followed by perhaps half as many more; and in fair supporting distance of these stalked with confident mien a single man! There seemed to me something indescribably ludicrous in the advance of this handful of men upon an army, albeit with their left flank protected by a forest. It does not so impress me now. They were the exposed flanks of three lines of infantry, each half a mile in length. In a moment our gunners had grappled with the nearest pieces, swung them half round, and were pouring streams of canister into the invaded wood. The infantry rose in masses, springing into line. Our threatened regiments stood like a wall, their loaded rifles at "ready," their bayonets hanging quietly in the scabbards. The right wing of my own regiment was thrown slightly backward to threaten the flank of the assault. The battered brigade away to the rear pulled itself together.

Then the storm burst. A great gray cloud seemed to spring out of the forest into the faces of the waiting battalions. It was received with a crash that made the very trees turn up their leaves. For one instant the assailants paused above their dead, then struggled forward, their bayonets glittering in the eyes that shone behind the smoke. One moment, and those unmoved men in blue would be impaled. What were they about? Why did they not fix bayonets? Were they stunned by their own volley? Their inaction was maddening! Another tremendous crash! — the rear rank had fired! Humanity, thank Heaven! is not made for this, and the shattered gray mass drew back a score of paces, opening a feeble fire. Lead had scored its old-time victory over steel; the heroic had broken its great heart against the commonplace. There are those who say that it is sometimes otherwise.

All this had taken but a minute of time, and now the second Confederate line swept down and poured in its fire. The line of blue staggered and gave way; in those two terrific volleys it seemed to have quite poured out its spirit. To this deadly work our reserve regiment now came up with a run. It was surprising to see it spitting fire with never a sound, for such was the infernal din that the ear could take in no more. This fearful scene was enacted within fifty paces of our toes, but we were rooted to the ground as if we had grown there. But now our commanding officer rode from behind us to the front, waved his hand with the courteous gesture that says *après vous*, and with a barely audible

cheer we sprang into the fight. Again the smoking front of gray re-
ceded, and again, as the enemy's third line emerged from its leafy
covert, it pushed forward across the piles of dead and wounded to
threaten with protruded steel. Never was seen so striking a proof of the
paramount importance of numbers. Within an area of three hundred
yards by fifty there struggled for front places no fewer than six regiments; and the accession of each, after the first collision, had it not
been immediately counterpoised, would have turned the scale.

As matters stood, we were now very evenly matched, and how long
we might have held out God only knows. But all at once something
appeared to have gone wrong with the enemy's left; our men had
somewhere pierced his line. A moment later his whole front gave way,
and springing forward with fixed bayonets we pushed him in utter
confusion back to his original line. Here, among the tents from which
Grant's people had been expelled the day before, our broken and
disordered regiments inextricably intermingled, and drunken with the
wine of triumph, dashed confidently against a pair of trim battalions,
provoking a tempest of hissing lead that made us stagger under its very
weight. The sharp onset of another against our flank sent us whirling
back with fire at our heels and fresh foes in merciless pursuit—who in
their turn were broken upon the front of the invalided brigade previously mentioned, which had moved up from the rear to assist in this
lively work.

As we rallied to reform behind our beloved guns and noted the
ridiculous brevity of our line — as we sank from sheer fatigue, and tried
to moderate the terrific thumping of our hearts—as we caught our
breath to ask who had seen such-and-such a comrade, and laughed
hysterically at the reply—there swept past us and over us into the
open field a long regiment with fixed bayonets and rifles on the right
shoulder. Another followed, and another; two—three—four! Heavens! where do all these men come from, and why did they not come
before? How grandly and confidently they go sweeping on like long
blue waves of ocean chasing one another to the cruel rocks! Involuntarily we draw in our weary feet beneath us as we sit, ready to spring up
and interpose our breasts when these gallant lines shall come back to us
across the terrible field, and sift brokenly through among the trees with
spouting fires at their backs. We still our breathing to catch the full
grandeur of the volleys that are to tear them to shreds. Minute after

minute passes and the sound does not come. Then for the first time we note that the silence of the whole region is not comparative, but absolute. Have we become stone deaf? See; here comes a stretcher-bearer, and there a surgeon! Good heavens! a chaplain!

The battle was indeed at an end.

XII

And this was, O so long ago! How they come back to me — dimly and brokenly, but with what a magic spell — those years of youth when I was soldiering! Again I hear the far warble of blown bugles. Again I see the tall, blue smoke of camp-fires ascending from the dim valleys of Wonderland. There steals upon my sense the ghost of an odor from pines that canopy the ambuscade. I feel upon my cheek the morning mist that shrouds the hostile camp unaware of its doom, and my blood stirs at the ringing rifle-shot of the solitary sentinel. Unfamiliar landscapes, glittering with sunshine or sullen with rain, come to me demanding recognition, pass, vanish and give place to others. Here in the night stretches a wide and blasted field studded with half-extinct fires burning redly with I know not what presage of evil. Again I shudder as I note its desolation and its awful silence. Where was it? To what monstrous inharmony of death was it the visible prelude?

O days when all the world was beautiful and strange; when unfamiliar constellations burned in the Southern midnights, and the mocking-bird poured out his heart in the moon-gilded magnolia; when there was something new under a new sun; will your fine, far memories ever cease to lay contrasting pictures athwart the harsher features of this later world, accentuating the ugliness of the longer and tamer life? Is it not strange that the phantoms of a blood-stained period have so airy a grace and look with so tender eyes? — that I recall with difficulty the danger and death and horrors of the time, and without effort all that was gracious and picturesque? Ah, Youth, there is no such wizard as thou! Give me but one touch of thine artist hand upon the dull canvas of the Present; gild for but one moment the drear and somber scenes of to-day, and I will willingly surrender another life than the one that I should have thrown away at Shiloh.

[1898; SOLE]

DEFENDING GENERAL BUELL[6]

The death of Gen. Don Carlos Buell[7] provoked hardly a ripple of interest. To many of the present generation he was hardly known as an historical figure. Yet he was a notable person in his day, and by many of the old Army men he was regarded as the ablest soldier of the Civil War. The whiskered pandours and the fierce hussars of the non-combatant contingent in Washington and elsewhere, the iron-handed Stanton[8] and his fiery following, thought that Buell's treatment of the Southern people had too much rose-water in it; many of his men and officers resented being put on guard over the property of their enemies, and the seraphim and cherubim of Abolition continually did cry. So his magnificent "Army of the Ohio" was taken away from him,[9] he was denied another opportunity and resigned before the close of the war; but if ever that turbulent time have a competent historian who had nothing to do with it the name of Don Carlos Buell will not need to be shouted in letters of brass to obtain an honorable mention.

Buell's most notable service was the rescue of Grant's army from the consequences of its commander's astonishing fatuity at Shiloh, or more accurately Pittsburg Landing. And in the ensuing controversy he showed literary qualities of the highest order.[10] One has only to read this controversy between Buell on one side and Grant[11] and Sherman[12] on the other to get an abiding consciousness of the man's immeasurable superiority to them in clarity of mind and conscience. Grant was

6. "Prattle," *San Francisco Examiner*, April 24, 1898. SOLE, 25–26.

7. Don Carlos Buell (1818–1898), Major-General commanding the Army of the Ohio. Bierce admired Buell over all other generals.

8. Edwin McMasters Stanton (1814–1869) served as Secretary of War from 1862 to 1869.

9. Stanton replaced Buell with George H. Thomas on October 24, 1862, for failing to press the attack after the battle of Perryville, Kentucky, on October 8. After a long investigation by a military board, Buell resigned his commission on June 1, 1864. SIFAKIS.

10. See Buell, "Shiloh Reviewed," *Battles and Leaders*, 1:487–536.

11. See Grant, "The Battle of Shiloh," 465–86.

12. Major-General William Tecumseh Sherman (1820–1891).

no more a match for him in logic and veracity than upon that memorable field he was for Sidney Johnston in arms.

The facts are simple. At the close of the first day's battle Grant's camps were held by the enemy and his army had been driven (withdrawn he says) to the river. Night had put an end to the fighting. Buell arrived that evening and crossing thirty thousand men attacked next morning. It required an all day's fight of incomparable severity for the united Federal armies to retake the lost ground and win a victory which was merely not a defeat. These facts are conceded by all — there is no dispute about them and they decide the question. Grant says he would have won without Buell, although with him he did no more than save himself. If that is true Buell's thirty thousand fresh troops counted for nothing, their labors and losses were needless, their assistance did not assist! That is the absurd position to which Grant's apologists are driven without their opponents having to make a single disputed statement. Let it be said in justice to them that they have never signified the faintest consciousness of the bog into which they have been herded.

TWO MILITARY EXECUTIONS

In the spring of the year 1862 General Buell's big army lay in camp, licking itself into shape for the campaign which resulted in the victory at Shiloh. It was a raw, untrained army, although some of its fractions had seen hard enough service, with a good deal of fighting, in the mountains of Western Virginia, and in Kentucky. The war was young and soldiering a new industry, imperfectly understood by the young American of the period, who found some features of it not altogether to his liking. Chief among these was that essential part of discipline, subordination. To one imbued from infancy with the fascinating fallacy that all men are born equal, unquestioning submission to authority is not easily mastered, and the American volunteer soldier in his "green and salad days" is among the worst known. That is how it happened that one of Buell's men, Private Bennett Story Greene, committed the indiscretion of striking his officer. Later in the war he would not have done that; like Sir Andrew Aguecheek, he would have "seen him damned" first. But time for reformation of his military manners was denied him: he was promptly arrested on complaint of the officer, tried by court-martial and sentenced to be shot.

"You might have thrashed me and let it go at that," said the condemned man to the complaining witness; "that is what you used to do at school, when you were plain Will Dudley and I was as good as you. Nobody saw me strike you; discipline would not have suffered much."

"Ben Greene, I guess you are right about that," said the lieutenant. "Will you forgive me? That is what I came to see you about."

There was no reply, and an officer putting his head in at the door of the guard-tent where the conversation had occurred, explained that the time allowed for the interview had expired. The next morning, when in the presence of the whole brigade Private Greene was shot to death by a squad of his comrades, Lieutenant Dudley turned his back upon the sorry performance and muttered a prayer for mercy, in which he himself was included.

A few weeks afterward, as Buell's leading division was being ferried over the Tennessee River to assist in succoring Grant's beaten army, night was coming on, black and stormy. Through the wreck of battle the division moved, inch by inch, in the direction of the enemy, who had withdrawn a little to reform his lines. But for the lightning the darkness was absolute. Never for a moment did it cease, and ever when the thunder did not crack and roar were heard the moans of the wounded among whom the men felt their way with their feet, and upon whom they stumbled in the gloom. The dead were there, too — there were dead a-plenty.

In the first faint gray of the morning, when the swarming advance had paused to resume something of definition as a line of battle, and skirmishers had been thrown forward, word was passed along to call the roll. The first sergeant of Lieutenant Dudley's company stepped to the front and began to name the men in alphabetical order. He had no written roll, but a good memory. The men answered to their names as he ran down the alphabet to G.

"Gorham."

"Here!"

"Grayrock."

"Here!"

The sergeant's good memory was affected by habit:

"Greene."

"Here!"

The response was clear, distinct, unmistakable!

A sudden movement, an agitation of the entire company front, as from an electric shock, attested the startling character of the incident. The sergeant paled and paused. The captain strode quickly to his side and said sharply:

"Call that name again."

Apparently the Society for Psychical Research is not first in the field of curiosity concerning the Unknown.

"Bennett Greene."

"Here!"

All faces turned in the direction of the familiar voice; the two men between whom in the order of stature Greene had commonly stood in line turned and squarely confronted each other.

"Once more," commanded the inexorable investigator, and once more came — a trifle tremulously — the name of the dead man:

"Bennett Story Greene."

"Here!"

At that instant a single rifle-shot was heard, away to the front, beyond the skirmish-line, followed, almost attended, by the savage hiss of an approaching bullet which, passing through the line, struck audibly, punctuating as with a full stop the captain's exclamation, "What the devil does it mean?"

Lieutenant Dudley pushed through the ranks from his place in the rear.

"It means this," he said, throwing open his coat and displaying a visibly broadening stain of crimson on his breast. His knees gave way; he fell awkwardly and lay dead.

A little later the regiment was ordered out of line to relieve the congested front, and through some misplay in the game of battle was not again under fire. Nor did Bennett Greene, expert in military executions, ever again signify his presence at one.

[1878; SOLE]

ON MILITARY EXECUTIONS[13]

I am reminded of an execution I once witnessed, at which a brace of miscreants assisted on the scaffold, and some thousands of not very sympathetic soldiers below it and about. It was in Murfreesboro, Tennessee, in war-time, and the fellows were hanged by the military for a murder of revolting atrocity, committed without orders. At the crucial moment one of them began a self-righteous assertion that he was "going home to Jesus." As the words left his mouth a railway engine standing near by uttered a loud and unmistakably derisive *Hoot — hoot!* It may have been accident, it may have been design; at any rate it expressed the "sense of the meeting" better than a leg's length of resolutions; and when the drop fell from beneath the feet of that pious assassin and his mate the ropes about their necks were actually kept slack for some seconds by the gusts of laughter ascending from below. They are the only persons I know in the other world who enjoyed the ghastly distinction of leaving this to the sound of inextinguishable merriment.

I once saw a cavalry soldier shot for desertion. He was seated *astride* his coffin, a black bandage about his eyes, his arms bound behind his back. The officer of the firing squad gave the commands "Ready-aim!" and a dozen loaded carbines were leveled at his breast. We heard him call out, up went the guns and the officer was seen to step forward and bend his ear to the man's lips. Then the officer stepped back, repeated the commands, and a second later the poor fellow was a thing of shreds and patches. "What did he say to you?" I afterward asked the officer. "Wanted to know if he couldn't have a saddle."

13. "Prattle," *Argonaut* 3 (December 21, 1878): 17. SOLE, 64.

[1898; CWAB, II]

AN AFFAIR OF OUTPOSTS

I

CONCERNING THE WISH TO BE DEAD

Two men sat in conversation. One was the Governor of the State. The year was 1861; the war was on and the Governor already famous for the intelligence and zeal with which he directed all the powers and resources of his State to the service of the Union.

"What! *you?*" the Governor was saying in evident surprise–"you too want a military commission? Really, the fifing and drumming must have effected a profound alteration in your convictions. In my character of recruiting sergeant I suppose I ought not to be fastidious, but" — there was a touch of irony in his manner–"well, have you forgotten that an oath of allegiance is required?"

"I have altered neither my convictions nor my sympathies," said the other, tranquilly. "While my sympathies are with the South, as you do me the honor to recollect, I have never doubted that the North was in the right. I am a Southerner in fact and in feeling, but it is my habit in matters of importance to act as I think, not as I feel."

The Governor was absently tapping his desk with a pencil; he did not immediately reply. After a while he said: "I have heard that there are all kinds of men in the world, so I suppose there are some like that, and doubtless you think yourself one. I've known you a long time and — pardon me — I don't think so."

"Then I am to understand that my application is denied?"

"Unless you can remove my belief that your Southern sympathies are in some degree a disqualification, yes. I do not doubt your good faith, and I know you to be abundantly fitted by intelligence and special training for the duties of an officer. Your convictions, you say, favor the Union cause, but I prefer a man with his heart in it. The heart is what men fight with."

"Look here, Governor," said the younger man, with a smile that had more light than warmth: "I have something up my sleeve — a qualification which I had hoped it would not be necessary to mention. A great military authority has given a simple recipe for being a good soldier:

'Try always to get yourself killed.' It is with that purpose that I wish to enter the service. I am not, perhaps, much of a patriot, but I wish to be dead."

The Governor looked at him rather sharply, then a little coldly. "There is a simpler and franker way," he said.

"In my family, sir," was the reply, "we do not do that — no Armisted has ever done that."

A long silence ensued and neither man looked at the other. Presently the Governor lifted his eyes from the pencil, which had resumed its tapping, and said:

"Who is she?"

"My wife."

The Governor tossed the pencil into the desk, rose and walked two or three times across the room. Then he turned to Armisted, who also had risen, looked at him more coldly than before and said: "But the man — would it not be better that he — could not the country spare him better than it can spare you? Or are the Armisteds opposed to 'the unwritten law'?"

The Armisteds, apparently, could feel an insult: the face of the younger man flushed, then paled, but he subdued himself to the service of his purpose.

"The man's identity is unknown to me," he said, calmly enough.

"Pardon me," said the Governor, with even less of visible contrition than commonly underlies those words. After a moment's reflection he added: "I shall send you to-morrow a captain's commission in the Tenth Infantry, now at Nashville, Tennessee. Good night."

"Good night, sir. I thank you."

Left alone, the Governor remained for a time motionless, leaning against his desk. Presently he shrugged his shoulders as if throwing off a burden. "This is a bad business," he said.

Seating himself at a reading-table before the fire, he took up the book nearest his hand, absently opening it. His eyes fell upon this sentence:

"When God made it necessary for an unfaithful wife to lie about her husband in justification of her own sins He had the tenderness to endow men with the folly to believe her."

He looked at the title of the book; it was, *His Excellency the Fool.*

He flung the volume into the fire.

II

HOW TO SAY WHAT IS WORTH HEARING

The enemy, defeated in two days of battle at Pittsburg Landing, had sullenly retired to Corinth, whence he had come. For manifest incompetence Grant, whose beaten army had been saved from destruction and capture by Buell's soldierly activity and skill, had been relieved of his command, which nevertheless had not been given to Buell, but to Halleck,[14] a man of unproved powers, a theorist, sluggish, irresolute. Foot by foot his troops, always deployed in line-of-battle to resist the enemy's bickering skirmishers, always entrenching against the columns that never came, advanced across the thirty miles of forest and swamp toward an antagonist prepared to vanish at contact, like a ghost at cockcrow. It was a campaign of "excursions and alarums," of reconnoissances and counter-marches, of cross-purposes and countermanded orders. For weeks the solemn farce held attention, luring distinguished civilians from fields of political ambition to see what they safely could of the horrors of war. Among these was our friend the Governor. At the headquarters of the army and in the camps of the troops from his State he was a familiar figure, attended by the several members of his personal staff, showily horsed, faultlessly betailored and bravely silk-hatted. Things of charm they were, rich in suggestions of peaceful lands beyond a sea of strife. The bedraggled soldier looked up from his trench as they passed, leaned upon his spade and audibly damned them to signify his sense of their ornamental irrelevance to the austerities of his trade.

"I think, Governor," said General Masterson one day, going into informal session atop of his horse and throwing one leg across the pommel of his saddle, his favorite posture–"I think I would not ride any farther in that direction if I were you. We've nothing out there but a

14. Henry Wager Halleck (1815–1872) was a career officer who wrote, among other books, *Elements of Military Art and Science* (1846). He commanded the Department of the Mississippi, taking direct command when Grant was relieved after the battle of Shiloh. In July 1862 Lincoln named Halleck as the Army General-in-Chief, a position he held until demoted when Grant took that position in 1864. Maybe the most unpopular man in the War Department, described by Secretary of the Navy Gideon Welles as a man who "plans nothing, suggests nothing, is good for nothing." SIFAKIS.

line of skirmishers. That, I presume, is why I was directed to put these siege guns here: if the skirmishers are driven in the enemy will die of dejection at being unable to haul them away — they're a trifle heavy."

There is reason to fear that the unstrained quality of this military humor dropped not as the gentle rain from heaven upon the place beneath the civilian's silk hat. Anyhow he abated none of his dignity in recognition.

"I understand," he said, gravely, "that some of my men are out there — a company of the Tenth, commanded by Captain Armisted. I should like to meet him if you do not mind."

"He is worth meeting. But there's a bad bit of jungle out there, and I should advise that you leave your horse and" — with a look at the Governor's retinue–"your other impedimenta."

The Governor went forward alone and on foot. In a half-hour he had pushed through a tangled undergrowth covering a boggy soil and entered upon firm and more open ground. Here he found a half-company of infantry lounging behind a line of stacked rifles. The men wore their accoutrements — their belts, cartridge-boxes, haversacks and canteens. Some lying at full length on the dry leaves were fast asleep: others in small groups gossiped idly of this and that; a few played at cards; none was far from the line of stacked arms. To the civilian's eye the scene was one of carelessness, confusion, indifference; a soldier would have observed expectancy and readiness.

At a little distance apart an officer in fatigue uniform, armed, sat on a fallen tree noting the approach of the visitor, to whom a sergeant, rising from one of the groups, now came forward.

"I wish to see Captain Armisted," said the Governor.

The sergeant eyed him narrowly, saying nothing, pointed to the officer, and taking a rifle from one of the stacks, accompanied him.

"This man wants to see you, sir," said the sergeant, saluting. The officer rose.

It would have been a sharp eye that would have recognized him. His hair, which but a few months before had been brown, was streaked with gray. His face, tanned by exposure, was seamed as with age. A long livid scar across the forehead marked the stroke of a sabre; one cheek was drawn and puckered by the work of a bullet. Only a woman of the loyal North would have thought the man handsome.

"Armisted — Captain," said the Governor, extending his hand, "do you not know me?"

"I know you, sir, and I salute you — as the Governor of my State."

Lifting his right hand to the level of his eyes he threw it outward and downward. In the code of military etiquette there is no provision for shaking hands. That of the civilian was withdrawn. If he felt either surprise or chagrin his face did not betray it.

"It is the hand that signed your commission," he said.

"And it is the hand — "

The sentence remains unfinished. The sharp report of a rifle came from the front, followed by another and another. A bullet hissed through the forest and struck a tree near by. The men sprang from the ground and even before the captain's high, clear voice was done intoning the command "At-ten-tion!" had fallen into line in rear of the stacked arms. Again — and now through the din of a crackling fusillade — sounded the strong, deliberate sing-song of authority: "Take . . . arms!" followed by the rattle of unlocking bayonets.

Bullets from the unseen enemy were now flying thick and fast, though mostly well spent and emitting the humming sound which signified interference by twigs and rotation in the plane of flight. Two or three of the men in the line were already struck and down. A few wounded men came limping awkwardly out of the undergrowth from the skirmish line in front; most of them did not pause, but held their way with white faces and set teeth to the rear.

Suddenly there was a deep, jarring report in front, followed by the startling rush of a shell, which passing overhead exploded in the edge of a thicket, setting afire the fallen leaves. Penetrating the din — seeming to float above it like the melody of a soaring bird — rang the slow, aspirated monotones of the captain's several commands, without emphasis, without accent, musical and restful as an evensong under the harvest moon. Familiar with this tranquilizing chant in moments of imminent peril, these raw soldiers of less than a year's training yielded themselves to the spell, executing its mandates with the composure and precision of veterans. Even the distinguished civilian behind his tree, hesitating between pride and terror, was accessible to its charm and suasion. He was conscious of a fortified resolution and ran away only when the skirmishers, under orders to rally on the reserve, came out of the woods like hunted hares and formed on the left of the stiff little line, breathing hard and thankful for the boon of breath.

III

THE FIGHTING OF ONE WHOSE HEART
WAS NOT IN THE QUARREL

Guided in his retreat by that of the fugitive wounded, the Governor struggled bravely to the rear through the "bad bit of jungle." He was well winded and a trifle confused. Excepting a single rifle-shot now and again, there was no sound of strife behind him; the enemy was pulling himself together for a new onset against an antagonist of whose numbers and tactical disposition he was in doubt. The fugitive felt that he would probably be spared to his country, and only commended the arrangements of Providence to that end, but in leaping a small brook in more open ground one of the arrangements incurred the mischance of a disabling sprain at the ankle. He was unable to continue his flight, for he was too fat to hop, and after several vain attempts, causing intolerable pain, seated himself on the earth to nurse his ignoble disability and deprecate the military situation.

A brisk renewal of the firing broke out and stray bullets came flitting and droning by. Then came the crash of two clean, definite volleys, followed by a continuous rattle, through which he heard the yells and cheers of the combatants, punctuated by thunderclaps of cannon. All this told him that Armisted's little command was bitterly beset and fighting at close quarters. The wounded men whom he had distanced began to straggle by on either hand, their numbers visibly augmented by new levies from the line. Singly and by twos and threes, some supporting comrades more desperately hurt than themselves, but all deaf to his appeals for assistance, they sifted through the underbrush and disappeared. The firing was increasingly louder and more distinct, and presently the ailing fugitives were succeeded by men who strode with a firmer tread, occasionally facing about and discharging their pieces, then doggedly resuming their retreat, reloading as they walked. Two or three fell as he looked, and lay motionless. One had enough of life left in him to make a pitiful attempt to drag himself to cover. A passing comrade paused beside him long enough to fire, appraised the poor devil's disability with a look and moved sullenly on, inserting a cartridge in his weapon.

In all this was none of the pomp of war—no hint of glory. Even in his distress and peril the helpless civilian could not forbear to contrast it with the gorgeous parades and reviews held in honor of himself—with the brilliant uniforms, the music, the banners, and the marching. It was an ugly and sickening business: to all that was artistic in his nature, revolting, brutal, in bad taste.

"Ugh!" he grunted, shuddering–"this is beastly! Where is the charm of it all? Where are the elevated sentiments, the devotion, the heroism, the—"

From a point somewhere near, in the direction of the pursuing enemy, rose the clear, deliberate sing-song of Captain Armisted.

"Stead-y, men—stead-y. Halt! Commence fir-ing."

The rattle of fewer than a score of rifles could be distinguished through the general uproar, and again that penetrating falsetto:

"Cease fir-ing. In re-treat. . . . maaarch!"

In a few moments this remnant had drifted slowly past the Governor, all to the right of him as they faced in retiring, the men deployed at intervals of a half-dozen paces. At the extreme left and a few yards behind came the captain. The civilian called out his name, but he did not hear. A swarm of men in gray now broke out of cover in pursuit, making directly for the spot where the Governor lay—some accident of the ground had caused them to converge upon that point: their line had become a crowd. In a last struggle for life and liberty the Governor attempted to rise, and looking back the captain saw him. Promptly, but with the same slow precision as before, he sang his commands:

"Skirm-ish-ers, halt!" The men stopped and according to rule turned to face the enemy.

"Ral-ly on the right!"—and they came in at a run, fixing bayonets and forming loosely on the man at that end of the line.

"Forward . . to save the Gov-ern-or of your State . . doub-le quick . . . maaarch!"

Only one man disobeyed this astonishing command! He was dead. With a cheer they sprang forward over the twenty or thirty paces between them and their task. The captain having a shorter distance to go arrived first—simultaneously with the enemy. A half-dozen hasty shots were fired at him, and the foremost man—a fellow of heroic stature, hatless and bare-breasted — made a vicious sweep at his head with a clubbed rifle. The officer parried the blow at the cost of a broken arm and drove his sword to the hilt into the behemoth's breast. As the body fell the weapon was wrenched from his hand and before he could pluck his revolver from the scabbard at his belt another man leaped upon him like a tiger, fastening both hands upon his throat and bearing him backward upon the prostrate Governor, still struggling to rise. This man was promptly spitted upon the bayonet of a Federal sergeant and his death-grip on the captain's throat loosened by a kick upon each wrist. When the captain had risen he was at the rear of his men, who had all passed over and around him and were thrusting fiercely at their more numerous but less coherent antagonists. Nearly all the rifles on both sides were empty and in the crush there was neither time nor room to reload. The Confederates were at a disadvantage in that most of them lacked bayonets; they fought by bludgeoning — and a clubbed rifle is a formidable arm. The sound of the conflict was a clatter, like that of the interlocking horns of battling bulls — now and then the pash of a crushed skull, an oath, or a grunt caused by the impact of a rifle's muzzle against the abdomen transfixed by its bayonet. Through an opening made by the fall of one of his men Captain Armisted sprang, with his dangling left arm; in his right hand a full-charged revolver, which he fired with rapidity and terrible effect into the thick of the gray crowd: but across the bodies of the slain the survivors in the front were pushed forward by their comrades in the rear till again they breasted the tireless bayonets. There were fewer bayonets now to breast — a beggarly half-dozen, all told. A few minutes more of this rough work — a little fighting back to back — and all would be over.

Suddenly a lively firing was heard on the right and the left: a fresh line of Federal skirmishers came forward at a run, driving before them those parts of the Confederate line that had been separated by staying the advance of the centre. And behind these new and noisy combatants, at a distance of two or three hundred yards, could be seen, indistinct among the trees a line-of-battle!

Instinctively before retiring, the crowd in gray made a tremendous rush upon its handful of antagonists, overwhelming them by mere momentum and, unable to use weapons in the crush, trampled them, stamped savagely on their limbs, their bodies, their necks, their faces;

then retiring with bloody feet across its own dead it joined the general rout and the incident was at an end.

IV

THE GREAT HONOR THE GREAT

The Governor, who had been unconscious, opened his eyes and stared about him, slowly recalling the day's events. A man in the uniform of a major was kneeling beside him; he was a surgeon. Grouped about were the civilian members of the Governor's staff, their faces expressing a natural solicitude regarding their offices. A little apart stood General Masterson addressing another officer and gesticulating with a cigar. He was saying: "It was the beautifulest fight ever made — by God, sir, it was great!"

The beauty and greatness were attested by a row of dead, trimly disposed, and another of wounded, less formally placed, restless, half-naked, but bravely bebandaged.

"How do you feel, sir?" said the surgeon. "I find no wound."

"I think I am all right," the patient replied, sitting up. "It is that ankle."

The surgeon transferred his attention to the ankle, cutting away the boot. All eyes followed the knife.

In moving the leg a folded paper was uncovered. The patient picked it up and carelessly opened it. It was a letter three months old, signed "Julia." Catching sight of his name in it he read it. It was nothing very remarkable — merely a weak woman's confession of unprofitable sin — the penitence of a faithless wife deserted by her betrayer. The letter had fallen from the pocket of Captain Armisted; the reader quietly transferred it to his own.

An aide-de-camp rode up and dismounted. Advancing to the Governor he saluted.

"Sir," he said, "I am sorry to find you wounded — the Commanding General has not been informed. He presents his compliments and I am directed to say that he has ordered for to-morrow a grand review of the reserve corps in your honor. I venture to add that the General's carriage is at your service if you are able to attend."

"Be pleased to say to the Commanding General that I am deeply touched by his kindness. If you have the patience to wait a few moments you shall convey a more definite reply."

He smiled brightly and glancing at the surgeon and his assistants added: "At present — if you will permit an allusion to the horrors of peace — I am 'in the hands of my friends.'"

The humor of the great is infectious; all laughed who heard.

"Where is Captain Armisted?" the Governor asked, not altogether carelessly.

The surgeon looked up from his work, pointing silently to the nearest body in the row of dead, the features discreetly covered with a handkerchief. It was so near that the great man could have laid his hand upon it, but he did not. He may have feared that it would bleed.

[1890; CWAB, II]

AN OCCURRENCE AT OWL CREEK BRIDGE

I

A man stood upon a railroad bridge in northern Alabama, looking down into the swift water twenty feet below. The man's hands were behind his back, the wrists bound with a cord. A rope closely encircled his neck. It was attached to a stout cross-timber above his head and the slack fell to the level of his knees. Some loose boards laid upon the sleepers supporting the metals of the railway supplied a footing for him and his executioners — two private soldiers of the Federal army, directed by a sergeant who in civil life may have been a deputy sheriff. At a short remove upon the same temporary platform was an officer in the uniform of his rank, armed. He was a captain. A sentinel at each end of the bridge stood with his rifle in the position known as "support," that is to say, vertical in front of the left shoulder, the hammer resting on the forearm thrown straight across the chest — a formal and unnatural position, enforcing an erect carriage of the body. It did not appear to be the duty of these two men to know what was occurring at the centre of the bridge; they merely blockaded the two ends of the foot planking that traversed it.

Beyond one of the sentinels nobody was in sight; the railroad ran straight away into a forest for a hundred yards, then, curving, was lost to view. Doubtless there was an outpost farther along. The other bank of the stream was open ground — a gentle acclivity topped with a stockade of vertical tree trunks, loopholed for rifles, with a single embrasure through which protruded the muzzle of a brass cannon commanding the bridge. Midway of the slope between bridge and fort were the spectators — a single company of infantry in line, at "parade rest," the butts of the rifles on the ground, the barrels inclining slightly backward against the right shoulder, the hands crossed upon the stock. A lieutenant stood at the right of the line, the point of his sword upon the ground, his left hand resting upon his right. Excepting the group of four at the centre of the bridge, not a man moved. The company faced the bridge, staring stonily, motionless. The sentinels, facing the banks of the stream, might have been statues to adorn the bridge. The captain stood with folded arms, silent, observing the work of his subordinates, but making no sign. Death is a dignitary who when he comes announced is to be received with formal manifestations of respect, even by those most familiar with him. In the code of military etiquette silence and fixity are forms of deference.

The man who was engaged in being hanged was apparently about thirty-five years of age. He was a civilian, if one might judge from his habit, which was that of a planter. His features were good—a straight nose, firm mouth, broad forehead, from which his long, dark hair was combed straight back, falling behind his ears to the collar of his well-fitting frock-coat. He wore a mustache and pointed beard, but no whiskers; his eyes were large and dark gray, and had a kindly expression which one would hardly have expected in one whose neck was in the hemp. Evidently this was no vulgar assassin. The liberal military code makes provision for hanging many kinds of persons, and gentlemen are not excluded.

The preparations being complete, the two private soldiers stepped aside and each drew away the plank upon which he had been standing. The sergeant turned to the captain, saluted and placed himself immediately behind that officer, who in turn moved apart one pace. These movements left the condemned man and the sergeant standing on the two ends of the same plank, which spanned three of the cross-ties of the bridge. The end upon which the civilian stood almost, but not quite, reached a fourth. This plank had been held in place by the weight of the captain; it was now held by that of the sergeant. At a signal from the former the latter would step aside, the plank would tilt and the condemned man go down between two ties. The arrangement commended itself to his judgment as simple and effective. His face had not been covered nor his eyes bandaged. He looked a moment at his "unsteadfast footing," then let his gaze wander to the swirling water of the stream racing madly beneath his feet. A piece of dancing driftwood caught his attention and his eyes followed it down the current. How slowly it appeared to move! What a sluggish stream!

He closed his eyes in order to fix his last thoughts upon his wife and children. The water, touched to gold by the early sun, the brooding mists under the banks at some distance down the stream, the fort, the soldiers, the piece of drift—all had distracted him. And now he became conscious of a new disturbance. Striking through the thought of his dear ones was a sound which he could neither ignore nor understand, a sharp, distinct, metallic percussion like the stroke of a blacksmith's hammer upon the anvil; it had the same ringing quality. He wondered what it was, and whether immeasurably distant or near by—it seemed both. Its recurrence was regular, but as slow as the tolling of a death knell. He awaited each stroke with impatience and—he knew not why—apprehension. The intervals of silence grew progressively longer; the delays became maddening. With their greater infrequency the sounds increased in strength and sharpness. They hurt his ear like the thrust of a knife; he feared he would shriek. What he heard was the ticking of his watch.

He unclosed his eyes and saw again the water below him. "If I could free my hands," he thought, "I might throw off the noose and spring into the stream. By diving I could evade the bullets and, swimming vigorously, reach the bank, take to the woods and get away home. My home, thank God, is as yet outside their lines; my wife and little ones are still beyond the invader's farthest advance."

As these thoughts, which have here to be set down in words, were flashed into the doomed man's brain rather than evolved from it the captain nodded to the sergeant. The sergeant stepped aside.

II

Peyton Farquhar was a well-to-do planter, of an old and highly respected Alabama family. Being a slave owner and like other slave owners a politician he was naturally an original secessionist and ardently devoted to the Southern cause. Circumstances of an imperious nature, which it is unnecessary to relate here, had prevented him from taking service with the gallant army that had fought the disastrous campaigns ending with the fall of Corinth, and he chafed under the inglorious restraint, longing for the release of his energies, the larger life of the soldier, the opportunity for distinction. That opportunity, he felt, would come, as it comes to all in war time. Meanwhile he did what he could. No service was too humble for him to perform in aid of the South, no adventure too perilous for him to undertake if consistent with the character of a civilian who was at heart a soldier, and who in good faith and without too much qualification assented to at least a part of the frankly villainous dictum that all is fair in love and war.

One evening while Farquhar and his wife were sitting on a rustic bench near the entrance to his grounds, a gray-clad soldier rode up to the gate and asked for a drink of water. Mrs. Farquhar was only too happy to serve him with her own white hands. While she was fetching the water her husband approached the dusty horseman and inquired eagerly for news from the front.

"The Yanks are repairing the railroads," said the man, "and are getting ready for another advance. They have reached the Owl Creek bridge, put it in order and built a stockade on the north bank. The commandant has issued an order, which is posted everywhere, declaring that any civilian caught interfering with the railroad, its bridges, tunnels or trains will be summarily hanged. I saw the order."

"How far is it to the Owl Creek bridge?" Farquhar asked.

"About thirty miles."

"Is there no force on this side the creek?"

"Only a picket post half a mile out, on the railroad, and a single sentinel at this end of the bridge."

"Suppose a man — a civilian and student of hanging — should elude the picket post and perhaps get the better of the sentinel," said Farquhar, smiling, "what could he accomplish?"

The soldier reflected. "I was there a month ago," he replied. "I observed that the flood of last winter had lodged a great quantity of driftwood against the wooden pier at this end of the bridge. It is now dry and would burn like tow."

The lady had now brought the water, which the soldier drank. He thanked her ceremoniously, bowed to her husband and rode away. An hour later, after nightfall, he repassed the plantation, going northward in the direction from which he had come. He was a Federal scout.

III

As Peyton Farquhar fell straight downward through the bridge he lost consciousness and was as one already dead. From this state he was awakened — ages later, it seemed to him — by the pain of a sharp pressure upon his throat, followed by a sense of suffocation. Keen, poignant agonies seemed to shoot from his neck downward through every fibre of his body and limbs. These pains appeared to flash along well-defined lines of ramification and to beat with an inconceivably rapid periodicity. They seemed like streams of pulsating fire heating him to an intolerable temperature. As to his head, he was conscious of nothing but a feeling of fullness — of congestion. These sensations were unaccompanied by thought. The intellectual part of his nature was already effaced; he had power only to feel, and feeling was torment. He was conscious of motion. Encompassed in a luminous cloud, of which he was now merely the fiery heart, without material substance, he swung through unthinkable arcs of oscillation, like a vast pendulum. Then all at once, with terrible suddenness, the light about him shot upward with the noise of a loud plash; a frightful roaring was in his ears, and all was cold and dark. The power of thought was restored; he knew that the rope had broken and he had fallen into the stream. There was no additional strangulation; the noose about his neck was already suffocating him and kept the water from his lungs. To die of hanging at the bottom of a river! — the idea seemed to him ludicrous. He opened his eyes in the darkness and saw above him a gleam of light, but how distant, how inaccessible! He was still sinking, for the light became fainter and fainter until it was a mere glimmer. Then it began to grow and brighten, and he knew that he was rising toward the surface — knew it with reluctance, for he was now very comfortable. "To be hanged and drowned," he thought, "that is not so bad; but I do not wish to be shot. No; I will not be shot; that is not fair."

He was not conscious of an effort, but a sharp pain in his wrist apprised him that he was trying to free his hands. He gave the struggle his attention, as an idler might observe the feat of a juggler, without interest in the outcome. What splendid effort! — what magnificent, what super-human strength! Ah, that was a fine endeavor! Bravo! The cord fell away; his arms parted and floated upward, the hands dimly seen on each side in the growing light. He watched them with a new interest as first one and then the other pounced upon the noose at his neck. They tore it away and thrust it fiercely aside, its undulations resembling those of a water-snake. "Put it back, put it back!" He thought he shouted these words to his hands, for the undoing of the noose had been succeeded by the direst pang that he had yet experienced. His neck ached horribly; his brain was on fire; his heart, which had been fluttering faintly, gave a great leap, trying to force itself out at his mouth. His whole body was racked and wrenched with an insupportable anguish! But his disobedient hands gave no heed to the command. They beat the water vigorously with quick, downward strokes, forcing him to the surface. He felt his head emerge; his eyes were blinded by the sunlight; his chest expanded convulsively, and with a supreme and crowning agony his lungs engulfed a great draught of air, which instantly he expelled in a shriek!

He was now in full possession of his physical senses. They were, indeed, preternaturally keen and alert. Something in the awful disturbance of his organic system had so exalted and refined them that they made record of things never before perceived. He felt the ripples upon his face and heard their separate sounds as they struck. He looked at the forest on the bank of the stream, saw the individual trees, the leaves and the veining of each leaf—saw the very insects upon them: the locusts, the brilliant-bodied flies, the gray spiders stretching their webs from twig to twig. He noted the prismatic colors in all the dewdrops upon a million blades of grass. The humming of the gnats that danced above the eddies of the stream, the beating of the dragon-flies' wings, the strokes of the water-spiders' legs, like oars which had lifted their boat—all these made audible music. A fish slid along beneath his eyes and he heard the rush of its body parting the water.

He had come to the surface facing down the stream; in a moment the visible world seemed to wheel slowly round, himself the pivotal point, and he saw the bridge, the fort, the soldiers upon the bridge, the captain, the sergeant, the two privates, his executioners. They were in silhouette against the blue sky. They shouted and gesticulated, pointing at him. The captain had drawn his pistol, but did not fire; the others were unarmed. Their movements were grotesque and horrible, their forms gigantic.

Suddenly he heard a sharp report and something struck the water smartly within a few inches of his head, spattering his face with spray. He heard a second report, and saw one of the sentinels with his rifle at his shoulder, a light cloud of blue smoke rising from the muzzle. The man in the water saw the eye of the man on the bridge gazing into his own through the sights of the rifle. He observed that it was a gray eye and remembered having read that gray eyes were keenest, and that all famous markmen had them. Nevertheless, this one had missed.

A counter-swirl had caught Farquhar and turned him half round; he was again looking into the forest on the bank opposite the fort. The sound of a clear, high voice in a monotonous singsong now rang out behind him and came across the water with a distinctness that pierced and subdued all other sounds, even the beating of the ripples in his ears. Although no soldier, he had frequented camps enough to know the dread significance of that deliberate, drawling, aspirated chant; the lieutenant on shore was taking a part in the morning's work. How coldly and pitilessly—with what an even, calm intonation, presaging, and enforcing tranquillity in the men —with what accurately measured intervals fell those cruel words:

"Attention, company! . . . Shoulder arms! . . . Ready! . . . Aim! . . . Fire!"

Farquhar dived—dived as deeply as he could. The water roared in his ears like the voice of Niagara, yet he heard the dulled thunder of the volley and, rising again toward the surface, met shining bits of metal, singularly flattened, oscillating slowly downward. Some of them touched him on the face and hands, then fell away, continuing their descent. One lodged between his collar and neck; it was uncomfortably warm and he snatched it out.

As he rose to the surface, gasping for breath, he saw that he had been a long time under water; he was perceptibly farther down stream — nearer to safety. The soldiers had almost finished reloading; the metal ramrods flashed all at once in the sunshine as they were drawn from the barrels, turned in the air, and thrust into their sockets. The two sentinels fired again, independently and ineffectually.

The hunted man saw all this over his shoulder; he was now swimming vigorously with the current. His brain was as energetic as his arms and legs; he thought with the rapidity of lightning.

"The officer," he reasoned, "will not make that martinet's error a second time. It is as easy to dodge a volley as a single shot. He has probably already given the command to fire at will. God help me, I cannot dodge them all!"

An appalling plash within two yards of him was followed by a loud, rushing sound, *diminuendo*, which seemed to travel back through the air to the fort and died in an explosion which stirred the very river to its deeps! A rising sheet of water curved over him, fell down upon him, blinded him, strangled him! The cannon had taken a hand in the game. As he shook his head free from the commotion of the smitten water he heard the deflected shot humming through the air ahead, and in an instant it was cracking and smashing the branches in the forest beyond.

"They will not do that again," he thought; "the next time they will use a charge of grape. I must keep my eye upon the gun; the smoke will apprise me — the report arrives too late; it lags behind the missile. That is a good gun."

Suddenly he felt himself whirled round and round — spinning like a top. The water, the banks, the forests, the now distant bridge, fort and men — all were commingled and blurred. Objects were represented by their colors only; circular horizontal streaks of color — that was all he saw. He had been caught in a vortex and was being whirled on with a velocity of advance and gyration that made him giddy and sick. In a few moments he was flung upon the gravel at the foot of the left bank of the stream — the southern bank — and behind a projecting point which concealed him from his enemies. The sudden arrest of his motion, the abrasion of one of his hands on the gravel, restored him, and he wept with delight. He dug his fingers into the sand, threw it over himself in handfuls and audibly blessed it. It looked like diamonds, rubies, emeralds; he could think of nothing beautiful which it did not resemble. The trees upon the bank were giant garden plants; he noted a definite order in their arrangement, inhaled the fragrance of their blooms. A strange, roseate light shone through the spaces among their trunks and the wind made in their branches the music of aeolian harps. He had no wish to perfect his escape — was content to remain in that enchanting spot until retaken.

A whiz and rattle of grapeshot among the branches high above his head roused him from his dream. The baffled cannoneer had fired him a random farewell. He sprang to his feet, rushed up the sloping bank, and plunged into the forest.

All that day he traveled, laying his course by the rounding sun. The forest seemed interminable; nowhere did he discover a break in it, not even a woodman's road. He had not known that he lived in so wild a region. There was something uncanny in the revelation.

By nightfall he was fatigued, footsore, famishing. The thought of his wife and children urged him on. At last he found a road which led him in what he knew to be the right direction, It was as wide and straight as a city street, yet it seemed untraveled. No fields bordered it, no dwelling anywhere. Not so much as the barking of a dog suggested human habitation. The black bodies of the trees formed a straight wall on both sides, terminating on the horizon in a point, like a diagram in a lesson in perspective. Overhead, as he looked up through this rift in the wood, shone great golden stars looking unfamiliar and grouped in strange constellations. He was sure they were arranged in some order which had a secret and malign significance. The wood on either side was full of singular noises, among which — once, twice, and again — he distinctly heard whispers in an unknown tongue.

His neck was in pain and lifting his hand to it he found it horribly swollen. He knew that it had a circle of black where the rope had bruised it. His eyes felt congested; he could no longer close them. His tongue was swollen with thirst; he relieved its fever by thrusting it forward from between his teeth into the cold air. How softly the turf had carpeted the untraveled avenue — he could no longer feel the roadway beneath his feet!

Doubtless, despite his suffering, he had fallen asleep while walking, for now he sees another scene — perhaps he has merely recovered from a delirium. He stands at the gate of his own home. All is as he left it, and all bright and beautiful in the morning sunshine. He must have traveled the entire night. As he pushes open the gate and passes up the wide white walk, he sees a flutter of female garments; his wife, looking fresh and cool and sweet, steps down from the veranda to meet him. At the bottom of the steps she stands waiting, with a smile of ineffable joy, an attitude of matchless grace and dignity. Ah, how beautiful she is! He springs forward with extended arms. As he is about to clasp her he feels a stunning blow upon the back of the neck; a blinding white light blazes all about him with a sound like the shock of a cannon — then all is darkness and silence!

Peyton Farquhar was dead; his body, with a broken neck, swung gently from side to side beneath the timbers of the Owl Creek bridge.

[1889; CWAB, II]

THE COUP DE GRÂCE

The fighting had been hard and continuous; that was attested by all the senses. The very taste of battle was in the air. All was now over; it remained only to succor the wounded and bury the dead — to "tidy up a bit," as the humorist of a burial squad put it. A good deal of "tidying up" was required. As far as one could see through the forests, among the splintered trees, lay wrecks of men and horses. Among them moved the stretcher-bearers, gathering and carrying away the few who showed signs of life. Most of the wounded had died of neglect while the right to minister to their wants was in dispute. It is an army regulation that the wounded must wait; the best way to care for them is to win the battle. It must be confessed that victory is a distinct advantage to a man requiring attention, but many do not live to avail themselves of it.

The dead were collected in groups of a dozen or a score and laid side by side in rows while the trenches were dug to receive them. Some, found at too great a distance from these rallying points, were buried where they lay. There was little attempt at identification, though in most cases, the burial parties being detailed to glean the same ground which they had assisted to reap, the names of the victorious dead were known and listed. The enemy's fallen had to be content with counting. But of that they got enough: many of them were counted several times, and the total, as given afterward in the official report of the victorious commander, denoted rather a hope than a result.

At some little distance from the spot where one of the burial parties had established its "bivouac of the dead," a man in the uniform of a Federal officer stood leaning against a tree. From his feet upward to his neck his attitude was that of weariness reposing; but he turned his head uneasily from side to side; his mind was apparently not at rest. He was perhaps uncertain in which direction to go; he was not likely to remain long where he was, for already the level rays of the setting sun straggled redly through the open spaces of the wood and the weary soldiers were quitting their task for the day. He would hardly make a night of it alone there among the dead. Nine men in ten whom you meet after a battle inquire the way to some fraction of the army — as if any one could know. Doubtless this officer was lost. After resting himself a moment he would presumably follow one of the retiring burial squads.

When all were gone he walked straight away into the forest toward the red west, its light staining his face like blood. The air of confidence with which he now strode along showed that he was on familiar ground; he had recovered his bearings. The dead on his right and on his left were unregarded as he passed. An occasional low moan from some sorely-stricken wretch whom the relief-parties had not reached, and who would have to pass a comfortless night beneath the stars with his thirst to keep him company, was equally unheeded. What, indeed, could the officer have done, being no surgeon and having no water?

At the head of a shallow ravine, a mere depression of the ground, lay a small group of bodies. He saw, and swerving suddenly from his course walked rapidly toward them. Scanning each one sharply as he passed, he stopped at last above one which lay at a slight remove from the others, near a clump of small trees. He looked at it narrowly. It seemed to stir. He stooped and laid his hand upon its face. It screamed.

The officer was Captain Downing Madwell, of a Massachusetts regiment of infantry, a daring and intelligent soldier, an honorable man.

In the regiment were two brothers named Halcrow—Caffal and Creede Halcrow. Caffal Halcrow was a sergeant in Captain Madwell's company, and these two men, the sergeant and the captain, were devoted friends. In so far as disparity of rank, difference in duties and considerations of military discipline would permit they were commonly together. They had, indeed, grown up together from childhood. A habit of the heart is not easily broken off. Caffal Halcrow had nothing military in his taste nor disposition, but the thought of separation from his friend was disagreeable; he enlisted in the company in which Madwell was second-lieutenant. Each had taken two steps upward in rank, but between the highest non-commissioned and the lowest commissioned officer the gulf is deep and wide and the old relation was maintained with difficulty and a difference.

Creede Halcrow, the brother of Caffal, was the major of the regiment—a cynical, saturnine man, between whom and Captain Madwell there was a natural antipathy which circumstances had nourished and strengthened to an active animosity. But for the restraining influence of their mutual relation to Caffal these two patriots would doubtless have endeavored to deprive their country of each other's services.

At the opening of the battle that morning the regiment was performing outpost duty a mile away from the main army. It was attacked and nearly surrounded in the forest, but stubbornly held its ground. During a lull in the fighting, Major Halcrow came to Captain Madwell. The two exchanged formal salutes, and the major said: "Captain, the colonel directs that you push your company to the head of this ravine and hold your place there until recalled. I need hardly apprise you of the dangerous character of the movement, but if you wish, you can, I suppose, turn over the command to your first-lieutenant. I was not, however, directed to authorize the substitution; it is merely a suggestion of my own, unofficially made."

To this deadly insult Captain Madwell coolly replied:

"Sir, I invite you to accompany the movement. A mounted officer would be a conspicuous mark, and I have long held the opinion that it would be better if you were dead."

The art of repartee was cultivated in military circles as early as 1862.

A half-hour later Captain Madwell's company was driven from its position at the head of the ravine, with a loss of one-third its number. Among the fallen was Sergeant Halcrow. The regiment was soon afterward forced back to the main line, and at the close of the battle was miles away. The captain was now standing at the side of his subordinate and friend.

Sergeant Halcrow was mortally hurt. His clothing was deranged; it seemed to have been violently torn apart, exposing the abdomen. Some of the buttons of his jacket had been pulled off and lay on the ground beside him and fragments of his other garments were strewn about. His leather belt was parted and had apparently been dragged from beneath him as he lay. There had been no great effusion of blood. The only visible wound was a wide, ragged opening in the abdomen. It was defiled with earth and dead leaves. Protruding from it was a loop of small intestine. In all his experience Captain Madwell had not seen a wound like this. He could neither conjecture how it was made nor explain the attendant circumstances — the strangely torn clothing, the parted belt, the besmirching of the white skin. He knelt and made a closer examination. When he rose to his feet, he turned his eyes in different directions as if looking for an enemy. Fifty yards away, on the crest of a low, thinly wooded hill, he saw several dark objects moving

about among the fallen men — a herd of swine. One stood with its back
to him, its shoulders sharply elevated. Its forefeet were upon a human
body, its head was depressed and invisible. The bristly ridge of its chine
showed black against the red west. Captain Madwell drew away his eyes
and fixed them again upon the thing which had been his friend.

The man who had suffered these monstrous mutilations was alive. At
intervals he moved his limbs; he moaned at every breath. He stared
blankly into the face of his friend and if touched screamed. In his giant
agony he had torn up the ground on which he lay; his clenched hands
were full of leaves and twigs and earth. Articulate speech was beyond
his power; it was impossible to know if he were sensible to anything but
pain. The expression of his face was an appeal; his eyes were full of
prayer. For what?

There was no misreading that look; the captain had too frequently
seen it in eyes of those whose lips had still the power to formulate it by
an entreaty for death. Consciously or unconsciously, this writhing fragment of humanity, this type and example of acute sensation, this handi-
work of man and beast, this humble, unheroic Prometheus, was implor-
ing everything, all, the whole non-ego, for the boon of oblivion. To the
earth and the sky alike, to the trees, to the man, to whatever took form
in sense or consciousness, this incarnate suffering addressed that silent
plea.

For what, indeed? For that which we accord to even the meanest
creature without sense to demand it, denying it only to the wretched of
our own race: for the blessed release, the rite of uttermost compassion,
the *coup de grâce*.

Captain Madwell spoke the name of his friend. He repeated it over
and over without effect until emotion choked his utterance. His tears
plashed upon the livid face beneath his own and blinded himself. He
saw nothing but a blurred and moving object, but the moans were more
distinct than ever, interrupted at briefer intervals by sharper shrieks.
He turned away, struck his hand upon his forehead, and strode from
the spot. The swine, catching sight of him, threw up their crimson
muzzles, regarding him suspiciously a second, and then with a gruff,
concerted grunt, raced away out of sight. A horse, its foreleg splintered
by a cannon-shot, lifted its head sidewise from the ground and neighed
piteously. Madwell stepped forward, drew his revolver and shot the
poor beast between the eyes, narrowly observing its death-struggle,

which, contrary to his expectation, was violent and long; but at last it lay still. The tense muscles of its lips, which had uncovered the teeth in a horrible grin, relaxed; the sharp, clean-cut profile took on a look of profound peace and rest.

Along the distant, thinly wooded crest to westward the fringe of sunset fire had now nearly burned itself out. The light upon the trunks of the trees had faded to a tender gray; shadows were in their tops, like great dark birds aperch. Night was coming and there were miles of haunted forest between Captain Madwell and camp. Yet he stood there at the side of the dead animal, apparently lost to all sense of his sur-roundings. His eyes were bent upon the earth at his feet; his left hand hung loosely at his side, his right still held the pistol. Presently he lifted his face, turned it toward his dying friend and walked rapidly back to his side. He knelt upon one knee, cocked the weapon, placed the muzzle against the man's forehead, and turning away his eyes pulled the trigger. There was no report. He had used his last cartridge for the horse.

The sufferer moaned and his lips moved convulsively. The froth that ran from them had a tinge of blood.

Captain Madwell rose to his feet and drew his sword from the scab-bard. He passed the fingers of his left hand along the edge from hilt to point. He held it out straight before him, as if to test his nerves. There was no visible tremor of the blade; the ray of bleak skylight that it reflected was steady and true. He stooped and with his left hand tore away the dying man's shirt, rose and placed the point of the sword just over the heart. This time he did not withdraw his eyes. Grasping the hilt with both hands, he thrust downward with all his strength and weight. The blade sank into the man's body — through his body into the earth; Captain Madwell came near falling forward upon his work. The dying man drew up his knees and at the same time threw his right arm across his breast and grasped the steel so tightly that the knuckles of the hand visibly whitened. By a violent but vain effort to withdraw the blade the wound was enlarged; a rill of blood escaped, running sinuously down into the deranged clothing. At that moment three men stepped silently forward from behind the clump of young trees which had concealed their approach. Two were hospital attendants and carried a stretcher.

The third was Major Creede Halcrow.

CHAPTER THREE

1863

A True War Story Is Never Moral,

Pride, a prime component of honor, courage, manhood, and duty, is one of the seven deadly sins. Bierce took great pleasure in exploring the limits of pride in his stories and newspaper articles. Embarrassment and fear itself are tied to pride as Civil War soldiers sought to prove themselves men in the face of imminent danger. Most overcame their fear in what historian Gerald Linderman has called "embattled courage." For soldiers who had joined early but still had not "seen the elephant"—a soldier's phrase for battle—and for new recruits and officers joining the war in 1863, embarrassment and fear were commonplace enough, especially when they encountered, joined, or led veteran soldiers. For Bierce, these concerns about the morality of honor, courage, duty, and pride are ultimately illusory. The greater truth of warfare is elemental: men fight, men suffer, men die. Whether they fight with courage, whether they suffer with honor, whether they prove their manhood in death—these ultimately mean nothing. Bierce foreshadowed Vietnam author Tim O'Brien's insight: A true war story is never moral.

In 1863, when the supply of volunteers failed to keep up with fate's "demand" for battlefield casualties, the U.S. government instituted a Conscription Act to draft civilians into the army. To cover demand, Lincoln issued his Emancipation Proclamation, freeing the slaves, but also opening military service to African American soldiers. Because these "new-be's" had to be drafted or were of a different race, they were viewed derisively by those who had joined when the war first opened. Bierce often wrote clearly about the differences between civilians untested in the face of the "Rebel yell" and bloodied men.

Bierce had a small respite from battle when the army settled into winter camp at Readyville, Tennessee, after the Stone's River battle. Bierce had only recently pinned on the gold bars of a second lieutenant when he replaced them on April 25 with silver bars. First Lieutenant Bierce did duty as a provost marshal, overseeing executions, as a scout seeking information for Hazen's brigade, and, finally, as a topographical engineer surveying terrain, finding routes, and drawing maps. Finally, on Midsummer's Day, the Army of the Cumberland formed into columns and marched off toward Chattanooga, an important railroad center and invasion route into Georgia. As the Federals approached, Confederate General Bragg fell back to Chickamauga Creek, Georgia, and when Rosecrans followed a bit too closely, Bragg reversed and, on September 19, hit hard into the Union lines, playing a sort of deadly hide and seek in the abundant dense woods and few open fields. Luck is an important part of battle and it was with the Confederates at Chickamauga. Rosecrans mistakenly removed one of his divisions (Wood's) from the very spot where a Confederate attack would come just minutes later. Rebels swept through the gap unmolested, cut the Union line, and swarmed against and behind isolated units. The Federal line fell apart with only George Thomas preventing a complete rout by holding firm on the left — and thereby gaining the sobriquet, "the Rock of Chickamauga." Still, it was the bloodiest two-day battle of the war, tolling Rosecrans's dead, wounded, and missing at 16,170, and Bragg's at 18,454. Miraculously, again, Bierce came through completely unscathed physically but deeply affected by what he had seen and done. His bravery compelled Hazen to ask and be granted permission to have Bierce, a man "among the very best in the service" permanently assigned to his staff for the duration of the war. From that position on staff, Bierce met or sat with Grant, Sherman, and other war leaders.

Bragg's army took up siege operations against the Federals, who, on September 20, placed themselves in a defensive posture at Chattanooga. Bragg placed his army on the high ground overlooking the town and the railroads, a mountainous line known as Missionary Ridge. Lincoln had appointed U. S. Grant to command all Union forces in the West and he quickly replaced Rosecrans with Thomas and sent 40,000 reinforcements under William Sherman and Joseph Hooker to raise the siege. Grant personally went to Chattanooga to push the offensive. On November 25, Sherman made repeated assaults on the Confederate position to no avail. Thomas's attack, with Hazen's brigade and the

Ninth Indiana in front, had better success, startling everyone — and became legendary in Civil War lore — when, without orders or coordination, the men irresistibly charged directly uphill in the center of the Confederate line and, somehow, broke through and secured the ridge for the Union. Hazen and Bierce were among the first ones over the breastworks, ordering Confederate cannon to be aimed and fired into the Rebel lines. Bragg retreated into Georgia and the Union army went into winter camp. Casualties seemed light these days at "only" 12,482: Union 5,815, Confederate 6,667.

Most narratives of battle leave out women and children and draw a picture of men charging and winning or retreating and losing. But battles happened in towns and in the open fields, plowed or planted with crops, and non-combatants were trapped by the suddenness of the encounters. We don't have a single study of what it was like for children to see the dead and wounded that covered the ground and filled the hospitals all over the South. Confederates especially fought near their homes, going home whenever possible to see about their loved ones or deserting. Spying became ever more commonplace the deeper the Federals penetrated into Dixie. As a staff officer, Bierce knew much of this face of war.

From *The Devil's Dictionary*

PHILOSOPHY, *n.* A route of many roads leading from nowhere to nothing.

CONSCIENCE, *n.* A morbid condition of the stomach, affecting the gray matter of the brain and producing a mental discord.

VALOR, *n.* A soldierly compound of vanity, duty and the gambler's hope.

"Why have you halted?" roared the commander of a division at Chickamauga, who had ordered a charge; "move forward, sir, at once."

"General," said the commander of the delinquent brigade, "I am persuaded that any further display of valor by my troops will bring them into collision with the enemy."

GUNPOWDER, *n.* An agency employed by civilized nations for the settlement of disputes which might become troublesome if left unadjusted.

REVEILLE, *n.* A signal to sleeping soldiers to dream of battlefields no more, but get up and have their blue noses counted.

ABATIS, *n.* Embarrassing circumstances placed outside a fort in order to augment the coy reluctance of the enemy.

n. Rubbish in front of a fort, to prevent the rubbish outside from molesting the rubbish inside.

MORAL, *adj.* Conforming to local and mutable standards of right. Having the quality of general expediency.

STONE'S RIVER[1]

A correspondent has directed my attention to some recent utterances of Mr. Jerome B. Cox,[2] concerning his services as commander of a field battery at the great battle of Stone's River, or Murfreesboro. Mr. Cox has had the vanity to join "the innumerable caravan" of "day-savers." The peculiarity of the day-saver is that, while he is but one of a mighty multitude each of whom believes himself to have "turned the tide of battle" by his personal efforts, he steadfastly ignores or passionately denies the existence (as day-savers) of all the rest. Captain Cox, it appears, saved the day at Stone's River by "mowing down" the enemy, who, with astonishing improvidence, came up to the mowing "nine battalions deep." "You can say," says Captain Cox, in conclusion of his story, "that our stubborn resistance changed the tide of victory and gave Rosecrans[3] time to rally his men and Bragg[4] got licked." Now I happen to be an eye-witness in this case: I saw the enemy's charge, the resistance, Captain Cox and all of it. Captain Cox was a brave and efficient officer: he fought his little battery with skill and discretion. But he was aided by several brigades of infantry which, veracity compels me to add, did most of the "mowing." In fact the incident was of such magnitude that Captain Cox and his guns cut a very small figure in it. And, after all, Bragg was not "licked" and the day was saved by the night.

It has seldom been my good fortune to meet a man who took part in a military engagement whose command did not signally distinguish itself in the action. The insupportable vanity which so easily persuades itself of its own importance in the scheme of the universe finds in the

1. "Prattle," *San Francisco Examiner*, May 5, 1889. SOLE, 26–27.

2. Jerome B. Cox, captain, commanded the Tenth Battery, Indiana Light Artillery, at Stone's River. SOLE, 318n.

3. William Starke Rosecrans (1819–1898) replaced Buell in the Army of the Cumberland (renamed from Army of the Ohio) and commanded from October 30, 1862 to October 20, 1863. BOATNER.

4. Lieutenant-General Braxton Bragg (1817–1876) commanded the Army of Tennessee at Stone's River and Chickamauga, being replaced after losing "impregnable" Missionary Ridge and Lookout Mountain to a frontal assault in which Bierce was in the lead. CONFED.

obscurity and tumult of battle its freest field and opportunity. This disagreeable phenomenon of self-magnification makes nearly all personal narrative of military service practically valueless. No battle of the civil war was so prolific of day-savers and tide-turners as the engagement at Stone's River. The history of that action is exceedingly simple. The two armies, nearly equal in strength, confronted one another on level ground at daybreak. As the Federal left was preparing to attack the Confederate right the Confederate left took the initiative and attacked the Federal right. By nightfall, which put an end to the engagement, the whole Federal line had been turned upon its left, as upon a hinge, till it lay at a right angle to its first direction. Yet I have heard at least a dozen commands of regiments, brigades and divisions of the beaten right make strenuous claims to the distinction of having resisted enough longer than the rest to save the army. Their conviction was undoubtedly shared by nearly every man and officer in their commands. The late Senator Miller,[5] whose brigade was driven from the field along with the others, always declared that its heroism stayed Bragg's whole army and wrested the victory from his hands. Two days later Bragg made a feeble attempt with six thousand men upon our left and rear. After it had been repulsed by our artillery alone, Miller's brigade and four or five others crossed a creek and assailed its retreat — to them an easy and almost bloodless operation. Miller was, I am convinced, fully persuaded that he again saved the army; and so persistently did his partisans repeat the tale that it became his chief public claim to political preferment. It was not until after his death that Mr. Cox ventured to stand forth in defense of the everlasting truth!

5. John Franklin Miller (1831–1886), colonel commanding the Third Brigade of the Army of the Cumberland. Later, U.S. senator from California, 1881– 86. BOATNER

[1908; CWAB, III]

A BAFFLED AMBUSCADE

Connecting Readyville and Woodbury was a good, hard turnpike nine or ten miles long. Readyville was an outpost of the Federal army at Murfreesboro; Woodbury had the same relation to the Confederate army at Tullahoma. For months after the big battle at Stone River these outposts were in constant quarrel, most of the trouble occurring, naturally, on the turnpike mentioned, between detachments of cavalry. Sometimes the infantry and artillery took a hand in the game by way of showing their good-will.

One night a squadron of Federal horse commanded by Major Seidel, a gallant and skillful officer, moved out from Readyville on an uncommonly hazardous enterprise requiring secrecy, caution and silence.

Passing the infantry pickets, the detachment soon afterward approached two cavalry videttes staring hard into the darkness ahead. There should have been three.

"Where is your other man?" said the major. "I ordered Dunning to be here tonight."

"He rode forward, sir," the man replied. "There was a little firing afterward, but it was a long way to the front."

"It was against orders and against sense for Dunning to do that," said the officer, obviously vexed. "Why did he ride forward?"

"Don't know, sir; he seemed mighty restless. Guess he was skeered."

When this remarkable reasoner and his companion had been absorbed into the expeditionary force, it resumed its advance. Conversation was forbidden; arms and accoutrements were denied the right to rattle. The horses tramping was all that could be heard and the movement was slow in order to have as little as possible of that. It was after midnight and pretty dark, although there was a bit of moon somewhere behind the masses of cloud.

Two or three miles along, the head of the column approached a dense forest of cedars bordering the road on both sides. The major commanded a halt by merely halting, and, evidently himself a bit "skeered," rode on alone to reconnoiter. He was followed, however, by his adjutant and three troopers, who remained a little distance behind and, unseen by him, saw all that occurred.

After riding about a hundred yards toward the forest, the major suddenly and sharply reined in his horse and sat motionless in the saddle. Near the side of the road, in a little open space and hardly ten paces away, stood the figure of a man, dimly visible and as motionless as he. The major's first feeling was that of satisfaction in having left his cavalcade behind; if this were an enemy and should escape he would have little to report. The expedition was as yet undetected.

Some dark object was dimly discernible at the man's feet; the officer could not make it out. With the instinct of the true cavalryman and a particular indisposition to the discharge of firearms, he drew his saber. The man on foot made no movement in answer to the challenge. The situation was tense and a bit dramatic. Suddenly the moon burst through a rift in the clouds and, himself in the shadow of a group of great oaks, the horseman saw the footman clearly, in a patch of white light. It was Trooper Dunning, unarmed and bareheaded. The object at his feet resolved itself into a dead horse, and at a right angle across the animal's neck lay a dead man, face upward in the moonlight.

"Dunning has had the fight of his life," thought the major, and was about to ride forward. Dunning raised his hand, motioning him back with a gesture of warning; then, lowering the arm, he pointed to the place where the road lost itself in the blackness of the cedar forest.

The major understood, and turning his horse rode back to the little group that had followed him and was already moving to the rear in fear of his displeasure, and so returned to the head of his command.

"Dunning is just ahead there," he said to the captain of his leading company. "He has killed his man and will have something to report."

Right patiently they waited, sabers drawn, but Dunning did not come. In an hour the day broke and the whole force moved cautiously forward, its commander not altogether satisfied with his faith in Private Dunning. The expedition had failed, but something remained to be done.

In the little open space off the road they found the fallen horse. At a right angle across the animal's neck face upward, a bullet in the brain, lay the body of Trooper Dunning, stiff as a statue, hours dead.

Examination disclosed abundant evidence that within a half hour the cedar forest had been occupied by a strong force of Confederate infantry — an ambuscade.

[1895; SOLE]

ON MILITARY PUNISHMENTS⁶

In an article on military punishments a writer in "Chambers' Journal" describes various brutalities practiced in the English army during the last century. Among them was that known as riding the wooden horse. For back the steed had a plank edge upward and the horseman was not permitted the luxury of stirrups, but in order that he might have a certain stability and augment the firmness of his session in the no saddle various material objects of a considerable weight were annexed to the ankles of him. We are assured with an almost audible sigh for the depravity of our forefathers that the remains of a wooden horse were standing on the parade at Portsmouth as lately as 1760. The wooden horse it will be observed differs from the ordinary domestic horse (*Equus penalis Hobarti*) even in death: its remains will stand alone, whereas the strongest man cannot stand those of the other beast.

Well, as lately as 1863 in this land of light and law the spectacle of a wooden horse carrying double or even triple was for weeks a familiar one to this present writer. Indeed, I have seen the animal serving as charger to as many as a half-dozen American warriors, the two legs of each thoughtfully provided with ballast of rock. This was at the little Tennessee village of Readyville, where I dare say tradition still babbles imperfect witness of the military phenomenon. I do not know if the wooden horse is still extant in American military life. If so it would seem singularly suited to the moral needs of the headless horseman of the retired list who are now so anxious to avert the horrors of peace by charging the British battleships. I am not sure but the fiery Dimond himself would, as a spectacular extravaganza, have an added picturesqueness if given an oaken mount; and in default of something better and heavier to keep him from falling off, I should not mind serving my country in the humble character of ballast by clinging to his legs.

6. "Prattle," *San Francisco Examiner*, December 29, 1895. SOLE, 27–28.

[1908; CWAB, III]

THREE AND ONE ARE ONE

In the year 1861 Barr Lassiter, a young man of twenty-two, lived with his parents and an elder sister near Carthage, Tennessee. The family were in somewhat humble circumstances, subsisting by cultivation of a small and not very fertile plantation. Owning no slaves, they were not rated among "the best people" of their neighborhood; but they were honest persons of good education, fairly well mannered and as respectable as any family could be if uncredentialed by personal dominion over the sons and daughters of Ham.[7] The elder Lassiter had that severity of manner that so frequently affirms an uncompromising devotion to duty, and conceals a warm and affectionate disposition. He was of the iron of which martyrs are made, but in the heart of the matrix had lurked a nobler metal, fusible at a milder heat, yet never coloring nor softening the hard exterior. By both heredity and environment something of the man's inflexible character had touched the other members of the family; the Lassiter home, though not devoid of domestic affection, was a veritable citadel of duty, and duty — ah, duty is as cruel as death!

When the war came on it found in the family, as in so many others in that State, a divided sentiment; the young man was loyal to the Union, the others savagely hostile. This unhappy division begot an insupportable domestic bitterness, and when the offending son and brother left home with the avowed purpose of joining the Federal army not a hand was laid in his, not a word of farewell was spoken, not a good wish followed him out into the world whither he went to meet with such spirit as he might whatever fate awaited him.

Making his way to Nashville, already occupied by the Army of General Buell, he enlisted in the first organization that he found, a Kentucky regiment of cavalry, and in due time passed through all the stages of military evolution from raw recruit to experienced trooper. A right

7. Generally, the biblical Ham, son of Noah — and the sons and daughters of Ham — were interpreted to be black, and were cursed by God to become slaves; the story of Ham constituted a crucial part of the proslavery argument in Antebellum years.

good trooper he was, too, although in his oral narrative from which this tale is made there was no mention of that; the fact was learned from his surviving comrades. For Barr Lassiter has answered "Here" to the sergeant whose name is Death.

Two years after he had joined it his regiment passed through the region whence he had come. The country thereabout had suffered severely from the ravages of war, having been occupied alternately (and simultaneously) by the belligerent forces, and a sanguinary struggle had occurred in the immediate vicinity of the Lassiter homestead. But of this the young trooper was not aware.

Finding himself in camp near his home, he felt a natural longing to see his parents and sister, hoping that in them, as in him, the unnatural animosities of the period had been softened by time and separation. Obtaining a leave of absence, he set foot in the late summer afternoon, and soon after the rising of the full moon was walking up the gravel path leading to the dwelling in which he had been born.

Soldiers in war age rapidly, and in youth two years are a long time. Barr Lassiter felt himself an old man, and had almost expected to find the place a ruin and a desolation. Nothing, apparently, was changed. At the sight of each dear and familiar object he was profoundly affected. His heart beat audibly, his emotion nearly suffocated him; an ache was in his throat. Unconsciously he quickened his pace until he almost ran, his long shadow making grotesque efforts to keep its place beside him.

The house was unlighted, the door open. As he approached and paused to recover control of himself his father came out and stood bare-headed in the moonlight.

"Father!" cried the young man, springing forward with outstretched hand — "Father!"

The elder man looked him sternly in the face, stood a moment motionless and without a word withdrew into the house. Bitterly disappointed, humiliated, inexpressibly hurt and altogether unnerved, the soldier dropped upon a rustic seat in deep dejection, supporting his head upon his trembling hand. But he would not have it so: he was too good a soldier to accept repulse as defeat. He rose and entered the house, passing directly to the "sitting-room."

It was dimly lighted by an uncurtained east window. On a low stool by the hearthside, the only article of furniture in the place, sat his mother, staring into a fireplace strewn with blackened embers and cold ashes.

He spoke to her — tenderly, interrogatively, and with hesitation, but she neither answered, nor moved, nor seemed in any way surprised. True, there had been time for her husband to apprise her of their guilty son's return. He moved nearer and was about to lay his hand upon her arm, when his sister entered from an adjoining room, looked him full in the face, passed him without a sign of recognition and left the room by a door that was partly behind him. He had turned his head to watch her, but when she was gone his eyes again sought his mother. She too had left the place.

Barr Lassiter strode to the door by which he had entered. The moonlight on the lawn was tremulous, as if the sward were a rippling sea. The trees and their black shadows shook as in a breeze. Blended with its borders, the gravel walk seemed unsteady and insecure to step on. This young soldier knew the optical illusions produced by tears. He felt them on his cheek, and saw them sparkle on the breast of his trooper's jacket. He left the house and made his way back to camp.

The next day, with no very definite intention, with no dominant feeling that he could rightly have named, he again sought the spot. Within a half-mile of it he met Bushrod Albro, a former playfellow and schoolmate, who greeted him warmly.

"I am going to visit my home," said the soldier.

The other looked at him rather sharply, but said nothing.

"I know," continued Lassiter, "that my folks have not changed, but — "

"There have been changes," Albro interrupted — "everything changes. I'll go with you if you don't mind. We can talk as we go."

But Albro did not talk.

Instead of a house they found only fire-blackened foundations of stone, enclosing an area of compact ashes pitted by rains.

Lassiter's astonishment was extreme.

"I could not find the right way to tell you," said Albro. "In the fight a year ago your house was burned by a Federal shell."

"And my family — where are they?"

"In Heaven, I hope. All were killed by the shell."

[1889; CWAB, II]

THE AFFAIR AT COULTER'S NOTCH

"Do you think, Colonel that your brave Coulter would like to put one of his guns in here?" the general asked.

He was apparently not altogether serious; it certainly did not seem a place where any artillerist, however brave, would like to put a gun. The colonel thought that possibly his division commander meant good-humoredly to intimate that in a recent conversation between them Captain Coulter's courage had been too highly extolled.

"General," he replied warmly, "Coulter would like to put a gun anywhere within reach of those people," with a motion of his hand in the direction of the enemy.

"It is the only place," said the general. He was serious, then.

The place was a depression, a "notch," in the sharp crest of a hill. It was a pass, and through it ran a turnpike, which reaching this highest point in its course by a sinuous ascent through a thin forest made a similar, though less steep, descent toward the enemy. For a mile to the left and a mile to the right, the ridge, though occupied by Federal infantry lying close behind the sharp crest and appearing as if held in place by atmospheric pressure, was inaccessible to artillery. There was no place but the bottom of the notch, and that was barely wide enough for the roadbed. From the Confederate side this point was commanded by two batteries posted on a slightly lower elevation beyond a creek, and a half-mile away. All the guns but one were masked by the trees of an orchard; that one — it seemed a bit of impudence — was on an open lawn directly in front of a rather grandiose building, the planter's dwelling. The gun was safe enough in its exposure — but only because the Federal infantry had been forbidden to fire. Coulter's Notch — it came to be called so — was not, that pleasant summer afternoon, a place where one would "like to put a gun."

Three or four dead horses lay there sprawling in the road, three or four dead men in a trim row at one side of it, and a little back, down the hill. All but one were cavalrymen belonging to the Federal advance. One was a quartermaster. The general commanding the division and the colonel commanding the brigade, with their staffs and escorts, had ridden into the notch to have a look at the enemy's guns — which had straightway obscured themselves in towering clouds of smoke. It was hardly profitable to be curious about guns which had the trick of the cuttlefish, and the season of observation had been brief. At its conclusion — a short remove backward from where it began — occurred the conversation already partly reported. "It is the only place," the general repeated thoughtfully, "to get at them."

The colonel looked at him gravely. "There is room for only one gun, General — one against twelve."

"That is true — for only one at a time," said the commander with something, like, yet not altogether like, a smile. "But then, your brave Coulter — a whole battery in himself."

The tone of irony was now unmistakable. It angered the colonel, but he did not know what to say. The spirit of military subordination is not favorable to retort, nor even to deprecation.

At this moment a young officer of artillery came riding slowly up the road attended by his bugler. It was Captain Coulter. He could not have been more than twenty-three years of age. He was of medium height, but very slender and lithe, and sat his horse with something of the air of a civilian. In face he was of a type singularly unlike the men about him; thin, high-nosed, gray-eyed, with a slight blond mustache, and long, rather straggling hair of the same color. There was an apparent negligence in his attire. His cap was worn with the visor a trifle askew; his coat was buttoned only at the sword-belt, showing a considerable expanse of white shirt, tolerably clean for that stage of the campaign. But the negligence was all in his dress and bearing; in his face was a look of intense interest in his surroundings. His gray eyes, which seemed occasionally to strike right and left across the landscape, like searchlights, were for the most part fixed upon the sky beyond the Notch; until he should arrive at the summit of the road there was nothing else in that direction to see. As he came opposite his division and brigade commanders at the roadside he saluted mechanically and was about to pass on. The colonel signed to him to halt.

"Captain Coulter," he said, "the enemy has twelve pieces over there on the next ridge. If I rightly understand the general, he directs that you bring up a gun and engage them."

There was a blank silence; the general looked stolidly at a distant regiment swarming slowly up the hill through rough undergrowth, like a torn and draggled cloud of blue smoke; the captain appeared not to have observed him. Presently the captain spoke, slowly and with apparent effort:

"On the next ridge, did you say, sir? Are the guns near the house?"

"Ah, you have been over this road before. Directly at the house."

"And it is—necessary—to engage them? The order is imperative?"

His voice was husky and broken. He was visibly paler. The colonel was astonished and mortified. He stole a glance at the commander. In that set, immobile face was no sign; it was as hard as bronze. A moment later the general rode away, followed by his staff and escort. The colonel, humiliated and indignant, was about to order Captain Coulter in arrest, when the latter spoke a few words in a low tone to his bugler, saluted, and rode straight forward into the Notch, where, presently, at the summit of the road, his field-glass at his eyes, he showed against the sky, he and his horse, sharply defined and statuesque. The bugler had dashed down the speed and disappeared behind a wood. Presently his bugle was heard singing in the cedars, and in an incredibly short time a single gun with its caisson, each drawn by six horses and manned by its full complement of gunners, came bounding and banging up the grade in a storm of dust, unlimbered under cover, and was run forward by hand to the fatal crest among the dead horses. A gesture of the captain's arm, some strangely agile movements of the men in loading, and almost before the troops along the way had ceased to hear the rattle of the wheels, a great white cloud sprang forward down the slope, and with a deafening report the affair at Coulter's Notch had begun.

It is not intended to relate in detail the progress and incidents of that ghastly contest—a contest without vicissitudes, its alternations only different degrees of despair. Almost at the instant when Captain Coulter's gun blew its challenging cloud twelve answering clouds rolled upward from among the trees about the plantation house, a deep multiple report roared back like a broken echo, and thenceforth to the end the Federal cannoneers fought their hopeless battle in an atmosphere of living iron whose thoughts were lightnings and whose deeds were death.

Unwilling to see the efforts which he could not aid and the slaughter which he could not stay, the colonel ascended the ridge at a point a quarter of a mile to the left, whence the Notch, itself invisible, but pushing up successive masses of smoke, seemed the crater of a volcano in thundering eruption. With his glass he watched the enemy's guns, noting as he could the effects of Coulter's fire — if Coulter still lived to direct it. He saw that the Federal gunners, ignoring those of the enemy's pieces whose positions could be determined by their smoke only, gave their whole attention to the one that maintained its place in the open — the lawn in front of the house. Over and about that hardy piece the shells exploded at intervals of a few seconds. Some exploded in the house, as could be seen by thin ascensions of smoke from the breached roof. Figures of prostrate men and horses were plainly visible.

"If our fellows are doing so good work with a single gun," said the colonel to an aide who happened to be nearest, "they must be suffering like the devil from twelve. Go down and present the commander of that piece with my congratulations on the accuracy of his fire."

Turning to his adjutant-general he said, "Did you observe Coulter's damned reluctance to obey orders?"

"Yes, sir, I did."

"Well, say nothing about it, please. I don't think the general will care to make any accusations. He will probably have enough to do in explaining his own connection with this uncommon way of amusing the rear-guard of a retreating enemy."

A young officer approached from below, climbing breathless up the acclivity. Almost before he had saluted, he gasped out:

"Colonel, I am directed by Colonel Harmon to say that the enemy's guns are within easy reach of our rifles, and most of them visible from several points along the ridge."

The brigade commander looked at him without a trace of interest in his expression. "I know it," he said quietly.

The young adjutant was visibly embarrassed. "Colonel Harmon would like to have permission to silence those guns," he stammered.

"So should I," the colonel said in the same tone. "Present my compliments to Colonel Harmon and say to him that the general's orders for the infantry not to fire are still in force."

The adjutant saluted and retired. The colonel ground his heel into the earth and turned to look again at the enemy's guns.

"Colonel," said the adjutant-general, "I don't know that I ought to say anything, but there is something wrong in all this. Do you happen to know that Captain Coulter is from the South?"

"No; *was* he, indeed?"

"I heard that last summer the division which the general then commanded was in the vicinity of Coulter's home—camped there for weeks, and—"

"Listen!" said the colonel, interrupting with an upward gesture. "Do you hear *that?*"

"That" was the silence of the Federal gun. The staff, the orderlies, the lines of infantry behind the crest—all had "heard," and were looking curiously in the direction of the crater, whence no smoke now ascended except desultory cloudlets from the enemy's shells. Then came the blare of a bugle, a faint rattle of wheels; a minute later the sharp reports recommenced with double activity. The demolished gun had been replaced with a sound one.

"Yes," said the adjutant-general, resuming his narrative, "the general made the acquaintance of Coulter's family. There was trouble—I don't know the exact nature of it—something about Coulter's wife. She is a red-hot Secessionist, as they all are, except Coulter himself, but she is a good wife and a high-bred lady. There was a complaint to army headquarters. The general was transferred to this division. It is odd that Coulter's battery should afterward have been assigned to it."

The colonel had risen from the rock upon which they had been sitting. His eyes were blazing with a generous indignation.

"See here, Morrison," said he, looking his gossiping staff officer straight in the face, "did you get that story from a gentleman or a liar?"

"I don't want to say how I got it, Colonel, unless it is necessary"—he was blushing a trifle—"but I'll stake my life upon its truth in the main."

The colonel turned toward a small knot of officers some distance away. "Lieutenant Williams!" he shouted.

One of the officers detached himself from the group and coming forward saluted, saying: "Pardon me, Colonel, I thought you had been informed. Williams is dead down there by the gun. What can I do, sir?"

Lieutenant Williams was the aide who had had the pleasure of conveying to the officer in charge of the gun his brigade commander's congratulations.

"Go," said the colonel, "and direct the withdrawal of that gun instantly. No—I'll go myself."

He strode down the declivity toward the rear of the Notch at a breakneck pace, over rocks and through brambles, followed by his little retinue in tumultuous disorder. At the foot of the declivity they mounted their waiting animals and took to the road at a lively trot, round a bend and into the Notch. The spectacle which they encountered there was appalling!

Within that defile, barely broad enough for a single gun, were piled the wrecks of no fewer than four. They had noted the silencing of only the last one disabled — there had been a lack of men to replace it quickly with another. The debris lay on both sides of the road; the men had managed to keep an open way between, through which the fifth piece was now firing. The men? — they looked like demons of the pit! All were hatless, all stripped to the waist, their reeking skins black with blotches of powder and spattered with gouts of blood. They worked like madmen, with rammer and cartridge, lever and lanyard. They set their swollen shoulders and bleeding hands against the wheels at each recoil and heaved the heavy gun back to its place. There were no commands; in that awful environment of whooping shot, exploding shells, shrieking fragments of iron, and flying splinters of wood, none could have been heard. Officers, if officers there were, were indistinguishable; all worked together — each while he lasted — governed by the eye. When the gun was sponged, it was loaded; when loaded, aimed and fired. The colonel observed something new to his military experience — something horrible and unnatural: the gun was bleeding at the mouth! In temporary default of water, the man sponging had dipped his sponge into a pool of comrade's blood. In all this work there was no clashing; the duty of the instant was obvious. When one fell, another, looking a trifle cleaner, seemed to rise from the earth in the dead man's tracks, to fall in his turn.

With the ruined guns lay the ruined men — alongside the wreckage, under it and atop of it; and back down the road — a ghastly procession! — crept on hands and knees such of the wounded as were able to move. The colonel — he had compassionately sent his cavalcade to the right about — had to ride over those who were entirely dead in order not to crush those who were partly alive. Into that hell he tranquilly held his way, rode up alongside the gun, and, in the obscurity of the last discharge, tapped upon the cheek the man holding the rammer — who straightway fell, thinking himself killed. A fiend seven times damned sprang out of the smoke to take his place, but paused and gazed up at the mounted officer with an unearthly regard, his teeth flashing between his black lips, his eyes, fierce and expanded, burning like coals beneath his bloody brow. The colonel made an authoritative gesture and pointed to the rear. The fiend bowed in token of obedience. It was Captain Coulter.

Simultaneously with the colonel's arresting sign, silence fell upon the whole field of action. The procession of missiles no longer streamed into that defile of death, for the enemy also had ceased firing. His army had been gone for hours, and the commander of his rear-guard, who had held his position perilously long in hope to silence the Federal fire, at that strange moment had silenced his own. "I was not aware of the breadth of my authority," said the colonel to anybody, riding forward to the crest to see what had really happened.

An hour later his brigade was in bivouac on the enemy's ground, and its idlers were examining, with something of awe, as the faithful inspect a saint's relics, a score of straddling dead horses and three disabled guns, all spiked. The fallen men had been carried away; their torn and broken bodies would have given too great satisfaction.

Naturally, the colonel established himself and his military family in the plantation house. It was somewhat shattered, but it was better than the open air. The furniture was greatly deranged and broken. Walls and ceilings were knocked away here and there, and a lingering odor of powder smoke was everywhere. The beds, the closets of women's clothing, the cupboards were not greatly damaged. The new tenants for a night made themselves comfortable, and the virtual effacement of Coulter's battery supplied them with an interesting topic.

During supper an orderly of the escort showed himself into the dining-room and asked permission to speak to the colonel.

"What is it, Barbour?" said that officer pleasantly, having overheard the request.

"Colonel, there is something wrong in the cellar; I don't know what — somebody there. I was down there rummaging about."

"I will go down and see," said a staff officer, rising.

"So will I," the colonel said; "let the others remain. Lead on, orderly."

They took a candle from the table and descended the cellar stairs, the orderly in visible trepidation. The candle made but a feeble light, but presently, as they advanced, its narrow circle of illumination revealed a human figure seated on the ground against the black stone wall which they were skirting, its knees elevated, its head bowed sharply forward. The face, which should have been seen in profile, was invisible, for the man was bent so far forward that his long hair concealed it;

and, strange to relate, the beard, of a much darker hue, fell in a great tangled mass and lay along the ground at his side. They involuntarily paused; then the colonel, taking the candle from the orderly's shaking hand, approached the man and attentively considered him. The long dark beard was the hair of a woman — dead. The dead woman clasped in her arms a dead babe. Both were clasped in the arms of the man, pressed against his breast, against his lips. There was blood in the hair of the woman, there was blood in the hair of the man. A yard away, near an irregular depression in the beaten earth which formed the cellar's floor — a fresh excavation with, a convex bit of iron, having jagged edges, visible in one of the sides — lay an infant's foot. The colonel held the light as high as he could. The floor of the room above was broken through, the splinters pointing at all angles downward. "This casemate is not bomb-proof," said the colonel gravely. It did not occur to him that his summing up of the matter had any levity in it.

They stood about the group awhile in silence; the staff officer was thinking of his unfinished supper, the orderly of what might possibly be in one of the casks on the other side of the cellar. Suddenly the man whom they had thought dead raised his head and gazed tranquilly into their faces. His complexion was coal black; the cheeks were apparently tattooed in irregular sinuous lines from the eyes downward. The lips, too, were white, like those of a stage Negro. There was blood upon his forehead.

The staff officer drew back a pace, the orderly two paces.

"What are you doing here, my man?" said the colonel, unmoved.

"This house belongs to me, sir," was the reply, civilly delivered.

"To you? Ah, I see! And these?"

"My wife and child. I am Captain Coulter."

[1892; SOLE]

DEFENDING REALISM II[8]

[Bierce here is responding to a review of *Tales of Soldiers and Civilians*. He begins the passage by quoting from a review in the New York *Sun*.] [The reviewer] goes on to say:

> Nor does there seem to us to be the appearance of truth or reason in some of the other tales. If the San Francisco physicians had got an ordinary undertaker to sit up with their dead man matters would have gone on with the utmost felicity; and if the officer in charge of the battery at Coulter's Notch had publicly explained the circumstances, we feel quite sure that he could have avoided the unpleasant duty of shooting cannon balls at his wife and child.

O what a thing it is to be an ass! No doubt the undertaker might do a number of things "with the utmost felicity," but my story was about a man unaccustomed to the society of the dead, who heard the corpse walking softly toward him in the darkness. If his death from fright lacks "the appearance of truth and reason," it can hardly be because an undertaker might have been braver. I will cheerfully confess that if my story had been different from what it was it might have been worse than it is. Regarding the officer at Coulter's Notch, I will confess, too, the probable efficacy of a "public explanation," whatever that might be in an army, though military subordination is not favorable to it. Unfortunately, though, for the relevancy of the suggestion I had chosen to write of an officer whose pride and sense of duty forbade him to explain. On the whole, I am of the conviction that my critic was at his best at first; he shines with a brighter splendor as a liar than as a fool, though in either character I should suppose he might cause a good deal of trouble to the fire department.

8. "Prattle," *San Francisco Examiner,* June 26, 1892. SOLE, 252–53.

[1883; CWAB, II]

GEORGE THURSTON

THREE INCIDENTS IN THE LIFE OF A MAN

George Thurston was a first lieutenant and aide-de-camp on the staff of Colonel Brough, commanding a Federal brigade. Colonel Brough was only temporarily in command, as senior colonel, the brigadier-general having been severely wounded and granted a leave of absence to recover. Lieutenant Thurston was, I believe, of Colonel Brough's regiment, to which, with his chief, he would naturally have been relegated had he lived till our brigade commander's recovery. The aide whose place Thurston took had been killed in battle; Thurston's advent among us was the only change in the *personnel* of our staff consequent upon the change in commanders. We did not like him; he was unsocial. This, however, was more observed by others than by me. Whether in camp or on the march, in barracks, in tents, or *en bivouac*, my duties as topographical engineer kept me working like a beaver — all day in the saddle and half the night at my drawing-table, platting my surveys. It was hazardous work; the nearer to the enemy's lines I could penetrate, the more valuable were my field notes and the resulting maps. It was a business in which the lives of men counted as nothing against the chance of defining a road or sketching a bridge. Whole squadrons of cavalry escort had sometimes to be sent thundering against a powerful infantry outpost in order that the brief time between the charge and the inevitable retreat might be utilized in sounding a ford or determining the point of intersection of two roads.

In some of the dark corners of England and Wales they have an immemorial custom of "beating the bounds" of the parish. On a certain day of the year the whole population turns out and travels in procession from one landmark to another on the boundary line. At the most important points lads are soundly beaten with rods to make them remember the place in after life. They become authorities. Our frequent engagements with the Confederate outposts, patrols, and scouting parties had, incidentally, the same educating value; they fixed in my memory a vivid and apparently imperishable picture of the locality — a picture serving instead of accurate field notes, which, indeed, it was not always convenient to take, with carbines cracking, sabers clashing, and horses plunging all about. These spirited encounters were observations entered in red.

One morning as I set out at the head of my escort on an expedition of more than the usual hazard Lieutenant Thurston rode up alongside and asked if I had any objection to his accompanying me, the colonel commanding having given him permission.

"None whatever," I replied rather gruffly; "but in what capacity will you go? You are not a topographical engineer, and Captain Burling commands my escort."

"I will go as a spectator," he said. Removing his sword-belt and taking the pistols from his holsters he handed them to his servant, who took them back to headquarters. I realized the brutality of my remark, but not clearly seeing my way to an apology, said nothing.

That afternoon we encountered a whole regiment of the enemy's cavalry in line and a field-piece that dominated a straight mile of the turnpike by which we had approached. My escort fought deployed in the woods on both sides, but Thurston remained in the center of the road, which at intervals of a few seconds was swept by gusts of grape and canister that tore the air wide open as they passed. He had dropped the rein on the neck of his horse and sat bolt upright in the saddle, with folded arms. Soon he was down, his horse torn to pieces. From the side of the road, my pencil and field book idle, my duty forgotten, I watched him slowly disengaging himself from the wreck and rising. At that instant, the cannon having ceased firing, a burly Confederate trooper on a spirited horse dashed like a thunderbolt down the road with drawn saber. Thurston saw him coming, drew himself up to his full height, and again folded his arms. He was too brave to retreat before the word, and my uncivil words had disarmed him. He was a spectator. Another moment and he would have been split like a mackerel, but a blessed bullet tumbled his assailant into the dusty road so near that the impetus sent the body rolling to Thurston's feet. That evening, while platting my hasty survey, I found time to frame an apology, which I think took the rude, primitive form of a confession that I had spoken like a malicious idiot.

A few weeks later a part of our army made an assault upon the enemy's left. The attack, which was made upon an unknown position and across unfamiliar ground, was led by our brigade. The ground was so broken and the underbrush so thick that all mounted officers and men were compelled to fight on foot — the brigade commander and his staff included. In the *mêlée* Thurston was parted from the rest of us, and we found him, horribly wounded, only when we had taken the enemy's last defense. He was some months in hospital at Nashville, Tennessee, but finally rejoined us. He said little about his misadventure, except that he had been bewildered and had strayed into the enemy's lines and been shot down; but from one of his captors, whom we in turn had captured, we learned the particulars. "He came walking right upon us as we lay in line," said the man. "A whole company of us instantly sprang up and leveled our rifles at his breast, some of them almost touching him. 'Throw down that sword and surrender, you damned Yank!' shouted some one in authority. The fellow ran his eyes along the line of rifle barrels, folded his arms across his breast, his right hand still clutching his sword, and deliberately replied, 'I will not.' If we had all fired he would have been torn to shreds. Some of us didn't. I didn't, for one; nothing could have induced me."

When one is tranquilly looking death in the eye and refusing him any concession one naturally has a good opinion of one's self. I don't know if it was this feeling that in Thurston found expression in a stiffish attitude and folded arms; at the mess table one day, in his absence, another explanation was suggested by our quartermaster, an irreclaim-able stammerer when the wine was in: "It's h-is w-ay of m-m-mastering a c-c-consti-t-tutional t-tendency to r-un aw-ay."

"What!" I flamed out, indignantly rising; "you intimate that Thurston is a coward — and in his absence?"

"If he w—ere a cow—wow-ard h—e w—wouldn't t-try to m-m-master it; and if he w—ere p-present I w-wouldn't d-d-dare to d-d-discuss it," was the mollifying reply.

This intrepid man, George Thurston, died an ignoble death. The brigade was in camp, with headquarters in a grove of immense trees. To an upper branch of one of these a venturesome climber had attached the two ends of a long rope and made a swing with a length of not less than one hundred feet. Plunging downward from a height of fifty feet, along the arc of a circle with such a radius, soaring to an equal altitude, pausing for one breathless instant, then sweeping dizzily backward — no one who has not tried it can conceive the terrors of such sport to the novice. Thurston came out of his tent one day and asked for instruction in the mystery of propelling the swing — the art of rising and sitting, which every boy has mastered. In a few moments he had acquired the trick and was swinging higher than the most experienced of us had dared. We shuddered to look at his fearful flights.

"St-t-top him," said the quartermaster, snailing lazily along from the mess-tent where he had been lunching; "h — e d-doesn't know that if h — e g-g-goes c-clear over h — e'll w-ind up the sw-ing."

With such energy was that strong man cannonading himself through the air that at each extremity of his increasing arc his body, standing in the swing, was almost horizontal. Should he once pass above the level of the rope's attachment he would be lost; the rope would slacken and he would fall vertically to a point as far below as he had gone above, and then the sudden tension of the rope would wrest it from his hands. All saw the peril — all cried out to him to desist, and gesticulated at him as, indistinct and with a noise like the rush of a cannon shot in flight, he swept past us through the lower reaches of his hideous oscillation. A woman standing at a little distance away fainted and fell unobserved. Men from the camp of a regiment near by ran in crowds to see, all shouting. Suddenly, as Thurston was on his upward curve, the shouts all ceased.

Thurston and the swing had parted — that is all that can be known; both hands at once had released the rope. The impetus of the light swing exhausted, it was falling back; the man's momentum was carrying him, almost erect, upward and forward, no longer in his arc, but with an outward curve. It could have been but an instant, yet it seemed an age. I cried out, or thought I cried out: "My God! will he never stop going up?" He passed close to the branch of a tree. I remember a feeling of delight as I thought he would clutch it and save himself. I speculated on the possibility of it sustaining his weight. He passed above it, and from my point of view was sharply outlined against the blue. At this distance of many years I can distinctly recall that image of a man in the sky, its head erect, its feet close together, its hands — I do not see its hands. All at once, with astonishing suddenness and rapidity, it turns clear over and pitches downward. There is another cry from the crowd, which has rushed instinctively forward. The man has become merely a whirling object, mostly legs. Then there is an indescribable sound — the sound of an impact that shakes the earth, and these men, familiar with death in its most awful aspects, turn sick. Many walk unsteadily away from the spot; others support themselves against the trunks of trees or sit at the roots. Death has taken an unfair advantage; he has struck with an unfamiliar weapon; he has executed a new and disquieting stratagem. We did not know that he had so ghastly resources, possibilities of terror so dismal.

Thurston's body lay on its back. One leg, bent beneath, was broken above the knee and the bone driven into the earth. The abdomen had burst; the bowels protruded. The neck was broken.

The arms were folded tightly across the breast.

[1893; CWAB, II]

THE STORY OF A CONSCIENCE

I

Captain Parrol Hartroy stood at the advanced post of his picket-guard, talking in low tones with the sentinel. This post was on a turn-pike which bisected the captain's camp, a half-mile in rear, though the camp was not in sight from that point. The officer was apparently giving the soldier certain instructions — was perhaps merely inquiring if all were quiet in front. As the two stood talking a man approached them from the direction of the camp, carelessly whistling, and was promptly halted by the soldier. He was evidently a civilian — a tall person, coarsely clad in the home-made stuff of yellow gray, called "butternut," which was men's only wear in the latter days of the Confederacy. On his head was a slouch felt hat, once white, from beneath which hung masses of uneven hair, seemingly unacquainted with either scissors or comb. The man's face was rather striking; a broad forehead, high nose, and thin cheeks, the mouth invisible in the full dark beard, which seemed as neglected as the hair. The eyes were large and had that steadiness and fixity of attention which so frequently mark a considering intel-ligence and a will not easily turned from its purpose — so say those physiognomists who have that kind of eyes. On the whole, this was a man whom one would be likely to observe and be observed by. He carried a walking-stick freshly cut from the forest and his ailing cowskin boots were white with dust.

"Show your pass," said the Federal soldier, a trifle more imperiously perhaps than he would have thought necessary if he had not been under the eye of his commander, who with folded arms looked on from the roadside.

" 'Lowed you'd rec'lect me, Gineral," said the wayfarer tranquilly, while producing the paper from the pocket of his coat. There was something in his tone — perhaps a faint suggestion of irony — which made his elevation of his obstructor to exalted rank less agreeable to that worthy warrior than promotion is commonly found to be. "You-all have to be purty pertickler, I reckon," he added, in a more conciliatory tone, as if in half-apology for being halted.

Having read the pass, with his rifle resting on the ground, the soldier handed the document back without a word, shouldered his weapon, and returned to his commander. The civilian passed on in the middle of the road, and when he had penetrated the circumjacent Confederacy a few yards resumed his whistling and was soon out of sight beyond an angle in the road, which at that point entered a thin forest. Suddenly the officer undid his arms from his breast, drew a revolver from his belt and sprang forward at a run in the same direction, leaving his sentinel in gaping astonishment at his post. After making to the various visible forms of nature a solemn promise to be damned, that gentleman resumed the air of stolidity which is supposed to be appropriate to a state of alert military attention.

II

Captain Hartroy held an independent command. His force consisted of a company of infantry, a squadron of cavalry, and a section of artillery, detached from the army to which they belonged, to defend an important defile in the Cumberland Mountains in Tennessee. It was a field officer's command held by a line officer promoted from the ranks, where he had quietly served until "discovered." His post was one of exceptional peril; its defense entailed a heavy responsibility and he had wisely been given corresponding discretionary powers, all the more necessary because of his distance from the main army, the precarious nature of his communications and the lawless character of the enemy's irregular troops infesting that region. He had strongly fortified his little camp, which embraced a village of a half-dozen dwellings and a country store, and had collected a considerable quantity of supplies. To a few resident civilians of known loyalty, with whom it was desirable to trade, and of whose services in various ways he sometimes availed himself, he had given written passes admitting them within his lines. It is easy to understand that an abuse of this privilege in the interest of the enemy might entail serious consequences. Captain Hartroy had made an order to the effect that any one so abusing it would be summarily shot.

While the sentinel had been examining the civilian's pass the captain had eyed the latter narrowly. He thought his appearance familiar and had at first no doubt of having given him the pass which had satisfied the sentinel. It was not until the man had got out of sight and hearing that his identity was disclosed by a revealing light from memory. With soldierly promptness of decision the officer had acted on the revelation.

III

To any but a singularly self-possessed man the apparition of an officer of the military forces, formidably clad, bearing in one hand a sheathed sword and in the other a cocked revolver, and rushing in furious pursuit, is no doubt disquieting to a high degree; upon the man to whom the pursuit was in this instance directed it appeared to have no other effect than somewhat to intensify his tranquillity. He might easily enough have escaped into the forest to the right or the left, but chose another course of action — turned and quietly faced the captain, saying as he came up: "I reckon ye must have something to say to me, which ye disremembered. What mout it be, neighbor?"

But the "neighbor" did not answer, being engaged in the unneighborly act of covering him with a cocked pistol.

"Surrender," said the captain as calmly as a slight breathlessness from exertion would permit, "or you die."

There was no menace in the manner of his demand; that was all in the matter and in the means of enforcing it. There was, too, something not altogether reassuring in the cold gray eyes that glanced along the barrel of the weapon. For a moment the two men stood looking at each other in silence; then the civilian, with no appearance of fear — with as great apparent unconcern as when complying with the less austere demand of the sentinel — slowly pulled from his pocket the paper which had satisfied that humble functionary and held it out, saying:

"I reckon this 'ere parss from Mister Hartroy is — "

"The pass is a forgery," the officer said, interrupting. "I am Captain Hartroy — and you are Dramer Brune."

It would have required a sharp eye to observe the slight pallor of the civilian's face at these words, and the only other manifestation attesting their significance was a voluntary relaxation of the thumb and fingers holding the dishonored paper, which, falling to the road, unheeded, was rolled by a gentle wind and then lay still, with a coating of dust, as in humiliation for the lie that it bore. A moment later the civilian, still looking unmoved into the barrel of the pistol, said:

"Yes, I am Dramer Brune, a Confederate spy, and your prisoner. I have on my person, as you will soon discover, a plan of your fort and its armament, a statement of the distribution of your men and their number, a map of the approaches, showing the positions of all your outposts. My life is fairly yours, but if you wish it taken in a more formal way than by your own hand, and if you are willing to spare me the indignity of marching into camp at the muzzle of your pistol, I promise you that I will neither resist, escape, nor remonstrate, but will submit to whatever penalty may be imposed."

The officer lowered his pistol, uncocked it, and thrust it into its place in his belt. Brune advanced a step, extending his right hand.

"It is the hand of a traitor and a spy," said the officer coldly, and did not take it. The other bowed.

"Come," said the captain, "let us go to camp; you shall not die until to-morrow morning."

He turned his back upon his prisoner, and these two enigmatical men retraced their steps and soon passed the sentinel, who expressed his general sense of things by a needless and exaggerated salute to his commander.

IV

Early on the morning after these events the two men, captor and captive, sat in the tent of the former. A table was between them on which lay, among a number of letters, official and private, which the captain had written during the night, the incriminating papers found upon the spy. That gentleman had slept through the night in an adjoining tent, unguarded. Both, having breakfasted, were now smoking.

"Mr. Brune," said Captain Hartroy, "you probably do not understand why I recognized you in your disguise, nor how I was aware of your name."

"I have not sought to learn, Captain," the prisoner said with quiet dignity.

"Nevertheless I should like you to know — if the story will not offend. You will perceive that my knowledge of you goes back to the autumn of 1861. At that time you were a private in an Ohio regiment — a brave

and trusted soldier. To the surprise and grief of your officers and comrades you deserted and went over to the enemy. Soon afterward you
were captured in a skirmish, recognized, tried by court-martial and
sentenced to be shot. Awaiting the execution of the sentence you were
confined, unfettered, in a freight car standing on a side track of a
railway."

"At Grafton, Virginia," said Brune, pushing the ashes from his cigar
with the little finger of the hand holding it, and without looking up.

"At Grafton, Virginia," the captain repeated. "One dark and stormy
night a soldier who had just returned from a long, fatiguing march was
put on guard over you. He sat on a cracker box inside the car, near the
door, his rifle loaded and the bayonet fixed. You sat in a corner and his
orders were to kill you if you attempted to rise."

"But if I *asked* to rise he might call the corporal of the guard."

"Yes. As the long silent hours wore away the soldier yielded to the
demands of nature: he himself incurred the death penalty by sleeping
at his post of duty."

"You did."

"What! you recognize me? you have known me all along?"

The captain had risen and was walking the floor of his tent, visibly
excited. His face was flushed, the grey eyes had lost the cold, pitiless
look which they had shown when Brune had seen them over the pistol
barrel; they had softened wonderfully.

"I knew you," said the spy, with his customary tranquillity, "the moment you faced me, demanding my surrender. In the circumstances it
would have been hardly becoming in me to recall these matters. I
am perhaps a traitor, certainly a spy; but I should not wish to seem a
suppliant."

The captain had paused in his walk and was facing his prisoner.
There was a singular huskiness in his voice as he spoke again.

"Mr. Brune, whatever your conscience may permit you to be, you
saved my life at what you must have believed the cost of your own. Until
I saw you yesterday when halted by my sentinel I believed you dead —
thought that you had suffered the fate which through my own crime
you might easily have escaped. You had only to step from the car and
leave me to take your place before the firing-squad. You had a divine
compassion. You pitied my fatigue. You let me sleep, watched over me,
and as the time drew near for the relief-guard to come and detect me

in my crime, you gently waked me. Ah, Brune, Brune, that was well done — that was great — that — "

The captain's voice failed him; the tears were running down his face and sparkled upon his beard and his breast. Resuming his seat at the table, he buried his face in his arms and sobbed. All else was silence.

Suddenly the clear warble of a bugle was heard sounding the "assembly." The captain started and raised his wet face from his arms; it had turned ghastly pale. Outside, in the sunlight, were heard the stir of the men falling into line; the voices of the sergeants calling the roll; the tapping of the drummers as they braced their drums. The captain spoke again:

"I ought to have confessed my fault in order to relate the story of your magnanimity; it might have procured you a pardon. A hundred times I resolved to do so, but shame prevented. Besides, your sentence was just and righteous. Well, Heaven forgive me! I said nothing, and my regiment was soon afterward ordered to Tennessee and I never heard about you."

"It was all right, sir," said Brune, without visible emotion; "I escaped and returned to my colors — the Confederate colors. I should like to add that before deserting from the Federal service I had earnestly asked a discharge, on the ground of altered convictions. I was answered by punishment."

"Ah, but if I had suffered the penalty of my crime — if you had not generously given me the life that I accepted without gratitude you would not be again in the shadow and imminence of death."

The prisoner started slightly and a look of anxiety came into his face. One would have said, too, that he was surprised. At that moment a lieutenant, the adjutant, appeared at the opening of the tent and saluted. "Captain," he said, "the battalion is formed."

Captain Hartroy had recovered his composure. He turned to the officer and said: "Lieutenant, go to Captain Graham and say that I direct him to assume command of the battalion and parade it outside the parapet. This gentleman is a deserter and a spy; he is to be shot to death in the presence of the troops. He will accompany you, unbound and unguarded."

While the adjutant waited at the door the two men inside the tent rose and exchanged ceremonious bows, Brune immediately retiring.

Half an hour later an old negro cook, the only person left in camp except the commander, was so startled by the sound of a volley of musketry that he dropped the kettle that he was lifting from a fire. But for his consternation and the hissing which the contents of the kettle made among the embers, he might also have heard, nearer at hand, the single pistol shot with which Captain Hartroy renounced the life which in conscience he could no longer keep.

In compliance with the terms of a note that he left for the officer who succeeded him in command, he was buried, like the deserter and spy, without military honors; and in the solemn shadow of the mountain which knows no more of war the two sleep well in long-forgotten graves.

[1891; CWAB, II]

PARKER ADDERSON, PHILOSOPHER

"Prisoner, what is your name?"

"As I am to lose it at daylight to-morrow morning it is hardly worth while concealing it. Parker Adderson."

"Your rank?"

"A somewhat humble one; commissioned officers are too precious to be risked in the perilous business of a spy. I am a sergeant."

"Of what regiment?"

"You must excuse me; my answer might, for anything I know, give you an idea of whose forces are in your front. Such knowledge as that is what I came into your lines to obtain, not to impart."

"You are not without wit."

"If you have the patience to wait you will find me dull enough to-morrow morning."

"How do you know that you are to die to-morrow morning?"

"Among spies captured by night that is the custom. It is one of the nice observances of the profession."

The general so far laid aside the dignity appropriate to a Confederate officer of high rank and wide renown as to smile. But no one in his power and out of his favor would have drawn any happy augury from that outward and visible sign of approval. It was neither genial nor infectious; it did not communicate itself to the other persons exposed to it — the caught spy who had provoked it and the armed guard who had brought him into the tent and now stood a little apart, watching his prisoner in the yellow candle-light. It was no part of that warrior's duty to smile; he had been detailed for another purpose. The conversation was resumed; it was in character a trial for a capital offense.

"You admit, then, that you are a spy — that you came into my camp, disguised as you are in the uniform of a Confederate soldier, to obtain information secretly regarding the numbers and disposition of my troops."

"Regarding, particularly, their numbers. Their disposition I already knew. It is morose."

The general brightened again; the guard, with a severer sense of his responsibility, accentuated the austerity of his expression and stood a trifle more erect than before. Twirling his gray slouch hat round and round upon his forefinger, the spy took a leisurely survey of his surroundings. They were simple enough. The tent was a common "wall tent," about eight feet by ten in dimensions, lighted by a single tallow candle stuck into the haft of a bayonet, which was itself stuck into a pine table at which the general sat, now busily writing and apparently forgetful of his unwilling guest. An old rag carpet covered the earthen floor; an older leather trunk, a second chair and a roll of blankets were about all else that the tent contained; in General Clavering's command Confederate simplicity and penury of "pomp and circumstance" had attained their highest development. On a large nail driven into the tent pole at the entrance was suspended a sword-belt supporting a long sabre, a pistol in its holster and, absurdly enough, a bowie-knife. Of that most unmilitary weapon it was the general's habit to explain that it was a souvenir of the peaceful days when he was a civilian.

It was a stormy night. The rain cascaded upon the canvas in torrents, with the dull, drum-like sound familiar to dwellers in tents. As the whooping blasts charged upon it the frail structure shook and swayed and strained at its confining stakes and ropes.

The general finished writing, folded the half-sheet of paper and spoke to the soldier guarding Adderson: "Here, Tassman, take that to the adjutant-general; then return."

"And the prisoner, General?" said the soldier, saluting, with an inquiring glance in the direction of that unfortunate.

"Do as I said," replied the officer, curtly.

The soldier took the note and ducked himself out of the tent. General Clavering turned his handsome face toward the Federal spy, looked him in the eyes, not unkindly, and said: "It is a bad night, my man."

"For me, yes."

"Do you guess what I have written?"

"Something worth reading, I dare say. And—perhaps it is my vanity—I venture to suppose that I am mentioned in it."

"Yes; it is a memorandum for an order to be read to the troops at *reveille* concerning your execution. Also some notes for the guidance of the provost-marshal in arranging the details of that event."

"I hope, General, the spectacle will be intelligently arranged, for I shall attend it myself."

"Have you any arrangements of your own that you wish to make? Do you wish to see a chaplain, for example?"

"I could hardly secure a longer rest for myself by depriving him of some of his."

"Good God, man! do you mean to go to your death with nothing but jokes upon your lips? Do you know that this is a serious matter?"

"How can I know that? I have never been dead in all my life. I have heard that death is a serious matter, but never from any of those who have experienced it."

The general was silent for a moment; the man interested, perhaps amused him — a type not previously encountered.

"Death," he said, "is at least a loss — a loss of such happiness as we have, and of opportunities for more."

"A loss of which we shall never be conscious can be borne with composure and therefore expected without apprehension. You must have observed, General, that of all the dead men with whom it is your soldierly pleasure to strew your path none shows signs of regret."

"If the being dead is not a regrettable condition, yet the becoming so — the act of dying — appears to be distinctly disagreeable to one who has not lost the power to feel."

"Pain is disagreeable, no doubt. I never suffer it without more or less discomfort. But he who lives longest is most exposed to it. What you call dying is simply the last pain — there is really no such thing as dying. Suppose, for illustration, that I attempt to escape. You lift the revolver that you are courteously concealing in your lap, and — "

The general blushed like a girl, then laughed softly, disclosing his brilliant teeth, made a slight inclination of his handsome head and said nothing. The spy continued: "You fire, and I have in my stomach what I did not swallow. I fall, but am not dead. After a half-hour of agony I am dead. But at any given instant of that half-hour I was either alive or dead. There is no transition period.

"When I am hanged to-morrow morning it will be quite the same; while conscious I shall be living; when dead, unconscious. Nature appears to have ordered the matter quite in my interest — the way that I should have ordered it myself. It is so simple," he added with a smile, "that it seems hardly worth while to he hanged at all."

At the finish of his remarks there was a long silence. The general sat impassive, looking into the man's face, but apparently not attentive to what had been said. It was as if his eyes had mounted guard over the prisoner while his mind concerned itself with other matters. Presently he drew a long, deep breath, shuddered, as one awakened from a dreadful dream, and exclaimed almost inaudibly: "Death is horrible!" — this man of death.

"It was horrible to our savage ancestors," said the spy, gravely, "because they had not enough intelligence to dissociate the idea of consciousness from the idea of the physical forms in which it is manfested — as an even lower order of intelligence, that of the monkey, for example, may be unable to imagine a house without inhabitants, and seeing a ruined hut fancies a suffering occupant. To us it is horrible because we have inherited the tendency to think it so, accounting for the notion by wild and fanciful theories of another world — as names of places give rise to legends explaining them and reasonless conduct to philosophies in justification. You can hang me, General, but there your power of evil ends; you cannot condemn me to heaven."

The general appeared not to have heard; the spy's talk had merely turned his thoughts into an unfamiliar channel, but there they pursued their will independently to conclusions of their own. The storm had ceased, and something of the solemn spirit of the night had imparted itself to his reflections, giving them the sombre tinge of a supernatural dread. Perhaps there was an element of prescience in it. "I should not like to die," he said — "not to-night."

He was interrupted — if, indeed, he had intended to speak further — by the entrance of an officer of his staff, Captain Hasterlick, the provost-marshal. This recalled him to himself; the absent look passed away from his face.

"Captain," he said, acknowledging the officer's salute, "this man is a Yankee spy captured inside our lines with incriminating papers on him. He has confessed. How is the weather?"

"The storm is over, sir, and the moon shining."

"Good; take a file of men, conduct him at once to the parade ground, and shoot him."

A sharp cry broke from the spy's lips. He threw himself forward, thrust out his neck, expanded his eyes, clenched his hands.

"Good God!" he cried hoarsely, almost inarticulately; "you do not mean that! You forget—I am not to die until morning."

"I have said nothing of morning," replied the general, coldly; "that was an assumption of your own. You die now."

"But, General, I beg—I implore you to remember; I am to hang! It will take some time to erect the gallows—two hours—an hour. Spies are hanged; I have rights under military law. For Heaven's sake, General, consider how short—"

"Captain, observe my directions."

The officer drew his sword and fixing his eyes upon the prisoner pointed silently to the opening of the tent. The prisoner hesitated; the officer grasped him by the collar and pushed him gently forward. As he approached the tent pole the frantic man sprang to it and with cat-like agility seized the handle of the bowie-knife, plucked the weapon from the scabbard and thrusting the captain aside leaped upon the general with the fury of a madman, hurling him to the ground and falling headlong upon him as he lay. The table was overturned, the candle extinguished and they fought blindly in the darkness. The provost-marshal sprang to the assistance of his superior officer and was himself prostrated upon the struggling forms. Curses and inarticulate cries of rage and pain came from the welter of limbs and bodies; the tent came down upon them and beneath its hampering and enveloping folds the struggle went on. Private Tassman, returning from his errand and dimly conjecturing the situation, threw down his rifle and laying hold of the flouncing canvas at random vainly tried to drag it off the men under it; and the sentinel who paced up and down in front, not daring to leave his beat though the skies should fall, discharged his rifle. The report alarmed the camp; drums beat the long roll and bugles sounded the assembly, bringing swarms of half-clad men into the moonlight, dressing as they ran, and falling into line at the sharp commands of their officers. This was well; being in line the men were under control; they stood at arms while the general's staff and the men of his escort brought order out of confusion by lifting off the fallen tent and pulling apart the breathless and bleeding actors in that strange contention.

Breathless, indeed, was one: the captain was dead; the handle of the bowie-knife, protruding from his throat, was pressed back beneath his chin until the end had caught in the angle of the jaw and the hand that delivered the blow had been unable to remove the weapon. In the dead man's hand was his sword, clenched with a grip that defied the strength of the living. Its blade was streaked with red to the hilt.

Lifted to his feet, the general sank back to the earth with a moan and fainted. Besides his bruises he had two sword-thrusts — one through the thigh, the other through the shoulder.

The spy had suffered the least damage. Apart from a broken right arm, his wounds were such only as might have been incurred in an ordinary combat with nature's weapons. But he was dazed and seemed hardly to know what had occurred. He shrank away from those attending him, cowered upon the ground and uttered unintelligible remonstrances. His face, swollen by blows and stained with gouts of blood, nevertheless showed white beneath his disheveled hair — as white as that of a corpse.

"The man is not insane," said the surgeon, preparing bandages and replying to a question; "he is suffering from fright. Who and what is he?"

Private Tassman began to explain. It was the opportunity of his life; he omitted nothing that could in any way accentuate the importance of his own relation to the night's events. When he had finished his story and was ready to begin it again nobody gave him any attention.

The general had now recovered consciousness. He raised himself upon his elbow, looked about him, and, seeing the spy crouching by a campfire, guarded, said simply:

"Take that man to the parade ground and shoot him."

"The general's mind wanders," said an officer standing near.

"His mind does *not* wander," the adjutant-general said. "I have a memorandum from him about this business; he had given that same order to Hasterlick" — with a motion of the hand toward the dead provost-marshal — "and, by God! it shall be executed."

Ten minutes later Sergeant Parker Adderson, of the Federal army, philosopher and wit, kneeling in the moonlight and begging incoherently for his life, was shot to death by twenty men. As the volley rang out upon the keen air of the midnight, General Clavering, lying white and still in the red glow of the camp-fire, opened his big blue eyes, looked pleasantly upon those about him and said: "How silent it all is!"

The surgeon looked at the adjutant-general, gravely and significantly. The patient's eyes slowly closed, and thus he lay for a few moments; then, his face suffused with a smile of ineffable sweetness, he said, faintly: "I suppose this must be death," and so passed away.

[1893; CWAB, II]

ONE OFFICER, ONE MAN

Captain Graffenreid stood at the head of his company. The regiment was not engaged. It formed a part of the front line-of-battle, which stretched away to the right with a visible length of nearly two miles through the open ground. The left flank was veiled by woods; to the right also the line was lost to sight, but it extended many miles. A hundred yards in rear was a second line; behind this, the reserve brigades and divisions in column. Batteries of artillery occupied the spaces between and crowned the low hills. Groups of horsemen — generals with their staffs and escorts, and field officers of regiments behind the colors — broke the regularity of the lines and columns. Numbers of these figures of interest had field-glasses at their eyes and sat motionless, stolidly scanning the country in front; others came and went at a slow canter, bearing orders. There were squads of stretcher-bearers, ambulances, wagon-trains with ammunition, and officers' servants in rear of all — of all that was visible — for still in rear of these, along the roads, extended for many miles all that vast multitude of non-combatants who with their various *impedimenta* are assigned to the inglorious but important duty of supplying the fighters' many needs.

An army in line-of-battle awaiting attack, or prepared to deliver it, presents strange contrasts. At the front are precision, formality, fixity, and silence. Toward the rear these characteristics are less and less conspicuous, and finally, in point of space, are lost altogether in confusion, motion and noise. The homogeneous becomes heterogeneous. Definition is lacking; repose is replaced by an apparently purposeless activity; harmony vanishes in hubbub, form in disorder. Commotion everywhere and ceaseless unrest. The men who do not fight are never ready.

From his position at the right of his company in the front rank, Captain Graffenreid had an unobstructed outlook toward the enemy. A half-mile of open and nearly level ground lay before him, and beyond it an irregular wood, covering a slight acclivity; not a human being anywhere visible. He could imagine nothing more peaceful than the appearance of that pleasant landscape with its long stretches of brown fields over which the atmosphere was beginning to quiver in the heat of the morning sun. Not a sound came from forest or field — not even the

barking of a dog or the crowing of a cock at the half-seen plantation
house on the crest among the trees. Yet every man in those miles of
men knew that he and death were face to face.

Captain Graffenreid had never in his life seen an armed enemy, and
the war in which his regiment was one of the first to take the field was
two years old. He had had the rare advantage of a military education,
and when his comrades had marched to the front he had been detached for administrative service at the capital of his State, where it was
thought that he could be most useful. Like a bad soldier he protested,
and like a good one obeyed. In close official and personal relations with
the governor of his State, and enjoying his confidence and favor, he
had firmly refused promotion and seen his juniors elevated above him.
Death had been busy in his distant regiment; vacancies among the field
officers had occurred again and again; but from a chivalrous feeling
that war's rewards belonged of right to those who bore the storm and
stress of battle he had held his humble rank and generously advanced
the fortunes of others. His silent devotion to principle had conquered
at last: he had been relieved of his hateful duties and ordered to the
front, and now, untried by fire, stood in the van of battle in command
of a company of hardy veterans, to whom he had been only a name, and
that name a by-word. By none — not even by those of his brother officers
in whose favor he had waived his rights — was his devotion to duty
understood. They were too busy to be just; he was looked upon as one
who had shirked his duty, until forced unwillingly into the field. Too
proud to explain, yet not too insensible to feel, he could only endure
and hope.

Of all the Federal Army on that summer morning none had accepted battle more joyously than Anderton Graffenreid. His spirit was
buoyant, his faculties were riotous. He was in a state of mental exalta-
tion and scarcely could endure the enemy's tardiness in advancing to
the attack. To him this was opportunity — for the result he cared nothing. Victory or defeat, as God might will; in one or in the other he
should prove himself a soldier and a hero; he should vindicate his
right to the respect of his men and the companionship of his brother
officers — to the consideration of his superiors. How his heart leaped in
his breast as the bugle sounded the stirring notes of the "assembly"!
With what a light tread, scarcely conscious of the earth beneath his feet,
he strode forward at the head of his company, and how exultingly he

noted the tactical dispositions which placed his regiment in the front line! And if perchance some memory came to him of a pair of dark eyes that might take on a tenderer light in reading the account of that day's doings, who shall blame him for the unmartial thought or count it a debasement of soldierly ardor?

Suddenly, from the forest a half-mile in front—apparently from among the upper branches of the trees, but really from the ridge beyond—rose a tall column of white smoke. A moment later came a deep, jarring explosion, followed—almost attended—by a hideous rushing sound that seemed to leap forward across the intervening space with inconceivable rapidity, rising from whisper to roar with too quick a gradation for attention to note the successive stages of its horrible progression! A visible tremor ran along the lines of men; all were startled into motion. Captain Graffenreid dodged and threw up his hands to one side of his head, palms outward. As he did so he heard a keen, ringing report, and saw on a hillside behind the line a fierce roll of smoke and dust—the shell's explosion. It had passed a hundred feet to his left! He heard, or fancied he heard, a low, mocking laugh and turning in the direction whence it came saw the eyes of his first lieutenant fixed upon him with an unmistakable look of amusement. He looked along the line of faces in the front ranks. The men were laughing. At him? The thought restored the color to his bloodless face—restored too much of it. His cheeks burned with a fever of shame.

The enemy's shot was not answered: the officer in command at that exposed part of the line had evidently no desire to provoke a cannonade. For the forbearance Captain Graffenreid was conscious of a sense of gratitude. He had not known that the flight of a projectile was a phenomenon of so appalling character. His conception of war had already undergone a profound change, and he was conscious that his new feeling was manifesting itself in visible perturbation. His blood was boiling in his veins; he had a choking sensation and felt that if he had a command to give it would be inaudible, or at least unintelligible. The hand in which he held his sword trembled; the other moved automatically, clutching at various parts of his clothing. He found a difficulty in standing still and fancied that his men observed it. Was it fear? He feared it was.

From somewhere away to the right came, as the wind served, a low, intermittent murmur like that of ocean in a storm—like that of a distant railway train — like that of wind among the pines — three sounds so nearly alike that the ear, unaided by the judgment, cannot distinguish them one from another. The eyes of the troops were drawn in that direction; the mounted officers turned their field-glasses that way. Mingled with the sound was an irregular throbbing. He thought it, at first, the beating of his fevered blood in his ears; next, the distant tapping of a bass drum.

"The ball is opened on the right flank," said an officer.

Captain Graffenreid understood: the sounds were musketry and artillery. He nodded and tried to smile. There was apparently nothing infectious in the smile.

Presently a light line of blue smoke-puffs broke out along the edge of the wood in front, succeeded by a crackle of rifles. There were keen, sharp hissings in the air, terminating abruptly with a thump near by. The man at Captain Graffenreid's side dropped his rifle; his knees gave way and he pitched awkwardly forward, falling upon his face. Somebody shouted "Lie down!" and the dead man was hardly distinguishable from the living. It looked as if those few rifle-shots had slain ten thousand men. Only the field officers remained erect; their concession to the emergency consisted in dismounting and sending their horses to the shelter of the low hills immediately in rear.

Captain Graffenreid lay alongside the dead man, from beneath whose breast flowed a little rill of blood. It had a faint, sweetish odor that sickened him. The face was crushed into the earth and flattened. It looked yellow already, and was repulsive. Nothing suggested the glory of a soldier's death nor mitigated the loathsomeness of the incident. He could not turn his back upon the body without facing away from his company.

He fixed his eyes upon the forest, where all again was silent. He tried to imagine what was going on there — the lines of troops forming to attack, the guns being pushed forward by hand to the edge of the open. He fancied he could see their black muzzles protruding from the undergrowth, ready to deliver their storm of missiles — such missiles as the one whose shriek had so unsettled his nerves. The distension of his eyes became painful; a mist seemed to gather before them; he could no longer see across the field, yet would not withdraw his gaze lest he see the dead man at his side.

The fire of battle was not now burning very brightly in this warrior's

soul. From inaction had come introspection. He sought rather to ana-
lyze his feelings than distinguish himself by courage and devotion.
The result was profoundly disappointing. He covered his face with his
hands and groaned aloud.

The hoarse murmur of battle grew more and more distinct upon the
right, the murmur had, indeed, become a roar, the throbbing, a thunder. The sounds had worked round obliquely to the front; evidently the
enemy's left was being driven back, and the propitious moment to
move against the salient angle of his line would soon arrive. The silence
and mystery in front were ominous; all felt that they boded evil to the
assailants.

Behind the prostrate lines sounded the hoofbeats of galloping
horses; the men turned to look. A dozen staff officers were riding to the
various brigade and regimental commanders, who had remounted. A
moment more and there was a chorus of voices, all uttering out of time
the same words—"Attention, battalion!" The men sprang to their feet
and were aligned by the company commanders. They awaited the word
"Forward!"—awaited, too, with beating hearts and set teeth the gusts
of lead and iron that were to smite them at their first movement in
obedience to that word. The word was not given; the tempest did not
break out. The delay was hideous, maddening! It unnerved like a respite at the guillotine.

Captain Graffenreid stood at the head of his company, the dead man
at his feet. He heard the battle on the right—rattle and crash of musketry, ceaseless thunder of cannon, desultory cheers of invisible combatants. He marked ascending clouds of smoke from distant forests. He
noted the sinister silence of the forest in front. These contrasting ex-
tremes affected the whole range of his sensibilities. The strain upon
his nervous organization was insupportable. He grew hot and cold by
turns. He panted like a dog, and then forgot to breathe until reminded
by vertigo.

Suddenly he grew calm. Glancing downward, his eyes had fallen
upon his naked sword, as he held it, point to earth. Foreshortened to
his view, it resembled somewhat, he thought, the short heavy blade of
the ancient Roman. The fancy was full of suggestion, malign, fateful,
heroic!

The sergeant in the rear rank, immediately behind Captain Graffenreid, now observed a strange sight. His attention drawn by an uncom-

mon movement made by the captain—a sudden reaching forward of the hands and their energetic withdrawal, throwing the elbows out, as in pulling an oar—he saw spring from between the officer's shoulders a bright point of metal which prolonged itself outward, nearly a half-arm's length—a blade! It was faintly streaked with crimson, and its point approached so near to the sergeant's breast, and with so quick a movement, that he shrank backward in alarm. That moment Captain Graffenreid pitched heavily forward upon the dead man and died.

A week later the major-general commanding the left corps of the Federal Army submitted the following official report:

"Sir: I have the honor to report, with regard to the action of the 19th inst., that owing to the enemy's withdrawal from my front to reinforce his beaten left, my command was not seriously engaged. My loss was as follows: Killed, one officer, one man."

ON CHICKAMAUGA[9]

Altogether apart from politics — which I abhor — I am sincerely sorry that Illinois "went" Republican, for that defeats General John M. Palmer,[10] the Democratic candidate for Governor. I knew General Palmer in the civil war and served in his division. He was a magnificent fellow in those days (the old man is about seventy-two now), courageous to the marrow in his bones, competent in command and with a perfectly ghastly frankness which kept every one about him in a white doubt as to what truth he would tell next. I believe he was the only commander on either side who ever made a mistake: he made a good one at the battle of Chickamauga. Yet the man's modesty was such that he did not at all glorify himself on account of it, but in his official report just mentioned it as he would have mentioned anything else that came under his observation, and precisely as if it were a common, every-day occurrence — something that constituted no distinction and no more than anybody could do. His words are these, the officers mentioned being commanders of brigades:

> Hazen had been relieved by General Turchin,[11] who had formed on Cruft's[12] left, and he (Hazen) had retired to fill his boxes and pro-

9. "Prattle," *San Francisco Examiner*, November 11, 1888. SOLE, 35–37.

10. General John McAuley Palmer (1817–1900) commanded the Second Division at Stone's River and Chickamauga. His status as a "war hero" — and Republican — led to his being elected governor of Illinois (1868–72) and, switching to the Democrats, U.S. senator (1891–97). He was a presidential candidate for the "Gold" Democrats in 1896 after most of his party went with the "Silver" candidate, William Jennings Bryan. He remade himself and the war in *Personal Recollections of John M. Palmer: The Story of an Earnest Life* (1901). BOATNER.

11. John Basil Turchin (1822–1901) fought in the Crimean War, immigrated from Russia in 1856, threw off the cumbersome name Ivan Vasilevitch Turchinioff, and joined the fight for the Union. Buell court-martialed Turchin for burning the town of Athens, Alabama, but Lincoln reinstated, then promoted, him. He was a division commander at Chickamauga and Missionary Ridge. BOATNER.

12. Major-General Charles Cruft (1826–1883) was wounded twice at Shiloh but returned to fight at Stone's River, Chickamauga, Chattanooga, Atlanta, and Nashville. SIFAKIS.

tect some artillery which was threatened from the rear. I then committed the error of directing Gross[13] to move to the right to engage in a severe fight going on in that direction.

There were greater soldiers than General Palmer, but as the author of the only error of the war which was not committed by the other fellow, he had, in my judgment, a just and reasonable claim to the distinction of governing Illinois, which is not much of a State anyhow.

While on the subject of great soldiers I may as well enlighten my editor about Colonel J. P. Jackson, the fiery soul who is accused of trying to incite a mob to hang a political opponent last Tuesday evening; the EXAMINER inquires who he is. In his civil capacity he is apparently a seller of experience to capitalists. As a warrior he says he "raised, equipped and commanded" the Twenty-third Kentucky Infantry during the war. When the panorama of the Battle of Missionary Ridge was first opened I had the pleasure of reading "Colonel" Jackson's glowing account of how he led that regiment up the ridge. The regiment was led up the ridge by Colonel James C. Foy, to whom I myself conveyed the order to go. I was in Hazen's brigade of Wood's division at that time and long before and after. I was an officer of Hazen's staff and naturally had to know the field-officers of the regiments. I knew those of the Twenty-third Kentucky, but I did not know Jackson, nor did I ever hear of him. It is my opinion that he was never a soldier at all or he would have known better than to make statements so easily refuted. He is not the only military impostor in California whose bubble of glory I can prick when so disposed. I have hitherto abstained because the bubbles are so gorgeous that I admire them myself.

Colonel Foy, who, by the way, was killed during the Atlanta campaign, was a good fellow and a brave man but not a very clear thinker, of which fact he seemed guiltily conscious. A few weeks before he was knocked over we were cautiously moving against the enemy's line, through a thick wood. Foy's little battalion got lost and I was sent to look it up. It was found about a half-mile away, utterly isolated and marching straight to kingdom come. Foy had not the faintest notion of

13. Palmer here means Major-General William Grose (1812–1900) who helped organize the Republican Party in Ohio. He was at Stone's River, Vicksburg, Chickamauga, Atlanta, Nashville. SIFAKIS.

where he came from, where he was nor where he was going to. "What are you doing here, Colonel?" I asked, biting my lips to keep from laughing. He looked at me for a moment in a helpless and bewildered way, then pulled on a grave face and replied: "O, I'm sort o' flankin' 'em."

[1889; CWAB, II]

CHICKAMAUGA

One sunny autumn afternoon a child strayed away from its rude home in a small field and entered a forest unobserved. It was happy in a new sense of freedom from control, happy in the opportunity of exploration and adventure; for this child's spirit, in bodies of its ancestors, had for thousands of years been trained to memorable feats of discovery and conquest — victories in battles whose critical moments were centuries, whose victors' camps were cities of hewn stone. From the cradle of its race it had conquered its way through two continents and passing a great sea had penetrated a third, there to be born to war and dominion as a heritage.

The child was a boy aged about six years, the son of a poor planter. In his younger manhood the father had been a soldier, had fought against naked savages and followed the flag of his country into the capital of a civilized race to the far South. In the peaceful life of a planter the warrior-fire survived; once kindled, it is never extinguished. The man loved military books and pictures and the boy had understood enough to make himself a wooden sword, though even the eye of his father would hardly have known it for what it was. This weapon he now bore bravely, as became the son of an heroic race, and pausing now and again in the sunny space of the forest assumed, with some exaggeration, the postures of aggression and defense that he had been taught by the engraver's art. Made reckless by the ease with which he overcame invisible foes attempting to stay his advance, he committed the common enough military error of pushing the pursuit to a dangerous extreme, until he found himself upon the margin of a wide but shallow brook, whose rapid waters barred his direct advance against the flying foe that had crossed with illogical ease. But the intrepid victor was not to be baffled; the spirit of the race which had passed the great sea burned unconquerable in that small breast and would not be denied. Finding a place where some bowlders in the bed of the stream lay but a step or a leap apart, he made his way across and fell again upon the rear-guard of his imaginary foe, putting all to the sword.

Now that the battle had been won, prudence required that he withdraw to his base of operations. Alas; like many a mightier conqueror, and like one, the mightiest, he could not

curb the lust for war,
Nor learn that tempted Fate will leave the loftiest star.[14]

Advancing from the bank of the creek he suddenly found himself confronted with a new and more formidable enemy: in the path that he was following, sat, bolt upright, with ears erect and paws suspended before it, a rabbit! With a startled cry the child turned and fled, he knew not in what direction, calling with inarticulate cries for his mother, weeping, stumbling, his tender skin cruelly torn by brambles, his little heart beating hard with terror—breathless, blind with tears—lost in the forest! Then, for more than an hour, he wandered with erring feet through the tangled undergrowth, till at last, overcome by fatigue, he lay down in a narrow space between two rocks, within a few yards of the stream and still grasping his toy sword, no longer a weapon but a companion, sobbed himself to sleep. The wood birds sang merrily above his head; the squirrels, whisking their bravery of tail, ran barking from tree to tree, unconscious of the pity of it, and somewhere far away was a strange, muffled thunder, as if the partridges were drumming in celebration of nature's victory over the son of her immemorial enslavers. And back at the little plantation, where white men and black were hastily searching the fields and hedges in alarm, a mother's heart was breaking for her missing child.

Hours passed, and then the little sleeper rose to his feet. The chill of the evening was in his limbs, the fear of the gloom in his heart. But he had rested, and he no longer wept. With some blind instinct which impelled to action he struggled through the undergrowth about him and came to a more open ground—on his right the brook, to the left a gentle acclivity studded with infrequent trees; over all, the gathering

14. From Byron's "Childe Harold's Pilgrimage":
    Oh, more or less than man—in high or low—
    Battling with nations, flying from the field;
    Now making monarchs' neck they footstool, now
    More than thy meanest soldier taught to yield;
    An Empire thou could'st crush, command, rebuild,
    But govern not thy pettiest passion, nor,
    However deeply in men's spirits skilled,
    Look through thine own, nor curb the lust of War,
    Nor learn that tempted Fate will leave the loftiest Star.
                                    (from Canto III)
Byron here is writing about Napoleon.

gloom of twilight. A thin, ghostly mist rose along the water. It frightened and repelled him; instead of recrossing, in the direction whence
he had come, he turned his back upon it, and went forward toward the
dark inclosing wood. Suddenly he saw before him a strange moving
object which he took to be some large animal—a dog, a pig—he could
not name it; perhaps it was a bear. He had seen pictures of bears, but
knew of nothing to their discredit and had vaguely wished to meet one.
But something in form or movement of this object—something in the
awkwardness of its approach—told him that it was not a bear, and
curiosity was stayed by fear. He stood still and as it came slowly on
gained courage every moment, for he saw that at least it had not the
long, menacing ears of the rabbit. Possibly his impressionable mind was
half conscious of something familiar in its shambling, awkward gait.
Before it had approached near enough to resolve his doubts he saw that
it was followed by another and another. To right and to left were many
more; the whole open space about him was alive with them—all moving toward the brook.

They were men. They crept upon their hands and knees. They used
their hands only, dragging their legs. They used their knees only, their
arms hanging idle at their sides. They strove to rise to their feet, but fell
prone in the attempt. They did nothing naturally, and nothing alike,
save only to advance foot by foot in the same direction. Singly, in pairs
and in little groups, they came on through the gloom, some halting
now and again while others crept slowly past them, then resuming their
movement. They came by dozens and by hundreds; as far on either
hand as one could see in the deepening gloom they extended and
the black wood behind them appeared to be inexhaustible. The very
ground seemed in motion toward the creek. Occasionally one who had
paused did not again go on, but lay motionless. He was dead. Some,
pausing, made strange gestures with their hands, erected their arms
and lowered them again, clasped their heads; spread their palms upward, as men are sometimes seen to do in public prayer.

Not all of this did the child note; it is what would have been noted
by an elder observer; he saw little but that these were men, yet crept
like babes. Being men, they were not terrible, though unfamiliarly clad.
He moved among them freely, going from one to another and peering
into their faces with childish curiosity. All their faces were singularly
white and many were streaked and gouted with red. Something in
this—something too, perhaps, in their grotesque attitudes and move-

ments—reminded him of the painted clown whom he had seen last summer in the circus, and he laughed as he watched them. But on and ever on they crept, these maimed and bleeding men, as heedless as he of the dramatic contrast between his laughter and their own ghastly gravity. To him it was a merry spectacle. He had seen his father's Negroes creep upon their hands and knees for his amusement—had ridden them so, "making believe" they were his horses. He now approached one of these crawling figures from behind and with an agile movement mounted it astride. The man sank upon his breast, recovered, flung the small boy fiercely to the ground as an unbroken colt might have done, then turned upon him a face that lacked a lower jaw—from the upper teeth to the throat was a great red gap fringed with hanging shreds of flesh and splinters of bone. The unnatural prominence of nose, the absence of chin, the fierce eyes, gave this man the appearance of a great bird of prey crimsoned in throat and breast by the blood of its quarry. The man rose to his knees, the child to his feet. The man shook his fist at the child; the child, terrified at last, ran to a tree near by, got upon the farther side of it and took a more serious view of the situation. And so the clumsy multitude dragged itself slowly and painfully along in hideous pantomime—moved forward down the slope like a swarm of great black beetles, with never a sound of going—in silence profound, absolute.

Instead of darkening, the haunted landscape began to brighten. Through the belt of trees beyond the brook shone a strange red light, the trunks and branches of the trees making a black lacework against it. It struck the creeping figures and gave them monstrous shadows, which caricatured their movements on the lit grass. It fell upon their faces, touching their whiteness with a ruddy tinge, accentuating the stains with which so many of them were freaked and maculated. It sparkled on buttons and bits of metal in their clothing. Instinctively the child turned toward the growing splendor and moved down the slope with his horrible companions; in a few moments had passed the foremost of the throng—not much of a feat, considering his advantages. He placed himself in the lead, his wooden sword still in hand, and solemnly directed the march, conforming his pace to theirs and occasionally turning as if to see that his forces did not straggle. Surely such a leader never before had such a following.

Scattered about upon the ground now slowly narrowing by the encroachment of this awful march to water, were certain articles to which, in the leader's mind, were coupled no significant associations: an occasional blanket, tightly rolled lengthwise, doubled and the ends bound together with a string; a heavy knapsack here, and there a broken rifle — such things, in short, as are found in the rear of retreating troops, the "spoor" of men flying from their hunters. Everywhere near the creek, which here had a margin of lowland, the earth was trodden into mud by the feet of men and horses. An observer of better experience in the use of his eyes would have noticed that these footprints pointed in both directions; the ground had been twice passed over — in advance and in retreat. A few hours before, these desperate, stricken men, with their more fortunate and now distant comrades, had penetrated the forest in thousands. Their successive battalions, breaking into swarms and re-forming in lines, had passed the child on every side — had almost trodden on him as he slept. The rustle and murmur of their march had not awakened him. Almost within a stone's throw of where he lay they had fought a battle; but all unheard by him were the roar of the musketry, the shock of the cannon, "the thunder of the captains and the shouting."[15] He had slept through it all, grasping his little wooden sword with perhaps a tighter clutch in unconscious sympathy with his martial environment, but as heedless of the grandeur of the struggle as the dead who had died to make the glory.

The fire beyond the belt of woods on the farther side of the creek, reflected to earth from the canopy of its own smoke, was now suffusing the whole landscape. It transformed the sinuous line of mist to the vapor of gold. The water gleamed with dashes of red, and red, too, were many of the stones protruding above the surface. But that was blood; the less desperately wounded had stained them in crossing. On them, too, the child now crossed with eager steps; he was going to the fire. As he stood upon the farther bank he turned about to look at the companions of his march. The advance was arriving at the creek. The stronger had already drawn themselves to the brink and plunged their faces into the flood. Three or four who lay without motion appeared to have no heads. At this the child's eyes expanded with wonder; even his hospitable understanding could not accept a phenomenon implying such vitality as that. After slaking their thirst these men had not had the strength to back away from the water, nor to keep their heads above it. They were drowned. In rear of these, the open spaces of the forest

15. See Job 39:25.

showed the leader as many formless figures of his grim command as at first; but not nearly so many were in motion. He waved his cap for their encouragement and smilingly pointed with his weapon in the direction of the guiding light — a pillar of fire to this strange exodus.

Confident of the fidelity of his forces, he now entered the belt of woods, passed through it easily in the red illumination, climbed a fence, ran across a field, turning now and again to coquet with his responsive shadow, and so approached the blazing ruin of a dwelling. Desolation everywhere! In all the wide glare not a living thing was visible. He cared nothing for that; the spectacle pleased, and he danced with glee in imitation of the wavering flames. He ran about, collecting fuel, but every object that he found was too heavy for him to cast in from the distance to which the heat limited his approach. In despair he flung in his sword — a surrender to the superior forces of nature. His military career was at an end.

Shifting his position, his eyes fell upon some outbuildings which had an oddly familiar appearance, as if he had dreamed of them. He stood considering them with wonder, when suddenly the entire plantation, with its inclosing forest, seemed to turn as if upon a pivot. His little world swung half around; the points of the compass were reversed. He recognized the blazing building as his own home!

For a moment he stood stupefied by the power of the revelation, then ran with stumbling feet, making a half-circuit of the ruin. There, conspicuous in the light of the conflagration, lay the dead body of a woman — the white face turned upward, the hands thrown out and clutched full of grass, the clothing deranged, the long dark hair in tangles and full of clotted blood. The greater part of the forehead was torn away. and from the jagged hole the brain protruded, overflowing the temple, a frothy mass of gray, crowned with clusters of crimson bubbles — the work of a shell.

The child moved his little hands, making wild, uncertain gestures. He uttered a series of inarticulate and indescribable cries — something between the chattering of an ape and the gobbling of a turkey — a startling, soulless, unholy sound, the language of a devil. The child was a deaf mute.

Then he stood motionless, with quivering lips, looking down upon the wreck.

[1898; CWAB, I]

A LITTLE OF CHICKAMAUGA

The history of that awful struggle is well known — I have not the intention to record it here, but only to relate some part of what I saw of it; my purpose not instruction, but entertainment.

I was an officer of the staff of a Federal brigade. Chickamauga was not my first battle by many, for although hardly more than a boy in years, I had served at the front from the beginning of the trouble, and had seen enough of war to give me a fair understanding of it. We knew well enough that there was to be a fight: the fact that we did not want one would have told us that, for Bragg always retired when we wanted to fight and fought when we most desired peace. We had manœuvred him out of Chattanooga, but had not manœuvred our entire army into it, and he fell back so sullenly that those of us who followed, keeping him actually in sight, were a good deal more concerned about effecting a junction with the rest of our army than to push the pursuit. By the time that Rosecrans had got his three scattered corps together we were a long way from Chattanooga, with our line of communication with it so exposed that Bragg turned to seize it. Chickamauga was a fight for possession of a road.

Back along this road raced Crittenden's corps,[16] with those of Thomas[17] and McCook,[18] which had not before traversed it. The whole army was moving by its left.

There was sharp fighting all along and all day, for the forest was so

16. Major-General Thomas Leonidas Crittenden (1819–1893) was son of U.S. Senator John J. Crittenden who, in 1860, proposed to extend the Missouri Compromise line to the Pacific — with slavery below and free-soil above the line — in a last effort to stop the Civil War. Senator Crittenden's other son, George, served as a major-general in the Confederate army. Thomas was part of those routed by Confederates at Chickamauga. SIFAKIS.

17. George H. Thomas (1816–1870) saved the Union army by his firm defense of Snodgrass Hill after Confederates had exploited a gap in the line after a fortuitous evacuation by the Union division under Wood. Thomas was forever after called the "Rock of Chickamauga" and replaced Rosecrans as head of the Army of the Cumberland. SIFAKIS.

18. Colonel Edward Moody McCook (1833–1909) commanded the Union's First Cavalry at Chickamauga. He was later promoted to major-general. SIFAKIS.

dense that the hostile lines came almost into contact before fighting was possible. One instance was particularly horrible. After some hours of close engagement my brigade, with foul pieces and exhausted cartridge boxes, was relieved and withdrawn to the road to protect several batteries of artillery — probably two dozen pieces — which commanded an open field in the rear of our line. Before our weary and virtually disarmed men had actually reached the guns the line in front gave way, fell back behind the guns and went on, the Lord knows whither. A moment later the field was gray with Confederates in pursuit. Then the guns opened fire with grape and canister and for perhaps five minutes — it seemed an hour — nothing could be heard but the infernal din of their discharge and nothing seen through the smoke but a great ascension of dust from the smitten soil. When all was over, and the dust cloud had lifted, the spectacle was too dreadful to describe. The Confederates were still there — all of them, it seemed — some almost under the muzzles of the guns. But not a man of all these brave fellows was on his feet, and so thickly were all covered with dust that they looked as if they had been reclothed in yellow.

"We bury our dead," said a gunner, grimly, though doubtless all were afterward dug out, for some were partly alive.

To a "day of danger" succeeded a "night of waking." The enemy, everywhere held back from the road, continued to stretch his line northward in the hope to overlap us and put himself between us and Chattanooga. We neither saw nor heard his movement, but any man with half a head would have known that he was making it, and we met it by a parallel movement to our left. By morning we had edged along a good way and thrown up rude intrenchments at a little distance from the road, on the threatened side. The day was not very far advanced when we were attacked furiously all along the line, beginning at the left. When repulsed, the enemy came again and again — his persistence was dispiriting. He seemed to be using against us the law of probabilities: of so many efforts one would eventually succeed.

One did, and it was my luck to see it win. I had been sent by my chief, General Hazen, to order up some artillery ammunition and rode away to the right and rear in search of it. Finding an ordnance train I obtained from the officer in charge a few wagons loaded with what I wanted, but he seemed in doubt as to our occupancy of the region across which I proposed to guide them. Although assured that I had just traversed it, and that it lay immediately behind Wood's division,[19] he insisted on riding to the top of the ridge behind which his train lay and overlooking the ground. We did so, when to my astonishment I saw the entire country in front swarming with Confederates; the very earth seemed to be moving toward us! They came on in thousands, and so rapidly that we had barely time to turn tail and gallop down the hill and away, leaving them in possession of the train, many of the wagons being upset by frantic efforts to put them about. By what miracle that officer had sensed the situation I did not learn, for we parted company then and there and I never again saw him.

By a misunderstanding Wood's division had been withdrawn from our line of battle just as the enemy was making an assault. Through the gap of half a mile the Confederates charged without opposition, cutting our army clean in two. The right divisions were broken up and with General Rosecrans in their midst fled how they could across the country, eventually bringing up in Chattanooga, whence Rosecrans telegraphed to Washington the destruction of the rest of his army. The rest of his army was standing its ground.

A good deal of nonsense used to be talked about the heroism of General Garfield,[20] who, caught in the rout of the right, nevertheless went back and joined the undefeated left under General Thomas. There was no great heroism in it; that is what every man should have done, including the commander of the army. We could hear Thomas's guns going — those of us who had ears for them — and all that was needful was to make a sufficiently wide detour and then move toward the sound. I did so myself, and have never felt that it ought to make me President. Moreover, on my way I met General Negley, and my duties as topographical engineer having given me some knowledge of the lay of the land offered to pilot him back to glory or the grave. I am sorry to say

19. Brigadier-General Thomas John Wood (1823–1906) commanded the division at Chickamauga that received the order by Rosecrans to move his men to fill a supposed gap in the line. Wood moved rapidly, but as it happened, just minutes before Confederates attacked the very spot he had been occupying. The result was the rout of the Union army, saved only by the actions of George H. Thomas. SIFAKIS.

20. Brigadier-General James Abram Garfield (1831–1881) was Rosecrans's chief of staff at Chickamauga and, in 1881, president of the United States. He campaigned on his war record.

my good offices were rejected a little uncivilly, which I charitably attributed to the general's obvious absence of mind. His mind, I think, was in Nashville, behind a breastwork.

Unable to find my brigade, I reported to General Thomas, who directed me to remain with him. He had assumed command of all the forces still intact and was pretty closely beset. The battle was fierce and continuous, the enemy extending his lines farther and farther around our right, toward our line of retreat. We could not meet the extension otherwise than by "refusing" our right flank and letting him inclose us; which but for gallant Gordon Granger[21] he would inevitably have done.

This was the way of it. Looking across the fields in our rear (rather longingly) I had the happy distinction of a discoverer. What I saw was the shimmer of sunlight on metal: lines of troops were coming in behind us! The distance was too great, the atmosphere too hazy to distinguish the color of their uniform, even with a glass. Reporting my momentous "find" I was directed by the general to go and see who they were. Galloping toward them until near enough to see that they were of our kidney I hastened back with the glad tidings and was sent again, to guide them to the general's position.

It was General Granger with two strong brigades of the reserve, moving soldier-like toward the sound of heavy firing. Meeting him and his staff I directed him to Thomas, and unable to think of anything better to do decided to go visiting. I knew I had a brother in that gang — an officer of an Ohio battery.[22] I soon found him near the head of a column, and as we moved forward we had a comfortable chat amongst such of the enemy's bullets as had inconsiderately been fired too high. The incident was a trifle marred by one of them unhorsing another officer of the battery, whom we propped against a tree and left. A few moments later Granger's force was put in on the right and the fighting was terrific!

By accident I now found Hazen's brigade — or what remained of it — which had made a half-mile march to add itself to the unrouted at the

21. Major-General Gordon Granger (1822–1876) commanded the Army of the Cumberland's Reserve Corps that helped Thomas "save" the army at Chickamauga.

22. Bierce's brother Albert was a lieutenant in Granger's Corps, serving with the Eighteenth Ohio Light Artillery. Bierce met him briefly on Snodgrass Hill. MORRIS, 60–61.

memorable Snodgrass Hill.[23] Hazen's first remark to me was an inquiry about that artillery ammunition that he had sent me for.

It was needed badly enough, as were other kinds: for the last hour or two of that interminable day Granger's were the only men that had enough ammunition to make a five minutes' fight. Had the Confederates made one more general attack we should have had to meet them with the bayonet alone. I don't know why they did not; probably they were short of ammunition. I know, though, that while the sun was taking its own time to set we lived through the agony of at least one death each, waiting for them to come on.

At last it grew too dark to fight. Then away to our left and rear some of Bragg's people set up "the rebel yell." It was taken up successively and passed round to our front, along our right and in behind us again, until it seemed almost to have got to the point whence it started. It was the ugliest sound that any mortal ever heard — even a mortal exhausted and unnerved by two days of hard fighting, without sleep, without rest, without food and without hope. There was, however, a space somewhere at the back of us across which that horrible yell did not prolong itself; and through that we finally retired in profound silence and dejection, unmolested.

To those of us who have survived the attacks of both Bragg and Time, and who keep in memory the dear dead comrades whom we left upon that fateful field, the place means much. May it mean something less to the younger men whose tents are now pitched where, with bended heads and clasped hands, God's great angels stood invisible among the heroes in blue and the heroes in gray, sleeping their last sleep in the woods of Chickamauga.

23. Made famous by being the rock upon which George Thomas stood in saving the army at Chickamauga.

MORE ON CHICKAMAUGA[24]

I have the following letter from a well-known physician of San Francisco:

"Dear sir — I read your article in 'The Examiner' on 'some personal recollections of Chickamauga' with a great deal of interest . . . from the fact that I had heard a description of that battle from a personal friend who was on the staff of General Jeff. C. Davis.[25] Your account differs from his in this particular: he characterizes Rosecrans' retreat with his staff from the battlefield as cowardly and ignominious in the extreme, of which you say nothing, possibly because Rosecrans so recently passed away.[26] I should be more than pleased, if this was not the case, to have you relate the battle more fully, telling us why and through whom it was so nearly lost, also through whom the army was saved, although I have always understood that it was through the consummate skill of General Thomas and his brave supporters."

Rosecrans' retirement from the field was not cowardly: he was caught in the rout of the right and naturally supposed that the entire army had given way. His error lay in accepting that view of the disaster without inquiry and endeavoring to repair his broken fortunes by holding the reorganized fugitives at Chattanooga instead of leading them back to the support of his unbeaten left. If that was impracticable he should at least have gone himself, though Thomas undoubtedly did better work without him. There is no reason to doubt that he acted on his best judgment, which, however, was never very good. Rosecrans was many kinds of a brilliant crank, but his personal courage was beyond ques-

---

24. "War Topics," *San Francisco Examiner*, May 8, 1898. SOLE, 33–34.

25. Brigadier-General Jefferson Columbus Davis (1828–1879) was appointed a colonel by a friend, Indiana Governor Oliver P. Morton. After Davis killed his superior officer in cold blood in the Galt House hotel in Louisville, charges were brought but never proven. Governor Morton told the War Department to reinstate him as a general officer in time for Stone's River and Chickamauga. FAUST.

26. Rosecrans's bad-luck order moving Wood's division cannot be attributed to poor generalship; however, his subsequent actions of retreating into the city of Chattanooga and letting the Confederate army take the high ground around the city and set siege to him brought Lincoln to replace him with George Thomas.

tion. The action was lost, as I explained, by withdrawal of Wood's division from its center just as the enemy was attacking. That was Rosecrans' fault, for his order, in obedience to which Wood withdrew, was made under an unpardonable misconception. Wood was directed to close on the right of another division, which was supposed to be next to him on the left. It was not, and in order to reach it he left the front line to move behind the troops intervening. Rosecrans had forgotten his own dispositions. Under these circumstances, Wood would have been justified in deferring obedience and apprising his commander of the situation. As to who saved the army there can be no two intelligent opinions: it was saved by the superb obstinacy of Thomas and the soldierly instinct of Gordon Granger in marching toward the sound of cannon.

[1911; SOLE]

LETTER TO
COLONEL ARCHIBALD GRACIE[27]

March 9, 1911

From the trouble that you took to consult me regarding certain phases of the battle of Chickamauga I infer that you are really desirous of the truth, and that your book is not to belong to that unhappily too large class of books written by "bad losers" for disparagement of antagonists.[28] Sympathies and antipathies are disabilities in an historian that are hard to overcome. That you believe yourself devoid of this disability I do not doubt; yet your strange views of Thomas, Granger and Brannan,[29] and some of the events in which they figured, are (to me) so obviously erroneous that I find myself unable to account for them on the hypothesis of an entirely open mind. All defeated peoples are "bad losers"—history supplies no examples to the contrary, though there are always individual exceptions. (General D. H. Hill[30] is an example of the "good loser," and, with reference to the battle of Chickamauga, the good winner. I assume your familiarity with his account of that action, and his fine tribute of admiration to some of the men whom he fought—Thomas and others.) The historians who have found, and will indubitably continue to find, general acceptance are those who have most generously affirmed the good faith and valor of their enemies. All this, however, you have of course considered. But consider it again.

27. Bierce to Archibald Gracie, March 9, 1911. Original in Bancroft Library, University of California-Berkeley. SOLE, 34–35.

28. Colonel Archibald Gracie Jr. (1858–1912) was the son of a Confederate general of the same name, who fought at Chickamauga. He wrote *The Truth about Chickamauga* (1911). Col. Gracie was one of the first-class passengers who got a seat in a lifeboat as the *Titanic* sank in 1912. SOLE, 320n.

29. Major-General John Milton Brannan (1819–1892) was one of the commanders whose army was routed at Chickamauga. He was reassigned from infantry to artillery and played a prominent part in the siege of Atlanta. FAUST.

30. Lieutenant-General Daniel Harvey Hill (1821–1889) wrote "Chickamauga: The Great Battle of the West," *Battles and Leaders*, 3:638–62. He also edited a monthly magazine in North Carolina, *The Land We Love* (1866–69), and a newspaper, *The Southern Home*. CONFED.

My very humble personal relation to the events at and about the Snodgrass house I partly explained to you, and you can get the rest from the little unmilitary sketch in the book that I lent you for the purpose. It seems to me that it gave me entirely adequate opportunities for observation. I passed almost the entire afternoon at and near the Snodgrass house, with nothing to do but look on, and, as a topographical officer, with some natural interest in, and knowledge of, "the lay of the land." Of my credibility as a witness you have of course no knowledge — no more than you can have of that of many others whom you quote, and must quote. But since you have asked for my views, I will set them down here a little more definitely than was possible in conversation, and you may take them for what they may seem to be worth.

I believe (and gave you some reasons for believing) that Granger did not arrive on the field until well along in the afternoon — I should say (with Hill — see *Battles and Leaders*) not earlier than three o'clock.

I believe that Hazen was already in the Snodgrass field when Granger arrived, and had detached the Ninth Indiana, which was then on the ridge west of the Snodgrass house; that it was among the men of that regiment that an ineffectual attempt was made to place a section of Aleshire's battery.[31] The facts that the section was commanded by my brother and that the Ninth Indiana was my regiment have given the incident unusual interest to me and tended to fix it in my mind.

There was at no time during the afternoon any organized body of troops occupying ground in the rear (north) of the Snodgrass house. Granger's were the only ones that even moved across it. We had no reserves — all our men were on the firing-line.

There is no hill, bald or otherwise, immediately to the north of the Snodgrass house. All is, and was then, open, level country for miles.

Hazen's fire was at no time directed toward what I think you call Horse-shoe Ridge. He faced due south and all his fire was in that direction.

The ridge immediately south of the Snodgrass house (I do not know if that is the one that you call Horse-shoe Ridge) was at no time, until after nightfall, occupied by the Confederates, nor was any other part of the ridges that our forces had held. Nobody was "driven" from this

31. Captain Charles C. Aleshire, Eighteenth Ohio Artillery, Reserve Corps.

position; all retired in perfect order in the evening, there having been no fighting here for a long time — I should say an hour or two.

I do not share the belief of some of the officers of my regiment that the regiment was intentionally "sacrificed" by General Brannan. There was no occasion, no need, to "sacrifice" anybody, for, as said above, we were not at all pressed. I mingled freely, naturally, with the officers and men of my regiment for many months afterward, at Chattanooga and elsewhere, yet never heard a hint of such a thing. Nor did I see anything in what you read me from your manuscript to fortify such a charge.

The commonly accepted account of the second day's battle on our right is true if my eyes were normal. We were defeated all right, cleanly and gallantly, but not as some of your "authorities" say.

[1882; SOLE]

GENERAL WOOD'S COMMAND[32]

The *Kreuz Zeitung*, according to a telegram, expresses a doubt if the Czar has a sufficiently powerful army to preserve the peace. The trouble is that his troops are not well armed. It is obvious that you can not prevent as much warfare with an old-fashioned muzzle-loading rifle that will not carry a hundred yards down hill as you can with an improved repeater with which you can pick off a dozen men a minute a quarter of a mile away. The Czar's artillery, too, is good for nothing in the way of peace-making; he ought to replace his old pot-metal cannon with some kind that will just mow down and stack up the fellows who believe in bloodshed.

I am here reminded of a command I once heard given in the civil war. There was a good deal of desultory skirmishing going on one day about a half mile from where General T. J. Wood[33] sat awaiting the issue of certain movements that were making to the right of his division. All at once a lively clatter of musketry broke out, and Wood, with marked impatience, turned to one of his brigade commanders, saying: "General, send a couple of regiments and your battery out there and put an end to that fighting."

---

32. "Prattle," *Wasp* 295 (March 31, 1882): 182. SOLE, 64.
33. See note 19.

[1886; SOLE]

GENERAL GRANT AND
THE POISONED CHALICE[34]

A deal of indignation is in course of discharge upon the memory of the late General Halleck[35] because he is said to have telegraphed to McClellan,[36] soon after the capture of Fort Donelson,[37] that Grant was "somewhere in the rear of his army, drunk." Defenders of Halleck are not lacking. They say he never sent such a telegram. They say that if he did he may honestly have erred. They say he was, anyhow, a competent commander—which is not so. They say this and they say that. So far, nobody seems to have thought to inquire if the telegram was true. For my part, I know of nothing in great military or civic abilities incompatible with a love of strong drink, nor any reason to suppose that a true patriot may not have the misfortune to be dissipated. Alexander the Great was a drunkard, and died of it. Webster was as often drunk as sober. The instances are numberless. When the nation's admiration of Grant, who was really an admirable soldier, shall have accomplished its fermentation and purged itself of toadyism, men of taste will not be ashamed to set it before their guests at a feast of reason. I present it as an intellectual tipple that one offers with an apology.

Old army men and old Californians need not be told that in Grant's early days of service he swallowed a good deal more than he chewed. With them the question whether he reformed before the battle at Donelson or afterward is not of sufficient importance to enlist their enthu-

34. "Prattle," *Wasp* 498 (February 13, 1886): 5. SOLE, 28–29.

35. See Chapter Two, note 14.

36. General George Brinton McClellan (1826–1885) won the battles of Rich Mountain and Carrick's Ford at the time the Union army lost at First Bull Run. Lincoln appointed McClellan commander of the Army of the Potomac. A skilled organizer, McClellan often refused to use the army he had built. Lincoln sacked him after he failed to follow up his victory at Antietam. McClellan was the Democratic candidate for president in 1864, an election that re-elected Lincoln. He justified his actions to himself in *McClellan's Own Story* (1887). FAUST.

37. The victory at Fort Donelson, February 13–16, 1862, combined with the one at Fort Henry gave the Union control of Kentucky and western Tennessee and made Lincoln first believe in Ulysses S. Grant. FAUST.

siasm on the one side or the other. My own observation — take it for what it is worth — is that it was some time afterward. As late as the battle of Mission Ridge (November 25, 1863) it was my privilege to be close to him for six or seven hours, on Orchard Knob — him and his staff and a variable group of other general and staff officers, including Thomas, Granger, Sheridan, Wood and Hazen. They looked upon the wine when it was red, these tall fellows — they bit glass. The poisoned chalice went about and about. Some of them did not kiss the dragon; my recollection is that Grant commonly did. I don't think he took enough to comfort the enemy — not more than I did myself from another bottle — but I was all the time afraid he would, which was ungenerous, for he did not appear at all afraid I would. This confidence touched me deeply.

Many times since then I have read with pleasure and approval the warmest praises of Grant's total abstinence from some of the gentlemen then and there present.

"Such virtues as we have
Our piety doth grace the gods withal."

These gentlemen were themselves total abstainers from the truth.

CHAPTER FOUR

War Is All Hell, 1864

After a year of hard campaigning at Stone's River, Chickamauga, and Missionary Ridge, veteran soldier Ambrose Bierce, still just twenty years old, was granted leave to spend Christmas 1863 at home in Warsaw, Indiana. He entertained his family and neighbors with stories too gruesome to believe, felt ill at ease around these "un-bloodied" civilians, and fell in love with Bernice "Fatima" Wright. He seemed to develop more than a little affection for her younger sister Clara as well, as revealed in the only surviving battlefield letter written by Bierce. The company of women and the meanings of life, home, normalcy, and future that they represented contrasted greatly with the universe of maleness and of war he had come to know. In February, Bierce returned to Tennessee.

Because of his victories at Vicksburg and Chattanooga, Ulysses Grant had gained President Lincoln's trust. When others criticized his tendency to drink too much or for being a "butcher" who threw away the lives of his men, Lincoln defended Grant, saying, "he fights." Lincoln had had poor luck with generals. In the showcase Army of the Potomac, he had changed commanders often: Irvin McDowell, George McClellan, Ambrose Burnside, Joseph Hooker, George McClellan (again), and George Meade. So confident was he that he had finally found his man, Lincoln commissioned Grant a lieutenant-general, a rank previously held only by George Washington. Grant personally took command of the Army of the Potomac in the east and named William Tecumseh Sherman to command the western armies.

Sherman set his army in motion from Chattanooga on May 5, with 104,000 veterans and 250 pieces of artillery with which "to make Georgia howl." Joseph Johnston and 65,000 Confederates would contest each foot of ground leading to Atlanta. Sherman and Grant knew that numbers favored the North and they made the contest a war of attrition where every dead body forecasted victory. Attrition demanded battles, but every time Sherman moved up, Johnston stepped back and established strong defenses. Sherman's temper—and the new plan—led him to make mistakes, but he was ultimately successful. On September 3, he telegraphed Lincoln that Atlanta had fallen after "one constant battle" since May 5.

The first battles in the "constant" fighting occurred at Resaca on May 13–15, Pickett's Mill on May 25–29, and Kennesaw Mountain on June 27. Bierce was active in them all, doing his duty even while detesting Sherman's bloody strategy. At Resaca, Sherman made a silly attack but came out even on casualties. Two weeks later at Pickett's Mill, Sherman ordered O. O. Howard—who was called "Uh Oh! Howard" by the soldiers for his long list of bad luck and failures—to strike the right end of Johnston's line. Hazen's brigade led the charge straight into an impossible position of massed artillery and overwhelming numbers of entrenched Confederates. This waste of Union lives was unjustifiable and Sherman never mentioned it in his official reports or memoirs. Historian Roy Morris called Sherman's silence a "Vietnam-like" coverup. Stunned by what he lived through at Pickett's Mill, Bierce wrote Clara Wright that "my turn will come." Two weeks later at Kennesaw Mountain in an impossible assault against an impregnable position, Bierce was shot in the head, a bullet lodging above and behind his left ear.

He was taken to a Chattanooga hospital before being sent home for thirty days' recuperation. In mid-September, he rejoined the army, now at Gaylesville, Alabama, and returned to his topographical duties in the brigade of Colonel Sidney Post of Thomas's Army of the Cumberland; his friend and commander, William Hazen, had been promoted, transferred, and marched to the sea with Sherman. Bierce continued to suffer from the head wound and in the campaign in Tennessee at the battles of Franklin and Nashville, from November 30 to December 15, he observed but did not participate in the fight. Christmas 1864 found him in camp for the last time.

From *The Devil's Dictionary*

COWARD, *n*. One who in a perilous emergency thinks with his legs.

MARTYR, *n*. One who moves along the line of least reluctance to a desired death.

PROJECTILE, *n*. The final arbiter in international disputes. . . . With the growth of prudence in military affairs the projectile came more and more into favor, and is now held in high esteem by the most courageous. Its capital defect is that it requires personal attendance at the point of propulsion.

MEDAL, *n*. A small metal disk given as a reward for virtues, attainments or services more or less authentic.

EPAULET, *n*. An ornamented badge, serving to distinguish a military officer from the enemy — that is to say, from the officer of lower rank to whom his death would give promotion.

Position of
HAZEN'S BRIGADE
AT RESACA.

A. G. Bierce

It & Act'g. Top. Engineer

Scale - Yds.
100   200

Traced in Adjutant General's Office.
From Original Records.

Bierce's map of "Position of Hazen's Brigade at Resaca." From General William B. Hazen,
Narrative of Military Service *(Boston: Ticknor, 1885), opp. p. 257.*

[1891; CWAB, II]

KILLED AT RESACA

The best soldier of our staff was Lieutenant Herman Brayle, one of the two aides-de-camp. I don't remember where the general picked him up; from some Ohio regiment, I think; none of us had previously known him, and it would have been strange if we had, for no two of us came from the same State, nor even from adjoining States. The general seemed to think that a position on his staff was a distinction that should be so judiciously conferred as not to beget any sectional jealousies and imperil the integrity of that part of the country which was still an integer. He would not even choose officers from his own command, but by some jugglery at department headquarters obtained them from other brigades. Under such circumstances, a man's services had to be very distinguished indeed to he heard of by his family and the friends of his youth; and "the speaking trump of fame" was a trifle hoarse from loquacity, anyhow. Lieutenant Brayle was more than six feet in height and of splendid proportions, with the light hair and gray-blue eyes which men so gifted usually find associated with a high order of courage. As he was commonly in full uniform, especially in action, when most officers are content to be less flamboyantly attired, he was a very striking and conspicuous figure. As to the rest, he had a gentleman's manners, a scholar's head, and a lion's heart. His age was about thirty.

We all soon came to like Brayle as much as we admired him, and it was with sincere concern that in the engagement at Stone's River — our first action after he joined us — we observed that he had one most objectionable and unsoldierly quality: he was vain of his courage. During all the vicissitudes and mutations of that hideous encounter, whether our troops were fighting in the open cotton fields, in the cedar thickets, or behind the railway embankment, he did not once take cover, except when sternly commanded to do so by the general, who usually had other things to think of than the lives of his staff officers — or those of his men, for that matter.

In every later engagement while Brayle was with us it was the same way. He would sit his horse like an equestrian statue, in a storm of bullets and grape, in the most exposed places — wherever, in fact, duty, requiring him to go, permitted him to remain — when, without trouble and with distinct advantage to his reputation for common sense, he might have been in such security as is possible on a battlefield in the brief intervals of personal inaction.

On foot, from necessity or in deference to his dismounted commander or associates, his conduct was the same. He would stand like a rock in the open when officers and men alike had taken to cover; while men older in service and years, higher in rank and of unquestionable intrepidity, were loyally preserving behind the crest of a hill lives infinitely precious to their country, this fellow would stand, equally idle, on the ridge, facing in the direction of the sharpest fire.

When battles are going on in open ground it frequently occurs that the opposing lines, confronting each other within a stone's throw for hours, hug the earth as closely as if they loved it. The line officers in their proper places flatten themselves no less, and the field officers, their horses all killed or sent to the rear, crouch beneath the infernal canopy of hissing lead and screaming iron without a thought of personal dignity.

In such circumstances the life of a staff officer of a brigade is distinctly "not a happy one," mainly because of its precarious tenure and the unnerving alternations of emotion to which he is exposed. From a position of that comparative security from which a civilian would ascribe his escape to a "miracle," he may be despatched with an order to some commander of a prone regiment in the front line — a person for the moment inconspicuous and not always easy to find without a deal of search among men somewhat preoccupied, and in a din in which question and answer alike must be imparted in the sign language. It is customary in such cases to duck the head and scuttle away on a keen run, an object of lively interest to some thousands of admiring marksmen. In returning — well, it is not customary to return.

Brayle's practice was different. He would consign his horse to the care of an orderly, — he loved his horse, — and walk quietly away on his perilous errand with never a stoop of the back, his splendid figure, accentuated by his uniform, holding the eye with a strange fascination. We watched him with suspended breath, our hearts in our mouths. On one occasion of this kind, indeed, one of our number, an impetuous stammerer, was so possessed by his emotion that he shouted at me:

"I'll b-b-bet you t-two d-d-dollars they d-drop him b-b-before he g-gets to that d-d-ditch!"

I did not accept the brutal wager; I thought they would.

Let me do justice to a brave man's memory; in all these needless exposures of life there was no visible bravado nor subsequent narration. In the few instances when some of us had ventured to remonstrate, Brayle had smiled pleasantly and made some light reply, which, however, had not encouraged a further pursuit of the subject. Once he said:

"Captain, if ever I come to grief by forgetting your advice, I hope my last moments will be cheered by the sound of your beloved voice breathing into my ear the blessed words, 'I told you so.'"

We laughed at the captain — just why we could probably not have explained — and that afternoon when he was shot to rags from an ambuscade Brayle remained by the body for some time, adjusting the limbs with needless care — there in the middle of a road swept by gusts of grape and canister! It is easy to condemn this kind of thing, and not very difficult to refrain from imitation, but it is impossible not to respect, and Brayle was liked none the less for the weakness which had so heroic an expression. We wished he were not a fool, but he went on that way to the end, sometimes hard hit, but always returning to duty about as good as new.

Of course, it came at last; he who ignores the law of probabilities challenges an adversary that is seldom beaten. It was at Resaca, in Georgia, during the movement that resulted in the taking of Atlanta. In front of our brigade the enemy's line of earthworks ran through open fields along a slight crest. At each end of this open ground we were close up to him in the woods, but the clear ground we could not hope to occupy until night, when darkness would enable us to burrow like moles and throw up earth. At this point our line was a quarter-mile away in the edge of a wood. Roughly, we formed a semicircle, the enemy's fortified line being the chord of the arc.

"Lieutenant, go tell Colonel Ward to work up as close as he can get cover, and not to waste much ammunition in unnecessary firing. You may leave your horse."

When the general gave this direction we were in the fringe of the forest, near the right extremity of the arc. Colonel Ward was at the left. The suggestion to leave the horse obviously enough meant that Brayle was to take the longer line, through the woods and among the men. Indeed, the suggestion was needless; to go by the short route meant absolutely certain failure to deliver the message. Before anybody could interpose, Brayle had cantered lightly into the field and the enemy's works were in crackling conflagration.

"Stop that damned fool!" shouted the general.

A private of the escort, with more ambition than brains, spurred forward to obey, and within ten yards left himself and his horse dead on the field of honor.

Brayle was beyond recall, galloping easily along, parallel to the enemy and less than two hundred yards distant. He was a picture to see! His hat had been blown or shot from his head, and his long, blond hair rose and fell with the motion of his horse. He sat erect in the saddle, holding the reins lightly in his left hand, his right hanging carelessly at his side. An occasional glimpse of his handsome profile as he turned his head one way or the other proved that the interest which he took in what was going on was natural and without affectation.

The picture was intensely dramatic, but in no degree theatrical. Successive scores of rifles spat at him viciously as he came within range, and our own line in the edge of the timber broke out in visible and audible defense. No longer regardful of themselves or their orders, our fellows sprang to their feet, and swarming into the open sent broad sheets of bullets against the blazing crest of the offending works, which poured an answering fire into their unprotected groups with deadly effect. The artillery on both sides joined the battle, punctuating the rattle and roar with deep, earth-shaking explosions and tearing the air with storms of screaming grape, which from the enemy's side splintered the trees and spattered them with blood, and from ours defiled the smoke of his arms with banks and clouds of dust from his parapet.

My attention had been for a moment drawn to the general combat, but now, glancing down the unobscured avenue between these two thunderclouds, I saw Brayle, the cause of the carnage. Invisible now from either side, and equally doomed by friend and foe, he stood in the shot-swept space, motionless, his face toward the enemy. At some little distance lay his horse. I instantly saw what had stopped him.

As topographical engineer I had, early in the day, made a hasty examination of the ground, and now remembered that at that point was a deep and sinuous gully, crossing half the field from the enemy's line, its general course at right angles to it. From where we now were it was invisible, and Brayle had evidently not known about it. Clearly,

it was impassable. Its salient angles would have afforded him absolute security if he had chosen to be satisfied with the miracle already
wrought in his favor and leapt into it. He could not go forward, he
would not turn back; he stood awaiting death. It did not keep him long
waiting.

By some mysterious coincidence, almost instantaneously as he fell,
the firing ceased, a few desultory shots at long intervals serving rather
to accentuate than break the silence. It was as if both sides had suddenly repented of their profitless crime. Four stretcher-bearers of ours,
following a sergeant with a white flag, soon afterward moved unmolested into the field, and made straight for Brayle's body. Several Confederate officers and men came out to meet them, and with uncovered
heads assisted them to take up their sacred burden. As it was borne
toward us we heard beyond the hostile works fifes and a muffled
drum — a dirge. A generous enemy honored the fallen brave.

Amongst the dead man's effects was a soiled Russia-leather pocket-
book. In the distribution of mementoes of our friend, which the general, as administrator, decreed, this fell to me.

A year after the close of the war, on my way to California, I opened
and idly inspected it. Out of an overlooked compartment fell a letter
without envelope or address. It was in a woman's, handwriting, and
began with words of endearment, but no name.

It had the following date line: "San Francisco, Cal., July 9, 1862."
The signature was "Darling," in marks of quotation. Incidentally, in the
body of the text, the writer's full name was given — Marian Mendenhall.

The letter showed evidence of cultivation and good breeding, but it
was an ordinary love letter, if a love letter can be ordinary. There was
not much in it, but there was something. It was this:

"Mr. Winters, whom I shall always hate for it, has been telling that at
some battle in Virginia, where he got his hurt, you were seen crouching
behind a tree. I think he wants to injure you in my regard, which he
knows the story would do if I believed it. I could bear to hear of my
soldier lover's death, but not of his cowardice."

These were the words which on that sunny afternoon, in a distant
region, had slain a hundred men. Is woman weak?

One evening I called on Miss Mendenhall to return the letter to her.
I intended, also, to tell her what she had done — but not that she did it.

I found her in a handsome dwelling on Rincon Hill. She was beautiful, well bred — in a word, charming.

"You knew Lieutenant Herman Brayle," I said, rather abruptly. "You know, doubtless, that he fell in battle. Among his effects was found this letter from you. My errand here is to place it in your hands."

She mechanically took the letter, glanced through it with deepening color, and then, looking at me with a smile, said:

"It is very good of you, though I am sure it was hardly worth while." She started suddenly and changed color. "This stain," she said, "is it — surely it is not — "

"Madam," I said, "pardon me, but that is the blood of the truest and bravest heart that ever beat."

She hastily flung the letter on the blazing coals. "Uh! I cannot bear the sight of blood!" she said. "How did he die?"

I had involuntarily risen to rescue that scrap of paper, sacred even to me, and now stood partly behind her. As she asked the question she turned her face about and slightly upward. The light of the burning letter was reflected in her eyes and touched her check with a tinge of crimson like the stain upon its page. I had never seen anything so beautiful as this detestable creature.

"He was bitten by a snake," I replied.

[1864, 1879; HAZEN]

Bierce's map of "Battle Ground of Pickett's Mill, May 27, 1864." From General William B. Hazen, Narrative of Military Service (Boston: Ticknor, 1885), opp. p. 251.

THE CRIME AT PICKETT'S MILL

There is a class of events which by their very nature, and despite any intrinsic interest that they may possess, are foredoomed to oblivion. They are merged in the general story of those greater events of which they were a part, as the thunder of a billow breaking on a distant beach is unnoted in the continuous roar. To how many having knowledge of the battles of our Civil War does the name Pickett's Mill suggest acts of heroism and devotion performed in scenes of awful carnage to accomplish the impossible? Buried in the official reports of the victors there are indeed imperfect accounts of the engagement: the vanquished have not thought it expedient to relate it. It is ignored by General Sherman in his memoirs, yet Sherman ordered it.[1] General Howard wrote an account of the campaign of which it was an incident, and dismissed it in a single sentence; yet General Howard planned it, and it was fought as an isolated and independent action under his eye. Whether it was so trifling an affair as to justify this inattention let the reader judge.[2]

The fight occurred on the 27th of May, 1864, while the armies of Generals Sherman and Johnston[3] confronted each other near Dallas, Georgia, during the memorable "Atlanta campaign." For three weeks we had been pushing the Confederates southward, partly by ma-

1. William Tecumseh Sherman, *The Memoirs of General William T. Sherman* (1875).

2. Major-General Oliver Otis Howard (1830–1909), a Medal of Honor winner, is credited with the loss at Chancellorsville, which he redeemed by selecting the battleground along Cemetery Hill at Gettysburg. After the war, he headed the Bureau of Refugees, Freedmen and Abandoned Lands, an agency that attempted to deal with the social disruption of freeing four million slaves. See his "The Struggle for Atlanta," *Battles and Leaders*, 4:298–325. On page 309, Howard wrote of another battle: "This battle was the reverse of mine at Pickett's Mill." FAUST.

3. General Joseph E. Johnston (1807–1891) commanded the Army of Northern Virginia until mid-1862 when he was replaced by Robert E. Lee. From December 1863 until July 1864, Johnston headed the Army of Tennessee as it opposed Sherman's advance toward Atlanta. He has been criticized for his defensive tactics. For Johnston's story, see his *Narrative of Military Operations Directed during the Late War Between the States* (1874). CONFED.

nœuvring, partly by fighting, out of Dalton, out of Resaca, through Adairsville, Kingston and Cassville. Each army offered battle everywhere, but would accept it only on its own terms. At Dallas Johnston made another stand and Sherman, facing the hostile line, began his customary manœuvring for an advantage. General Wood's division of Howard's[4] corps occupied a position opposite the Confederate right. Johnston finding himself on the 26th overlapped by Schofield,[5] still farther to Wood's left, retired his right (Polk)[6] across a creek, whither we followed him into the woods with a deal of desultory bickering, and at nightfall had established the new lines at nearly a right angle with the old — Schofield reaching well around and threatening the Confederate rear.

The civilian reader must not suppose when he reads accounts of military operations in which relative positions of the forces are defined, as in the foregoing passages, that these were matters of general knowledge to those engaged. Such statements are commonly made, even by those high in command, in the light of later disclosures, such as the enemy's official reports. It is seldom, indeed, that a subordinate officer knows anything about the disposition of the enemy's forces — except that it is unamiable — or precisely whom he is fighting. As to the rank and file, they can know nothing more of the matter than the arms they carry. They hardly know what troops are upon their own right or left the length of a regiment away. If it is a cloudy day they are ignorant even of the points of the compass. It may be said, generally, that a soldier's knowledge of what is going on about him is coterminous with his official relation to it and his personal connection with it; what is going on in front of him he does not know at all until he learns it afterward.

At nine o'clock on the morning of the 27th Wood's division was withdrawn and replaced by Stanley's.[7] Supported by Johnson's division, it moved at ten o'clock to the left, in the rear of Schofield, a distance of

4. See Chapter Three, notes 13 and 21.

5. Major-General John McAllister Schofield (1831–1906) commanded the Army of the Ohio during Sherman's campaign against Atlanta. He served briefly as Secretary of War in Andrew Johnson's cabinet. FAUST.

6. Lieutenant-General Leonidas Polk (1806–1874). CONFED.

7. Major-General David Sloane Stanley (1828–1902) led the cavalry for the Army of Ohio during the 1863 campaign from Lookout Mountain to Atlanta. FAUST.

four miles through a forest, and at two o'clock in the afternoon had reached a position where General Howard believed himself free to move in behind the enemy's forces and attack them in the rear, or at least, striking them in the flank, crush his way along their line in the direction of its length, throw them into confusion and prepare an easy victory for a supporting attack in front. In selecting General Howard for this bold adventure General Sherman was doubtless not unmindful of Chancellorsville, where Stonewall Jackson[8] had executed a similar manœuvre for Howard's instruction. Experience is a normal school: it teaches how to teach.

There are some differences to be noted. At Chancellorsville it was Jackson who attacked; at Pickett's Mill, Howard. At Chancellorsville it was Howard who was assailed; at Pickett's Mill, Hood. The significance of the first distinction is doubled by that of the second.

The attack, it was understood, was to be made in column of brigades, Hazen's[9] brigade of Wood's division leading. That such was at least Hazen's understanding I learned from his own lips during the movement, as I was an officer of his. But after a march of less than a mile an hour and a further delay of three hours at the end of it to acquaint the enemy of our intention to surprise him, our single shrunken brigade of fifteen hundred men was sent forward without support to double up the army of General Johnston. "We will put in Hazen and see what success he has." In these words of General Wood to General Howard we were first apprised of the true nature of the distinction about to be conferred upon us.

8. Lieutenant-General Thomas Jonathon Jackson (1824–1863) was one of the most romantic and heroic figures of the war. Some have written that the loss of this single man lost the war for the South. His flanking movement at Chancellorsville is still widely heralded as the boldest movement of the war, enabling a much weaker Confederate force to defeat the Union army under Joseph Hooker. Jackson struck fully into the unprepared defenses of O. O. Howard, routing them. Jackson was killed by a volley of fire from his own men. His wife, Mary Anna Jackson, added to his fame by publishing *Memoirs of "Stonewall" Jackson* (1895). CONFED.

9. Brigadier-General William Babcock Hazen (1830–1887) grew up in Hiram, Ohio, along with his childhood friend and future president James A. Garfield. He commanded Bierce's regiment from its initial muster through the campaign against Atlanta. Bierce came to respect Hazen above all other soldiers in the war. See also note 11. FAUST.

General W. B. Hazen, a born fighter, an educated soldier, after the war Chief Signal Officer of the Army and now long dead, was the best hated man that I ever knew, and his very memory is a terror to every unworthy soul in the service. His was a stormy life: he was in trouble all round. Grant, Sherman, Sheridan[10] and a countless multitude of the less eminent luckless had the misfortune, at one time and another, to incur his disfavor, and he tried to punish them all. He was always — after the war — the central figure of a court-martial or a Congressional inquiry, was accused of everything, from stealing to cowardice, was banished to obscure posts, "jumped on" by the press, traduced in public and in private, and always emerged triumphant.[11] While Signal Officer, he went up against the Secretary of War and put him to the controversial sword. He convicted Sheridan of falsehood, Sherman of barbarism, Grant of inefficiency. He was aggressive, arrogant, tyrannical, honorable, truthful, courageous — a skillful soldier, a faithful friend and one of the most exasperating of men. Duty was his religion, and like the Moslem he proselyted with the sword. His missionary efforts were directed chiefly against the spiritual darkness of his superiors in rank, though he would turn aside from pursuit of his erring commander to set a chicken-thieving orderly astride a wooden horse, with a heavy stone attached to each foot. "Hazen," said a brother brigadier, "is a synonym of insubordination." For my commander and my friend, my master in the art of war, now unable to answer for himself, let this fact answer: when he heard Wood say they would put him in and see what success he would have in defeating an army — when he saw Howard assent — he uttered never a word, rode to the head of his feeble brigade

10. General Philip Henry Sheridan (1831–1888) was prominent at Stone's River, Chickamauga, and Chattanooga, where he commanded the line that charged up Missionary Ridge. For that audacity, Grant put him in charge of the cavalry for the Army of the Potomac from which he took up a total war campaign in the Shenandoah Valley. He wrote of himself and others in *Personal Memoirs* (1888). BOATNER.

11. After the war, Hazen served prominently in the West and, later, as head of the U.S. Weather Bureau, was involved in the disastrous arctic expedition of A. W. Greely. Hazen was court-martialed after he was outspoken in blaming Secretary of War Robert Lincoln for failing to send a rescue mention to Greely. Hazen also created controversy by his steadfast defense of General Buell and through his memoir, *A Narrative of Military Service* (1885). See note 9. BOATNER.

and patiently awaited the command to go. Only by a look which I knew how to read did he betray his sense of the criminal blunder.

The enemy had now had seven hours in which to learn of the movement and prepare to meet it. General Johnston says:

"The Federal troops extended their intrenched line (we did not intrench) so rapidly to their left that it was found necessary to transfer Cleburne's[12] division to Hardee's[13] corps to our right, where it was formed on the prolongation of Polk's[14] line."

General Hood,[15] commanding the enemy's right corps, says:

"On the morning of the 27th the enemy were known to be rapidly extending their left, attempting to turn my right as they extended. Cleburne was deployed to meet them, and at half-past five P.M. a very stubborn attack was made on this division, extending to the right, where Major-General Wheeler[16] with his cavalry division was engaging them. The assault was continued with great determination upon both Cleburne and Wheeler."

That, then, was the situation: a weak brigade of fifteen hundred

---

12. Major-General Patrick Ronayne Cleburne (1828–1864) fought at Stone's River, protected the Confederate retreat from Missionary Ridge, and distinguished himself at Pickett's Mill and, generally, during the entire Atlanta defense. CONFED.

13. Lieutenant-General William Joseph Hardee (1815–1873) wrote the standard manual used to train U.S. and Confederate soldiers, *Rifle and Light Infantry Tactics* (1855). He commanded the corps defending — with Patrick Cleburne — Bragg's defeated and retreating army after Missionary Ridge. Hardee was prominent in the defense of Atlanta. CONFED.

14. Brigadier-General Lucius Eugene Polk (1833–1892) fought under Patrick Cleburne from Shiloh to Atlanta. CONFED.

15. Lieutenant-General John Bell Hood (1831–1879) is best known for his brave but often rash attacks on the enemy. Known as a fighter, Hood replaced Johnston after the latter's defensive tactics put him in disfavor with Jefferson Davis. Hood destroyed Johnston's army in aggressive attacks against strong Union positions at Atlanta. He tells a different story in *Advance and Retreat* (1880). CONFED.

16. Major-General Joseph Wheeler (1836–1906) commanded the Confederate cavalry in Mississippi, Tennessee, and Georgia. By May 1864, he was the highest-ranking CSA cavalryman, lucky to be alive after having sixteen horses shot from under him in battles. He wrote the manual for cavalry training, *Cavalry Tactics* (1863). After the war, he served sixteen years representing Alabama in the U.S. Congress. CONFED.

men, with masses of idle troops behind in the character of audience, waiting for the word to march a quarter-mile up hill through almost impassable tangles of underwood, along and across precipitous ravines, and attack breastworks constructed at leisure and manned with two divisions of troops as good as themselves. True, we did not know all this, but if any man on that ground besides Wood and Howard expected a "walkover" his must have been a singularly hopeful disposition. As topographical engineer it had been my duty to make a hasty examination of the ground in front. In doing so I had pushed far enough forward through the forest to hear distinctly the murmur of the enemy awaiting us, and this had been duly reported; but from our lines nothing could be heard but the wind among the trees and the songs of birds. Some one said it was a pity to frighten them, but there would necessarily be more or less noise. We laughed at that: men awaiting death on the battlefield laugh easily, though not infectiously.

The brigade was formed in four battalions, two in front and two in rear. This gave us a front of about two hundred yards. The right front battalion was commanded by Colonel R. L. Kimberly of the 41st Ohio, the left by Colonel O. H. Payne of the 124th Ohio, the rear battalions by Colonel J. C. Foy, 23d Kentucky, and Colonel W. W. Berry, 5th Kentucky—all brave and skillful officers, tested by experience on many fields. The whole command (known as the Second Brigade, Third Division, Fourth Corps) consisted of no fewer than nine regiments, reduced by long service to an average of less than two hundred men each. With full ranks and only the necessary details for special duty we should have had some eight thousand rifles in line.

We moved forward. In less than one minute the trim battalions had become simply a swarm of men struggling through the undergrowth of the forest, pushing and crowding. The front was irregularly serrated, the strongest and bravest in advance, the others following in fan-like formations, variable and inconstant, ever defining themselves anew. For the first two hundred yards our course lay along the left bank of a small creek in a deep ravine, our left battalions sweeping along its steep slope. Then we came to the fork of the ravine. A part of us crossed below, the rest above, passing over both branches, the regiments inextricably intermingled, rendering all military formation impossible. The color-bearers kept well to the front with their flags, closely furled, aslant backward over their shoulders. Displayed, they would have been torn to rags by the boughs of the trees. Horses were all sent to the rear; the general and staff and all the field officers toiled along on foot as best they could. "We shall halt and form when we get out of this," said an aide-de-camp.

Suddenly there were a ringing rattle of musketry, the familiar hissing of bullets, and before us the interspaces of the forest were all blue with smoke. Hoarse, fierce yells broke out of a thousand throats. The forward fringe of brave and hardy assailants was arrested in its mutable extensions; the edge of our swarm grew dense and dearly defined as the foremost halted, and the rest pressed forward to align themselves beside them, all firing. The uproar was deafening; the air was sibilant with streams and sheets of missiles. In the steady, unvarying roar of small-arms the frequent shock of the cannon was rather felt than heard, but the gusts of grape which they blew into that populous wood were audible enough, screaming among the trees and cracking against their stems and branches. We had, of course, no artillery to reply.

Our brave color-bearers were now all in the forefront of battle in the open, for the enemy had cleared a space in front of his breastworks. They held the colors erect, shook out their glories, waved them forward and back to keep them spread, for there was no wind. From where I stood, at the right of the line — we had "halted and formed," indeed — I could see six of our flags at one time. Occasionally one would go down, only to be instantly lifted by other hands.

I must here quote again from General Johnston's[17] account of this engagement, for nothing could more truly indicate the resolute nature of the attack than the Confederate belief that it was made by the whole Fourth Corps, instead of one weak brigade:

"The Fourth Corps came on in deep order and assailed the Texans with great vigor, receiving their close and accurate fire with the fortitude always exhibited by General Sherman's troops in the actions of this campaign. . . . The Federal troops approached within a few yards of the Confederates, but at last were forced to give way by their storm of well-directed bullets, and fell back to the shelter of a hollow near and behind them. They left hundreds of corpses within twenty paces of the Confederate line. When the United States troops paused in their advance within fifteen paces of the Texan front rank one of their color-

17. See note 3.

bearers planted his colors eight or ten feet in front of his regiment, and was instantly shot dead. A soldier sprang forward to his place and fell also as he grasped the color-staff. A second and third followed successively, and each received death as speedily as his predecessors. A fourth, however, seized and bore back the object of soldierly devotion."

Such incidents have occurred in battle from time to time since men began to venerate the symbols of their cause, but they are not commonly related by the enemy. If General Johnston had known that his veteran divisions were throwing their successive lines against fewer than fifteen hundred men his glowing tribute to his enemy's valor could hardly have been more generously expressed. I can attest the truth of his soldierly praise: I saw the occurrence that he relates and regret that I am unable to recall even the name of the regiment whose colors were so gallantly saved.

Early in my military experience I used to ask myself how it was that brave troops could retreat while still their courage was high. As long as a man is not disabled he can go forward; can it be anything but fear that makes him stop and finally retire? Are there signs by which he can infallibly know the struggle to be hopeless? In this engagement, as in others, my doubts were answered as to the fact; the explanation is still obscure. In many instances which have come under my observation, when hostile lines of infantry engage at close range and the assailants afterward retire, there was a "dead-line" beyond which no man advanced but to fall. Not a soul of them ever reached the enemy's front to be bayoneted or captured. It was a matter of the difference of three or four paces — too small a distance to affect the accuracy of aim. In these affairs no aim is taken at individual antagonists; the soldier delivers his fire at the thickest mass in his front. The fire is, of course, as deadly at twenty paces as at fifteen; at fifteen as at ten. Nevertheless, there is the "dead-line," with its well-defined edge of corpses — those of the bravest. Where both lines are fighting without cover — as in a charge met by a counter-charge — each has its "dead-line," and between the two is a clear space — neutral ground, devoid of dead, for the living cannot reach it to fall there.

I observed this phenomenon at Pickett's Mill. Standing at the right of the line I had an unobstructed view of the narrow, open space across which the two lines fought. It was dim with smoke, but not greatly obscured: the smoke rose and spread in sheets among the branches of the trees. Most of our men fought kneeling as they fired, many of them behind trees, stones and whatever cover they could get, but there were considerable groups that stood. Occasionally one of these groups, which had endured the storm of missiles for moments without perceptible reduction, would push forward, moved by a common despair, and wholly detach itself from the line. In a second every man of the group would be down. There had been no visible movement of the enemy, no audible change in the awful, even roar of the firing — yet all were down. Frequently the dim figure of an individual soldier would be seen to spring away from his comrades, advancing alone toward that fateful interspace, with leveled bayonet. He got no farther than the farthest of his predecessors. Of the "hundreds of corpses within twenty paces of the Confederate line," I venture to say that a third were within fifteen paces, and not one within ten.

It is the perception — perhaps unconscious — of this inexplicable phenomenon that causes the still unharmed, still vigorous and still courageous soldier to retire without having come into actual contact with his foe. He sees, or feels, that he cannot. His bayonet is a useless weapon for slaughter; its purpose is a moral one. Its mandate exhausted, he sheathes it and trusts to the bullet. That failing, he retreats. He has done all that he could do with such appliances as he has.

No command to fall back was given, none could have been heard. Man by man, the survivors withdrew at will, sifting through the trees into the cover of the ravines, among the wounded who could drag themselves back; among the skulkers whom nothing could have dragged forward. The left of our short line had fought at the corner of a cornfield, the fence along the right side of which was parallel to the direction of our retreat. As the disorganized groups fell back along this fence on the wooded side, they were attacked by a flanking force of the enemy moving through the field in a direction nearly parallel with what had been our front. This force, I infer from General Johnston's account, consisted of the brigade of General Lowrey,[18] or two Arkansas regiments under Colonel Baucum. I had been sent by General Hazen to that point and arrived in time to witness this formidable movement. But already our retreating men, in obedience to their officers, their courage

18. Brigadier-General Mark Perrin Lowrey (1828–1885) fought with the Army of Tennessee from 1862 to 1865. CONFED

and their instinct of self-preservation, had formed along the fence and opened fire. The apparently slight advantage of the imperfect cover and the open range worked its customary miracle: the assault, a singularly spiritless one, considering the advantages it promised and that it was made by an organized and victorious force against a broken and retreating one, was checked. The assailants actually retired, and if they afterward renewed the movement they encountered none but our dead and wounded.

The battle, as a battle, was at an end, but there was still some slaughtering that it was possible to incur before nightfall; and as the wreck of our brigade drifted back through the forest we met the brigade (Gibson's) [19] which, had the attack been made in column, as it should have been, would have been but five minutes behind our heels, with another five minutes behind its own. As it was, just forty-five minutes had elapsed, during which the enemy had destroyed us and was now ready to perform the same kindly office for our successors. Neither Gibson nor the brigade which was sent to his "relief" as tardily as he to ours accomplished, or could have hoped to accomplish, anything whatever. I did not note their movements, having other duties, but Hazen in his "Narrative of Military Service" says:

"I witnessed the attack of the two brigades following my own, and none of these (troops) advanced nearer than one hundred yards of the enemy's works. They went in at a run, and as organizations were broken in less than a minute." [20]

Nevertheless their losses were considerable, including several hundred prisoners taken from a sheltered place whence they did not care to rise and run. The entire loss was about fourteen hundred men, of whom nearly one-half fell killed and wounded in Hazen's brigade in less than thirty minutes of actual fighting.

General Johnston says:

"The Federal dead lying near our line were counted by many persons, officers and soldiers. According to these counts there were seven hundred of them."

This is obviously erroneous, though I have not the means at hand to ascertain the true number. I remember that we were all astonished

19. Colonel William Harvey Gibson (?–1894). BOATNER.
20. See note 11.

at the uncommonly large proportion of dead to wounded—a consequence of the uncommonly close range at which most of the fighting
was done.[21]

The action took its name from a water-power mill near by. This was
on a branch of a stream having, I am sorry to say, the prosaic name of
Pumpkin Vine Creek. I have my own reasons for suggesting that the
name of that water-course be altered to Sunday-School Run.

21. Wood's Division lost approximately 1,400 dead and wounded to Cleburne's 450.

[1894; SOLE]

ON GENERAL O. O. HOWARD[22]

The *Magazine of American History* is to be revived, with General O. O. Howard as editor. General Howard's hardihood in accentuating his connection with American history transcends the limits of human effrontery and passes into the circumcluding domain of infinite gall. This military Quaker, spirited sheeply and skilled in the tactics of confusion and the strategy of retreat, will hardly try to keep up with his pen the place in American history that he won with his heels. I do not mean to affirm a lack of courage in General Howard; his crayfish charges were due to a lukewarm support on the part of the enemy — whose woeful state of sin caused him the liveliest and most prayerful concern. The piety of the man is touching. When struck by a spent bullet he would knuckle down upon his Marybones and thank the God of Battles for letting him off with all his limbs; when his arm went he made a handsome acknowledgment of the divine goodness in thinking him worthy to keep his life. If he had incurred a bellyful of grapeshot he would have expended his last breath in gratitude for the safety of his hat. Of his patriotism there can be no question: this is a country of religious cant, and he loves it — a land of holy snuffle and he will fight for it as long as it has an enemy out of sight and hearing. He is about to retire, however, being sixty-four years old. If he had been born sixty-four years old it would have been greatly to the advantage of his military reputation outside church circles, and would have saved us two years of war.

I once had the honor to serve as a staff officer under this consummate master of the art of needless defeat, and he made the critical Confederate eye familiar with my back — which is not handsome. I said then that I would get even if spared, and Heaven having spared me for the good work, these remarks are in part performance of that pious vow. This explanation seems proper in order that they may be taken with whatever allowances the reader may think right and just in a matter not devoid of personal feeling. I should be sorry indeed to discredit any of my private animosities by disguising them as history.

22. "Prattle," *San Francisco Examiner*, October 7, 1894. SOLE, 44–45.

Down in Georgia is a little forest where the blood of six hundred of my fifteen hundred battlemates utters a mute demand for recognition and place in this revenge. It took them only twenty minutes to fall, but it has taken General Howard thirty years to ignore their hopeless heroism, and he has not finished. He was probably the only officer present who expected a different result; but as humble testimony to the sustaining power of religion, I am bound to confess that he has borne his disappointment with a more unfailing cheerfulness than the rest of us have felt in the memory of our fulfilled expectations. *Vale,* General Howard! — may you live forever! And may every unctuous smile of your life cover a warm and comfortable consciousness of your soldierly generosity in enriching American history with *one line* about the affair at Pickett's Mill.

[1900; Sole]

ON PRAYER IN BATTLE[23]

If a man is good he thinks all men are more or less worthy; if bad he makes all mankind co-defendants. That comes of looking into his own heart and fancying that he surveys the world. Naturally the Rev. W. S. Hubbell, Chaplain in the Loyal Legion,[24] is a praying man, as befits him. When in trouble he asks God to help him out. So he assumes that all others do the same. At a recent meeting of a Congregational Club to do honor to General Howard on that gentleman's seventieth birthday (may he have a seventy-first) Dr. Hubbell said: "I bear personal testimony that if ever a man prays in his life it is in the midst of battle."

My personal testimony is the other way. I have been in a good many battles, and in my youth I used some times to pray — when in trouble. But I never prayed in battle. I was always too much preoccupied to think about it. Probably Dr. Hubbell was misled by hearing in the battle the sacred Name spoken on all sides with great frequency and fervency. And probably he was too busy with his own devotions to observe, or, observing, did not understand the mystic word that commonly followed — which, as nearly as I can recollect, was "Dammit."

23. "The Passing Show," *San Francisco Examiner*, December 2, 1900. SOLE, 65–66.

24. The Military Order of the Loyal Legion of the United States was founded in Philadelphia on April 15, 1865, and open to all former Union officers who pledged to be "minutemen" coming to the aid of their country if the rebellion started up again. The Loyal Legion became a social club where members remembered their participation in the war and kept its memory alive. FAUST.

[1864; SOLE]

MY DEAR CLARΛ[25]

Hd.Qrs. 2nd Brig. 3d Div. 4th A.C.
Ackworth, Ga., June 8th, 1864

My Dear Clara:[26]

Will you be very much displeased to hear from me by letter?

If I thought so I would never touch pen again. 'Tis true you never asked me to write to you, but the knowledge that I still live cannot be unwelcome to one who professed to regard me as a *friend*. I don't know Clare what the word *friend* means to you who have so many, but to *me* friendship has a meaning deeper than the definition of Webster or Worcester. And my friendship for you is a feeling which no language can define. Do you call this flattery? If so you do not know me and I forgive you.

I have not written to you before, but my neglect was not caused by indifference. I knew Tima would sometimes mention my name to you. But I want to hear from you very much; not because you will tell me of Tima,[27] but of yourself. You always seemed to think, Clare, that I never cared for you except as Tima's sister — a sort of necessary evil. (*Vide*— our carriage ride by Eagle lake.) Is it necessary for me to say you were unjust to me? No, Clare, except our sweet Tima, I love you better than any one on this earth.

Perhaps this is not right; — perhaps my mother and sister should be first in my affections, — but so it is.

I am getting very tired of my present life and weary of the profession of arms. Not because of its horrors or dangers; not because its hardships affect me, but because I wish to be with you and my darling. The pleasant weeks with you, so like a dream, have nearly spoiled the soldier to make the — pensive individual.

Ask Tima why I get no more letters from her. Have I offended her? I

---

25. Bierce to Clara Wright; SOLE, 45–47. See also Carey McWilliams, "Ambrose Bierce and His First Love," *Bookman* 75 (June–July 1932): 257–58.

26. Clara Wright, younger sister to Bierce's girlfriend, Fatima Wright, of Warsaw, Indiana. SOLE, 45.

27. Bernice "Fatima" Wright of Warsaw, Indiana. Very little is known about the relationship of Bierce and Wright.

may have written something as heartless and cruel as I used to say to her. If I have I hope she will forgive me. Her last letter was dated May 11th.

Do you think that there is a probability of my letters getting into other hands than hers? Please tell me for the thought troubles me very much. Oh, if I could be with you both again my measure of happiness would be full. I do not see how I could have been so unhappy as I sometimes was when with you.

But I ought rather to be thankful for being allowed so much happiness with you — so much more than I deserved — than to repine at the fate which withholds more. I hardly expect ever to see you again, and perhaps it is better so. Every day some one is struck down who is so much better than I. Since leaving Cleveland Tenn. my brigade has lost nearly one third its numbers killed and wounded.

Among these were so many good men who could ill be spared from the army and the world. And yet I am left. But my turn will come in time. Oh, how pleasant would death be were it for you and Tima, instead of for my country — for a cause which may be right and may be wrong. Do you think I lack patriotism for talking this way? Perhaps so. Soldiers are not troubled with that sort of stuff.

May I talk to you about D —? Do you love him yet? or think you do?

Is that a blunt question? You know you told me you did once. Please answer it.

Oh, I wish I could help you. You who have been so good to me. But my hands are tied. I can only warn you. There is a metal among the rocks here which viewed at a distance has all the appearances of gold. A close inspection shows it to be the basest dross. You are an admirer of pebbles I believe.

Do tell me all about yourself and Tima. What books you read, what society you have, and if you have lots of fun. Capt. Webster desired to be remembered to you and Tima if I ever wrote you. By the way is Jo Williams at W.? The less you have to do with him the better you will please me. If you require reasons I will give them. Do you know my mother yet, and does Tima call on her as she promised me? How is Lyde C.?

Now Clare if you don't write to me at once I shall take it as proof that you don't wish to hear from me again.

Give my kindest regards to 'Slissa and the girls.

Take my darling in your arms, and kiss her a thousand times for me. With more love than I can tell, I am

Your friend

A. G. Bierce

P.S. Do you hear from Ol? I can get no word from him.

B—

It is raining very hard and I am very lonely. In looking over my valise just now I found tucked away snugly a little embroidered handkerchief. Do you remember it? Then there were also some little pebbles; common looking things enough, but each one is transparent, and looking into it I see two tiny figures with skirts just *slightly* elevated, showing such delicate little — feet, stepping along the soft sand, and picking up these little nothings for me. What delicate little tracks they leave behind them. But these tracks will all be erased by the next rain. Not so the impressions left on the hard and stony soil of my heart. Every examination shows me how some mischievous persons have crept into the garden of my soul, and tracked it up worse than a melon patch by school-boys.

But not one of the little tracks shall be blotted out by the rude gardener Time. The amount of it all is, Clare, that I love you and Tima so I can't find language to tell it.

I just wish I could pass my whole life with you both, and have nothing to do but give myself up to the delicious intoxication of your society. For that, I would renounce the whole world and all the ties of kindred; throw away every ambition or aim in life, and make a fool of myself in the most approved style generally.

Brady.

[1891; CWAB, II]

ONE OF THE MISSING

Jerome Searing, a private soldier of General Sherman's army, then confronting the enemy at and about Kennesaw Mountain, Georgia, turned his back upon a small group of officers with whom he had been talking in low tones, stepped across a light line of earthworks, and disappeared in a forest. None of the men in line behind the works had said a word to him, nor had he so much as nodded to them in passing, but all who saw understood that this brave man had been intrusted with some perilous duty. Jerome Searing, though a private, did not serve in the ranks; he was detailed for service at division headquarters, being borne upon the rolls as an orderly. "Orderly" is a word covering a multitude of duties. An orderly may be a messenger, a clerk, an officer's servant—anything. He may perform services for which no provision is made in orders and army regulations. Their nature may depend upon his aptitude, upon favor, upon accident. Private Searing, an incomparable marksman, young, hardy, intelligent and insensible to fear, was a scout. The general commanding his division was not content to obey orders blindly without knowing what was in his front, even when his command was not on detached service, but formed a fraction of the line of the army; nor was he satisfied to receive his knowledge of his *vis-à-vis* through the customary channels; he wanted to know more than he was apprised of by the corps commander and the collisions of pickets and skirmishers. Hence Jerome Searing, with his extraordinary daring, his woodcraft, his sharp eyes, and truthful tongue. On this occasion his instructions were simple: to get as near the enemy's lines as possible and learn all that he could.

In a few moments he had arrived at the picket-line, the men on duty there lying in groups of two and four behind little banks of earth scooped out of the slight depression in which they lay, their rifles protruding from the green boughs with which they had masked their small defenses. The forest extended without a break toward the front, so solemn and silent that only by an effort of the imagination could it be conceived as populous with armed men, alert and vigilant—a forest formidable with possibilities of battle. Pausing a moment in one of these rifle-pits to apprise the men of his intention Searing crept stealthily forward on his hands and knees and was soon lost to view in a dense thicket of underbrush.

"That is the last of him," said one of the men; "I wish I had his rifle; those fellows will hurt some of us with it."

Searing crept on, taking advantage of every accident of ground and growth to give himself better cover. His eyes penetrated everywhere, his ears took note of every sound. He stilled his breathing, and at the cracking of a twig beneath his knee stopped his progress and hugged the earth. It was slow work, but not tedious; the danger made it exciting, but by no physical signs was the excitement manifest. His pulse was as regular, his nerves were as steady as if he were trying to trap a sparrow.

"It seems a long time," he thought, "but I cannot have come very far; I am still alive."

He smiled at his own method of estimating distance, and crept forward. A moment later he suddenly flattened himself upon the earth and lay motionless, minute after minute. Through a narrow opening in the bushes he had caught sight of a small mound of yellow clay — one of the enemy's rifle-pits. After some little time he cautiously raised his head, inch by inch, then his body upon his hands, spread out on each side of him, all the while intently regarding the hillock of clay. In another moment he was upon his feet, rifle in hand, striding rapidly forward with little attempt at concealment. He had rightly interpreted the signs, whatever they were; the enemy was gone.

To assure himself beyond a doubt before going back to report upon so important a matter, Searing pushed forward across the line of abandoned pits, running from cover to cover in the more open forest, his eyes vigilant to discover possible stragglers. He came to the edge of a plantation — one of those forlorn, deserted homesteads of the last years of the war, upgrown with brambles, ugly with broken fences and desolate with vacant buildings having blank apertures in place of doors and windows. After a keen reconnoissance from the safe seclusion of a clump of young pines Searing ran lightly across a field and through an orchard to a small structure which stood apart from the other farm buildings, on a slight elevation. This he thought would enable him to overlook a large scope of country in the direction that he supposed the enemy to have taken in withdrawing. This building, which had originally consisted of a single room elevated upon four posts about ten feet high, was now little more than a roof; the floor had fallen away, the joists and planks loosely piled on the ground below or resting on end at various angles, not wholly torn from their fastenings above. The supporting posts were themselves no longer vertical. It looked as if the whole edifice would go down at the touch of a finger.

Concealing himself in the debris of joists and flooring Searing looked across the open ground between his point of view and a spur of Kennesaw Mountain, a half-mile away. A road leading up and across this spur was crowded with troops—the rear-guard of the retiring enemy, their gun-barrels gleaming in the morning sunlight.

Searing had now learned all that he could hope to know. It was his duty to return to his own command with all possible speed and report his discovery. But the gray column of Confederates toiling up the mountain road was singularly tempting. His rifle—an ordinary "Springfield," but fitted with a globe sight and hair-trigger—would easily send its ounce and a quarter of lead hissing into their midst. That would probably not affect the duration and result of the war, but it is the business of a soldier to kill. It is also his habit if he is a good soldier. Searing cocked his rifle and "set" the trigger.

But it was decreed from the beginning of time that Private Searing was not to murder anybody that bright summer morning, nor was the Confederate retreat to be announced by him. For countless ages events had been so matching themselves together in that wondrous mosaic to some parts of which, dimly discernible, we give the name of history, that the acts which he had in will would have marred the harmony of the pattern. Some twenty-five years previously the Power charged with the execution of the work according to the design had provided against that mischance by causing the birth of a certain male child in a little village at the foot of the Carpathian Mountains, had carefully reared it, supervised its education, directed its desires into a military channel, and in due time made it an officer of artillery. By the concurrence of an infinite number of favoring influences and their preponderance over an infinite number of opposing ones, this officer of artillery had been made to commit a breach of discipline and flee from his native country to avoid punishment. He had been directed to New Orleans (instead of New York), where a recruiting officer awaited him on the wharf. He was enlisted and promoted, and things were so ordered that he now commanded a Confederate battery some two miles along the line from where Jerome Searing, the Federal scout, stood cocking his rifle. Nothing had been neglected—at every step in the progress of both these men's lives, and in the lives of their contemporaries and ancestors, and in the lives of the contemporaries of their ancestors, the right thing had been done to bring about the desired result. Had anything in all this vast concatenation been overlooked Private Searing might have fired on the retreating Confederates that morning, and would perhaps have missed. As it fell out, a Confederate captain of artillery, having nothing better to do while awaiting his turn to pull out and be off, amused himself by sighting a field-piece obliquely to his right at what he mistook for some Federal officers on the crest of a hill, and discharged it. The shot flew high of its mark.

As Jerome Searing drew back the hammer of his rifle and with his eyes upon the distant Confederates considered where he could plant his shot with the best hope of making a widow or an orphan or a childless mother,—perhaps all three, for Private Searing, although he had repeatedly refused promotion, was not without a certain kind of ambition,—he heard a rushing sound in the air, like that made by the wings of a great bird swooping down upon its prey. More quickly than he could apprehend the gradation, it increased to a hoarse and horrible roar, as the missile that made it sprang at him out of the sky, striking with a deafening impact one of the posts supporting the confusion of timbers above him, smashing it into matchwood, and bringing down the crazy edifice with a loud clatter, in clouds of blinding dust!

When Jerome Searing recovered consciousness he did not at once understand what had occurred. It was, indeed, some time before he opened his eyes. For a while he believed that he had died and been buried, and he tried to recall some portions of the burial service. He thought that his wife was kneeling upon his grave, adding her weight to that of the earth upon his breast. The two of them, widow and earth, had crushed his coffin. Unless the children should persuade her to go home he would not much longer be able to breathe. He felt a sense of wrong. "I cannot speak to her," he thought; "the dead have no voice; and if I open my eyes I shall get them full of earth."

He opened his eyes. A great expanse of blue sky, rising from a fringe of the tops of trees. In the foreground, shutting out some of the trees, a high, dun mound, angular in outline and crossed by an intricate, patternless system of straight lines; the whole an immeasurable distance away — a distance so inconceivably great that it fatigued him, and he closed his eyes. The moment that he did so he was conscious of an insufferable light. A sound was in his ears like the low, rhythmic thunder of a distant sea breaking in successive waves upon the beach, and out of this noise, seeming a part of it, or possibly coming from beyond it, and intermingled with its ceaseless undertone, came the articulate words:

"Jerome Searing, you are caught like a rat in a trap — in a trap, trap, trap."

Suddenly there fell a great silence, a black darkness, an infinite tranquillity, and Jerome Searing, perfectly conscious of his rathood, and well assured of the trap that he was in, remembering all and no-wise alarmed, again opened his eyes to reconnoitre, to note the strength of his enemy, to plan his defense.

He was caught in a reclining posture, his back firmly supported by a solid beam. Another lay across his breast, but he had been able to shrink a little away from it so that it no longer oppressed him, though it was immovable. A brace joining it at an angle had wedged him against a pile of boards on his left, fastening the arm on that side. His legs, slightly parted and straight along the ground, were covered upward to the knees with a mass of debris which towered above his narrow horizon. His head was as rigidly fixed as in a vise; he could move his eyes, his chin — no more. Only his right arm was partly free. "You must help us out of this," he said to it. But he could not get it from under the heavy timber athwart his chest, nor move it outward more than six inches at the elbow.

Searing was not seriously injured, nor did he suffer pain. A smart rap on the head from a flying fragment of the splintered post, incurred simultaneously with the frightfully sudden shock to the nervous system, had momentarily dazed him. His term of unconsciousness, including the period of recovery, during which he had had the strange fancies, had probably not exceeded a few seconds, for the dust of the wreck had not wholly cleared away as he began an intelligent survey of the situation.

With his partly free right hand he now tried to get hold of the beam that lay across, but not quite against, his breast. In no way could he do so. He was unable to depress the shoulder so as to push the elbow beyond that edge of the timber which was nearest his knees; failing in that, he could not raise the forearm and hand to grasp the beam. The brace that made an angle with it downward and backward prevented him from doing anything in that direction, and between it and his body the space was not half so wide as the length of his forearm. Obviously he could not get his hand under the beam nor over it; the hand could not, in fact, touch it at all. Having demonstrated his inability, he desisted, and began to think whether he could reach any of the débris piled upon his legs.

In surveying the mass with a view to determining that point, his attention was arrested by what seemed to be a ring of shining metal immediately in front of his eyes. It appeared to him at first to surround some perfectly black substance, and it was somewhat more than a half inch in diameter. It suddenly occurred to his mind that the blackness was simply shadow and that the ring was in fact the muzzle of his rifle protruding from the pile of debris. He was not long in satisfying himself that this was so—if it was a satisfaction. By closing either eye he could look a little way along the barrel—to the point where it was hidden by the rubbish that held it. He could see the one side, with the corresponding eye, at apparently the same angle as the other side with the other eye. Looking with the right eye, the weapon seemed to be directed at a point to the left of his head, and vice versa. He was unable to see the upper surface of the barrel, but could see the under surface of the stock at a slight angle. The piece was, in fact, aimed at the exact centre of his forehead.

In the perception of this circumstance, in the recollection that just previously to the mischance of which this uncomfortable situation was the result he had cocked the rifle and set the trigger so that a touch would discharge it, Private Searing was affected with a feeling of uneasiness. But that was as far as possible from fear; he was a brave man, somewhat familiar with the aspect of rifles from that point of view, and of cannon too. And now he recalled, with something like amusement, an incident of his experience at the storming of Missionary Ridge, where, walking up to one of the enemy's embrasures from which he had seen a heavy gun throw charge after charge of grape among the assailants he had thought for a moment that the piece had been withdrawn; he could see nothing in the opening but a brazen circle. What that was he had understood just in time to step aside as it pitched another peck of iron down that swarming slope. To face firearms is one

of the commonest incidents in a soldier's life — firearms, too, with ma-
levolent eyes blazing behind them. That is what a soldier is for. Still,
Private Searing did not altogether relish the situation, and turned away
his eyes.

After groping, aimless, with his right hand for a time he made an
ineffectual attempt to release his left. Then he tried to disengage his
head, the fixity of which was the more annoying from his ignorance of
what held it. Next he tried to free his feet, but while exerting the
powerful muscles of his legs for that purpose it occurred to him that a
disturbance of the rubbish which held them might discharge the rifle;
how it could have endured what had already befallen it he could not
understand, although memory assisted him with several instances in
point. One in particular he recalled, in which in a moment of mental
abstraction he had clubbed his rifle and beaten out another gentleman's brains, observing afterward that the weapon which he had been
diligently swinging by the muzzle was loaded, capped, and at full
cock — knowledge of which circumstance would doubtless have cheered
his antagonist to longer endurance. He had always smiled in recalling
that blunder of his "green and salad days" as a soldier, but now he did
not smile. He turned his eyes again to the muzzle of the rifle and for a
moment fancied that it had moved; it seemed somewhat nearer.

Again he looked away. The tops of the distant trees beyond the
bounds of the plantation interested him: he had not before observed
how light and feathery they were, nor how darkly blue the sky was, even
among their branches, where they somewhat paled it with their green;
above him it appeared almost black. "It will be uncomfortably hot
here," he thought, "as the day advances. I wonder which way I am
looking."

Judging by such shadows as he could see, he decided that his face
was due north; he would at least not have the sun in his eyes, and
north — well, that was toward his wife and children.

"Bah!" he exclaimed aloud, "what have they to do with it?"

He closed his eyes. "As I can't get out I may as well go to sleep. The
rebels are gone and some of our fellows are sure to stray out here
foraging. They'll find me."

But he did not sleep. Gradually he became sensible of a pain in his
forehead — a dull ache, hardly perceptible at first, but growing more
and more uncomfortable. He opened his eyes and it was gone — closed

them and it returned. "The devil!" he said, irrelevantly, and stared again at the sky. He heard the singing of birds, the strange metallic note of the meadow lark, suggesting the clash of vibrant blades. He fell into pleasant memories of his childhood, played again with his brother and sister, raced across the fields, shouting to alarm the sedentary larks, entered the sombre forest beyond and with timid steps followed the faint path to Ghost Rock, standing at last with audible heart-throbs before the Dead Man's Cave and seeking to penetrate its awful mystery. For the first time he observed that the opening of the haunted cavern was encircled by a ring of metal. Then all else vanished and left him gazing into the barrel of his rifle as before. But whereas before it had seemed nearer, it now seemed an inconceivable distance away, and all the more sinister for that. He cried out and, startled by something in his own voice — the note of fear — lied to himself in denial: "If I don't sing out I may stay here till I die."

He now made no further attempt to evade the menacing stare of the gun barrel. If he turned away his eyes an instant it was to look for assistance (although he could not see the ground on either side the ruin), and he permitted them to return, obedient to the imperative fascination. If he closed them it was from weariness, and instantly the poignant pain in his forehead — the prophecy and menace of the bullet — forced him to reopen them.

The tension of nerve and brain was too severe; nature came to his relief with intervals of unconsciousness. Reviving from one of these he became sensible of a sharp, smarting pain in his right hand, and when he worked his fingers together, or rubbed his palm with them, he could feel that they were wet and slippery. He could not see the hand, but he knew the sensation; it was running blood. In his delirium he had beaten it against the jagged fragments of the wreck, had clutched it full of splinters. He resolved that he would meet his fate more manly. He was a plain, common soldier, had no religion and not much philosophy; he could not die like a hero, with great and wise last words, even if there had been some one to hear them, but he could die "game," and he would. But if he could only know when to expect the shot!

Some rats which had probably inhabited the shed came sneaking and scampering about. One of them mounted the pile of debris that held the rifle; another followed and another. Searing regarded them at first with indifference, then with friendly interest; then, as the thought flashed into his bewildered mind that they might touch the trigger of his rifle, he cursed them and ordered them to go away. "It is no business of yours," he cried.

The creatures went away; they would return later, attack his face, gnaw away his nose, cut his throat — he knew that, but he hoped by that time to be dead.

Nothing could now unfix his gaze from the little ring of metal with its black interior. The pain in his forehead was fierce and incessant. He felt it gradually penetrating the brain more and more deeply, until at last its progress was arrested by the wood at the back of his head. It grew momentarily more insufferable: he began wantonly beating his lacerated hand against the splinters again to counteract that horrible ache. It seemed to throb with a slow, regular recurrence, each pulsation sharper than the preceding, and sometimes he cried out, thinking he felt the fatal bullet. No thoughts of home, of wife and children, of country, of glory. The whole record of memory was effaced. The world had passed away — not a vestige remained. Here in this confusion of timbers and boards is the sole universe. Here is immortality in time — each pain an everlasting life. The throbs tick off eternities.

Jerome Searing, the man of courage, the formidable enemy, the strong, resolute warrior, was as pale as a ghost. His jaw was fallen; his eyes protruded; he trembled in every fibre; a cold sweat bathed his entire body; he screamed with fear. He was not insane — he was terrified.

In groping about with his torn and bleeding hand he seized at last a strip of board, and, pulling, felt it give way. It lay parallel with his body, and by bending his elbow as much as the contracted space would permit, he could draw it a few inches at a time. Finally it was altogether loosened from the wreckage covering his legs; he could lift it clear of the ground its whole length. A great hope came into his mind: perhaps he could work it upward, that is to say backward, far enough to lift the end and push aside the rifle; or, if that were too tightly wedged, so place the strip of board as to deflect the bullet. With this object he passed it backward inch by inch, hardly daring to breathe lest that act somehow defeat his intent, and more than ever unable to remove his eyes from the rifle, which might perhaps now hasten to improve its waning opportunity. Something at least had been gained: in the occupation of his mind in this attempt at self-defense he was less sensible of the pain in his head and had ceased to wince. But he was still dreadfully frightened and his teeth rattled like castanets.

The strip of board ceased to move to the suasion of his hand. He tugged at it with all his strength, changed the direction of its length all he could, but it had met some extended obstruction behind him and the end in front was still too far away to clear the pile of debris and reach the muzzle of the gun. It extended, indeed, nearly as far as the trigger guard, which, uncovered by the rubbish, he could imperfectly see with his right eye. He tried to break the strip with his hand, but had no leverage. In his defeat, all his terror returned, augmented tenfold. The black aperture of the rifle appeared to threaten a sharper and more imminent death in punishment of his rebellion. The track of the bullet through his head ached with an intenser anguish. He began to tremble again.

Suddenly he became composed. His tremor subsided. He clenched his teeth and drew down his eyebrows. He had not exhausted his means of defense; a new design had shaped itself in his mind — another plan of battle. Raising the front end of the strip of board, he carefully pushed it forward through the wreckage at the side of the rifle until it pressed against the trigger guard. Then he moved the end slowly outward until he could feel that it had cleared it, then, closing his eyes, thrust it against the trigger with all his strength! There was no explosion; the rifle had been discharged as it dropped from his hand when the building fell. But it did its work.

Lieutenant Adrian Searing, in command of the picket-guard on that part of the line through which his brother Jerome had passed on his mission, sat with attentive ears in his breastwork behind the line. Not the faintest sound escaped him; the cry of a bird, the barking of a squirrel, the noise of the wind among the pines — all were anxiously noted by his overstrained sense. Suddenly, directly in front of his line, he heard a faint, confused rumble, like the clatter of a falling building translated by distance. The lieutenant mechanically looked at his watch. Six o'clock and eighteen minutes. At the same moment an officer approached him on foot from the rear and saluted.

"Lieutenant," said the officer, "the colonel directs you to move forward your line and feel the enemy if you find him. If not, continue the advance until directed to halt. There is reason to think that the enemy has retreated."

The lieutenant nodded and said nothing; the other officer retired. In a moment the men, apprised of their duty by the non-commissioned officers in low tones, had deployed from their rifle-pits and were moving forward in skirmishing order, with set teeth and beating hearts.

This line of skirmishers sweeps across the plantation toward the mountain. They pass on both sides of the wrecked building, observing nothing. At a short distance in their rear their commander comes. He casts his eyes curiously upon the ruin and sees a dead body half buried in ill boards and timbers. It is so covered with dust that its clothing is Confederate gray. Its face is yellowish white; the cheeks are fallen in, the temples sunken, too, with sharp ridges about them, making the forehead forbiddingly narrow; the upper lip, slightly lifted, shows the white teeth, rigidly clenched. The hair is heavy with moisture, the face as wet as the dewy grass all about. From his point of view the officer does not observe the rifle; the man was apparently killed by the fall of the building.

"Dead a week," said the officer curtly, moving on and absently pulling out his watch as if to verify his estimate of time. Six o'clock and forty minutes.

[1888; CWAB, II]

A SON OF THE GODS

A STUDY IN THE PRESENT TENSE

A breezy day and a sunny landscape. An open country to right and left and forward; behind, a wood. In the edge of this wood, facing the open but not venturing into it, long lines of troops, halted. The wood is alive with them, and full of confused noises — the occasional rattle of wheels as a battery of artillery goes into position to cover the advance; the hum and murmur of the soldiers talking; a sound of innumerable feet in the dry leaves that strew the interspaces among the trees; hoarse commands of officers. Detached groups of horsemen are well in front — not altogether exposed — many of them intently regarding the crest of a hill a mile away in the direction of the interrupted advance. For this powerful army, moving in battle order through a forest, has met with a formidable obstacle — the open country. The crest of that gentle hill a mile away has a sinister look; it says, Beware! Along it runs a stone wall extending to left and right a great distance. Behind the wall is a hedge; behind the hedge are seen the tops of trees in rather straggling order. Among the trees — what? It is necessary to know.

Yesterday, and for many days and nights previously, we were fighting somewhere; always there was cannonading, with occasional keen rattlings of musketry, mingled with cheers, our own or the enemy's, we seldom knew, attesting some temporary advantage. This morning at daybreak the enemy was gone. We have moved forward across his earthworks, across which we have so often vainly attempted to move before, through the debris of his abandoned camps, among the graves of his fallen, into the woods beyond.

How curiously we had regarded everything! How odd it all had seemed! Nothing had appeared quite familiar; the most commonplace objects — an old saddle, a splintered wheel, a forgotten canteen — everything had related something of the mysterious personality of those strange men who had been killing us. The soldier never becomes wholly familiar with the conception of his foes as men like himself; he cannot divest himself of the feeling that they are another order of beings, differently conditioned, in an environment not altogether of the earth. The smallest vestiges of them rivet his attention and engage his interest. He thinks of them as inaccessible; and, catching an unexpected glimpse of them, they appear farther away, and therefore larger, than they really are — like objects in a fog. He is somewhat in awe of them.

From the edge of the wood leading up the acclivity are the tracks of horses and wheels — the wheels of cannon. The yellow grass is beaten down by the feet of infantry. Clearly they have passed this way in thousands; they have not withdrawn by the country roads. This is significant — it is the difference between retiring and retreating.

That group of horsemen is our commander, his staff and escort. He is facing the distant crest, holding his field-glass against his eyes with both hands, his elbows needlessly elevated. It is a fashion; it seems to dignify the act; we are all addicted to it. Suddenly he lowers the glass and says a few words to those about him. Two or three aides detach themselves from the group and canter away into the woods, along the lines in each direction. We did not hear his words, but we know them: "Tell General X. to send forward the skirmish line." Those of us who have been out of place resume our positions; the men resting at ease straighten themselves and the ranks are reformed without a command. Some of us staff officers dismount and look at our saddle girths; those already on the ground remount.

Galloping rapidly along in the edge of the open ground comes a young officer on a snow-white horse. His saddle blanket is scarlet. What a fool! No one who has ever been in action but remembers how naturally every rifle turns toward the man on a white horse; no one but has observed how a bit of red enrages the bull of battle. That such colors are fashionable in military life must be accepted as the most astonishing of all the phenomena of human vanity. They would seem to have been devised to increase the death-rate.

This young officer is in full uniform, as if on parade. He is all agleam with bullion — a blue-and-gold edition of the Poetry of War. A wave of derisive laughter runs abreast of him all along the line. But how handsome he is! — with what careless grace he sits his horse!

He reins up within a respectful distance of the corps commander and salutes. The old soldier nods familiarly; he evidently knows him. A brief colloquy between them is going on; the young man seems to be preferring some request which the elder one is indisposed to grant. Let us ride a little nearer. Ah! too late — it is ended. The young officer salutes again, wheels his horse, and rides straight toward the crest of the hill!

A thin line of skirmishers, the men deployed at six paces or so apart, now pushes from the wood into the open. The commander speaks to his bugler, who claps his instrument to his lips. *Tra-la-la! Tra-la-la!* The skirmishers halt in their tracks.

Meantime the young horseman has advanced a hundred yards. He is riding at a walk, straight up the long slope, with never a turn of the head. How glorious! Gods! what would we not give to be in his place — with his soul! He does not draw his sabre; his right hand hangs easily at his side. The breeze catches the plume in his hat and flutters it smartly. The sunshine rests upon his shoulder-straps, lovingly, like a visible benediction. Straight on he rides. Ten thousand pairs of eyes are fixed upon him with an intensity that he can hardly fail to feel; ten thousand hearts keep quick time to the inaudible hoofbeats of his snowy steed. He is not alone — he draws all souls after him. But we remember that we laughed! On and on, straight for the hedge-lined wall, he rides. Not a look backward. O, if he would but turn — if he could but see the love, the adoration, the atonement!

Not a word is spoken; the populous depths of the forest still murmur with their unseen and unseeing swarm, but all along the fringe is silence. The burly commander is an equestrian statue of himself. The mounted staff officers, their field-glasses up, are motionless all. The line of battle in the edge of the wood stands at a new kind of "attention," each man in the attitude in which he was caught by the consciousness of what is going on. All these hardened and impenitent man-killers, to whom death in its awfulest forms is a fact familiar to their every-day observation; who sleep on hills trembling with the thunder of great guns, dine in the midst of streaming missiles, and play at cards among the dead faces of their dearest friends — all are watching with suspended breath and beating hearts the outcome of an act involving the life of one man. Such is the magnetism of courage and devotion.

If now you should turn your head you would see a simultaneous movement among the spectators — a start, as if they had received an electric shock — and looking forward again to the now distant horseman you would see that he has in that instant altered his direction and is riding at an angle to his former course. The spectators suppose the sudden deflection to be caused by a shot, perhaps a wound; but take his field-glass and you will observe that he is riding toward a break in the wall and hedge. He means, if not killed, to ride through and overlook the country beyond.

You are not to forget the nature of this man's act; it is not permitted to you to think of it as an instance of bravado, nor, on the other hand, a needless sacrifice of self. If the enemy has not retreated he is in force on that ridge. The investigator will encounter nothing less than a line of battle; there is no need of pickets, videttes, skirmishers, to give warning of our approach; our attacking lines will be visible, conspicuous, exposed to an artillery fire that will shave the ground the moment they break from cover, and for half the distance to a sheet of rifle bullets in which nothing can live. In short, if the enemy is there, it would be madness to attack him in front; he must be manœuvred out by the immemorial plan of threatening his line of communication, as necessary to his existence as to the diver at the bottom of the sea his air tube. But how ascertain if the enemy is there? There is but one way, — somebody must go and see. The natural and customary thing to do is to send forward a line of skirmishers. But in this case they will answer in the affirmative with all their lives; the enemy, crouching in double ranks behind the stone wall and in cover of the hedge, will wait until it is possible to count each assailant's teeth. At the first volley a half of the questioning line will fall, the other half before it can accomplish the predestined retreat. What a price to pay for gratified curiosity! At what a dear rate an army must sometimes purchase knowledge! "Let me pay all," says this gallant man — this military Christ!

There is no hope except the hope against hope that the crest is clear. True, he might prefer capture to death. So long as he advances, the line will not fire — why should it? He can safely ride into the hostile ranks and become a prisoner of war. But this would defeat his object. It would not answer our question; it is necessary either that he return unharmed or be shot to death before our eyes. Only so shall we know how to act. If captured — why, that might have been done by a half-dozen stragglers.

Now begins an extraordinary contest of intellect between a man and an army. Our horseman, now within a quarter of a mile of the crest, suddenly wheels to the left and gallops in a direction parallel to it. He has caught sight of his antagonist; he knows all. Some slight advantage of ground has enabled him to overlook a part of the line. If he were here he could tell us in words. But that is now hopeless; he must make the best use of the few minutes of life remaining to him, by compelling the enemy himself to tell us as much and as plainly as possible — which naturally, that discreet power is reluctant to do. Not a rifleman in those crouching ranks, not a cannoneer at those masked and shotted guns, but knows the needs of the situation, the imperative duty of forbearance. Besides, there has been time enough to forbid them all to fire. True, a single rifle-shot might drop him and be no great disclosure. But firing is infectious — and see how rapidly he moves, with never a pause except as he whirls his horse about to take a new direction, never directly backward toward us, never directly forward toward his executioners. All this is visible through the glass; it seems occurring within pistol-shot; we see all but the enemy, whose presence, whose thoughts, whose motives we infer. To the unaided eye there is nothing but a black figure on a white horse, tracing slow zigzags against the slope of a distant hill — so slowly they seem almost to creep.

Now — the glass again — he has tired of his failure, or sees his error, or has gone mad; he is dashing directly forward at the wall, as if to take it at a leap, hedge and all! One moment only and he wheels right about and is speeding like the wind straight down the slope — toward his friends, toward his death! Instantly the wall is topped with a fierce roll of smoke for a distance of hundreds of yards to right and left. This is as instantly dissipated by the wind, and before the rattle of the rifle reaches us he is down. No, he recovers his seat; he has but pulled his horse upon its haunches. They are up and away! A tremendous cheer bursts from our ranks, relieving the insupportable tension of our feelings. And the horse and its rider? Yes, they are up and away. Away, indeed — they are making directly to our left, parallel to the now steadily blazing and smoking wall. The rattle of the musketry is continuous, and every bullet's target is that courageous heart.

Suddenly a great bank of white smoke pushes upward from behind the wall. Another and another — a dozen roll up before the thunder of the explosions and the humming of the missiles reach our ears and the missiles themselves come bounding through clouds of dust into our covert, knocking over here and there a man and causing a temporary distraction, a passing thought of self.

The dust drifts away. Incredible! — that enchanted horse and rider have passed a ravine and are climbing another slope to unveil another conspiracy of silence, to thwart the will of another armed host. Another moment and that crest too is in eruption. The horse rears and strikes the air with its forefeet. They are down at last. But look again — the man has detached himself from the dead animal. He stands erect, motionless, holding his sabre in his right hand straight above his head. His face is toward us. Now he lowers his hand to a level with his face and moves it outward, the blade of the sabre describing a downward curve. It is a sign to us, to the world, to posterity. It is a hero's salute to death and history.

Again the spell is broken; our men attempt to cheer; they are choking with emotion; they utter hoarse, discordant cries; they clutch their weapons and press tumultuously forward into the open. The skirmishers, without orders, against orders, are going forward at a keen run, like hounds unleashed. Our cannon speak and the enemy's now open in full chorus; to right and left as far as we can see, the distant crest, seeming now so near, erects its towers of cloud and the great shot pitch roaring down among our moving masses. Flag after flag of ours emerges from the wood, line after line sweeps forth, catching the sunlight on its burnished arms. The rear battalions alone are in obedience; they preserve their proper distance from the insurgent front.

The commander has not moved. He now removes his field-glass from his eyes and glances to the right and left. He sees the human current flowing on either side of him and his huddled escort, like tide waves parted by a rock. Not a sign of feeling in his face; he is thinking. Again he directs his eyes forward; they slowly traverse that malign and awful crest. He addresses a calm word to his bugler. *Tra-la-la! Tra-la-la!* The injunction has an imperiousness which enforces it. It is repeated by all the bugles of all the subordinate commanders; the sharp metallic notes assert themselves above the hum of the advance and penetrate the sound of the cannon. To halt is to withdraw. The colors move slowly back; the lines face about and sullenly follow, bearing their wounded, the skirmishers return, gathering up the dead.

Ah, those many, many needless dead! That great soul whose beautiful body is lying over yonder, so conspicuous against the sere hillside — could it not have been spared the bitter consciousness of a vain devotion? Would one exception have marred too much the pitiless perfection of the divine, eternal plan?

DEFENDING REALISM III[28]

Among examples of "literary criticism" which I joy to collect for no better reason than that they relate to my books are some in which I cannot fail to discern the hand of a frowning Providence put forth to humble my proud spirit. Beneath the following, from "Life," I bend my corrigible neck like a rose detected in an attempt to associate with cabbages:

"The younger American writers are doing some very artistic killing in their stories. Stephen Crane,[29] Robert W. Chambers,[30] Ambrose Bierce, E. W. Thomson,[31] Owen Wister[32] and Richard Harding Davis[33] have all tried their hands at blood-spilling with the accessories of war. They are clever young men who never smelt powder burnt in battle, but they have a certain realistic faculty of making the reader see what they have only imagined. Whether Kipling[34] started them on their career of

28. "Concerning Wit and Humor," *San Francisco Examiner*, March 1, 1897. SOLE, 253–54.

29. Stephen Crane (1871–1900), American writer best known for his widely read Civil War novel *The Red Badge of Courage*. Crane, born after the war was over, claimed that what he knew about the battlefield he had learned on his high-school football team.

30. Robert William Chambers (1865–1933). Prolific American novelist, his more than 80 books include novels set during the American Revolution, the War of 1812, the Mexican-American War, the Civil War, and World War I.

31. Edward William Thomson (1849–1924). Canadian journalist, fiction writer, poet, and ardent admirer of Abraham Lincoln, Thomson ran away from his home in Toronto to join the Army of the Potomac in 1864. His war stories include "The Ride by Night," set in the Civil War, and "The Swartz Diamond," set in the Boer War.

32. Owen Wister (1860–1938). American author, best known for his western novel *The Virginian* (1902).

33. Richard Harding Davis (1864–1916). Son of Rebecca Harding Davis, this American novelist and short story writer is the author of *Soldiers of Fortune* (1897).

34. Rudyard Kipling (1865–1936). English author of many works chronicling British imperialism, notably in India. His works include *Barrack-Room Ballads* (1892) and *Soldiers Three* (1888).

revolution and slaughter, or whether it was something in the air that struck them all about the same time, is not quite clear." Etc.

To which I venture to add, in corroboration, the facts following: (1) I am an older man than any young man in America. (2) The fragrance of "powder burnt in battle" has many times reminded me of my preference for that of roasted critic. (3) The stories that this gentleman had in mind were published (and reviewed in more than four hundred of the magazines and newspapers of this country and Europe) before Mr. Kipling had been heard of outside the editorial rooms of "The Mulligachutney Bango." If my esteemed reviewer will add these facts to his esteemed review he will enhance its value by as much as two cents.

By the way, it commonly occurs that in my poor little battle-yarns the incidents that come in for special reprobation by the critics as "improbable" and even "impossible" are transcripts from memory — things that actually occurred before my eyes. In mentioning a certain story of mine the curio that "censures letters" in "Life" supplies an added instance:

"It is a great thing to watch the 'Son of the Gods' ride out to his sure death like a stage hero. It is magnificent, but it is not war."

Well, I saw that thing done, just as related. True, the "Son" escaped whole, but he "rode out" all right, and if matters had been as we all believed them to be, and as he thought them himself, he would have been shot to rags.

Let me not be unfair. My critic's civilian training has led him into the lamentable error of censuring me, but with reference to the other story-tellers whom he names his reprehension is singularly intelligent — he could not have overdamned them if he had tried. This admission, I take it, is commendably just. 'Egad, it is magnanimous!

[1888; CWAB, I]

FOUR DAYS IN DIXIE

During a part of the month of October, 1864, the Federal and Confederate armies of Sherman and Hood respectively, having performed
a surprising and resultless series of marches and countermarches since
the fall of Atlanta, confronted each other along the separating line of
the Coosa River in the vicinity of Gaylesville, Alabama. Here for several
days they remained at rest — at least most of the infantry and artillery
did; what the cavalry was doing nobody but itself ever knew or greatly
cared. It was an interregnum of expectancy between two regimes of
activity.

I was on the staff of Colonel McConnell,[35] who commanded an infantry brigade in the absence of its regular commander. McConnell was a
good man, but he did not keep a very tight rein upon the half dozen
restless and reckless young fellows who (for his sins) constituted his
"military family." In most matters we followed the trend of our desires,
which commonly ran in the direction of adventure — it did not greatly
matter what kind. In pursuance of this policy of escapades, one bright
Sunday morning Lieutenant Cobb, an aide-de-camp, and I mounted
and set out to "seek our fortunes," as the story books have it. Striking
into a road of which we knew nothing except that it led toward the river,
we followed it for a mile or such a matter, when we found our advance
interrupted by a considerable creek, which we must ford or go back. We
consulted a moment and then rode at it as hard as we could, possibly in
the belief that a high momentum would act as it does in the instance of
a skater passing over thin ice. Cobb was fortunate enough to get across
comparatively dry, but his hapless companion was utterly submerged.
The disaster was all the greater from my having on a resplendent new
uniform, of which I had been pardonably vain. Ah, what a gorgeous
new uniform it never was again!

A half-hour devoted to wringing my clothing and dry-charging my
revolver, and we were away. A brisk canter of a half-hour under the
arches of the trees brought us to the river, where it was our ill luck to

35. Colonel Henry Kumler McConnell (?–1898). SOLE, 323, n.91.

find a boat and three soldiers of our brigade. These men had been for several hours concealed in the brush patiently watching the opposite bank in the amiable hope of getting a shot at some unwary Confederate, but had seen, none. For a great distance up and down the stream on the other side, and for at least a mile back from it, extended cornfields. Beyond the cornfields, on slightly higher ground, was a thin forest, with breaks here and there in its continuity, denoting plantations, probably. No houses were in sight, and no camps. We knew that it was the enemy's ground, but whether his forces were disposed along the slightly higher country bordering the bottom lands, or at strategic points miles back, as ours were, we knew no more than the least curious private in our army. In any case the river line would naturally be picketed or patrolled. But the charm of the unknown was upon us: the mysterious exerted its old-time fascination, beckoning to us from that silent shore so peaceful and dreamy in the beauty of the quiet Sunday morning. The temptation was strong and we fell. The soldiers were as eager for the hazard as we, and readily volunteered for the madmen's enterprise. Concealing our horses in a cane-brake, we unmoored the boat and rowed across unmolested.

Arrived at a kind of "landing" on the other side, our first care was so to secure the boat under the bank as to favor a hasty re-embarking in case we should be so unfortunate as to incur the natural consequence of our act; then, following an old road through the ranks of standing corn, we moved in force upon the Confederate position, five strong, with an armament of three Springfield rifles and two Colt's revolvers. We had not the further advantage of music and banners. One thing favored the expedition, giving it an apparent assurance of success: it was well officered — an officer to each man and a half.

After marching about a mile we came into a neck of woods and crossed an intersecting road which showed no wheel-tracks, but was rich in hoof-prints. We observed them and kept right on about our business, whatever that may have been. A few hundred yards farther brought us to a plantation bordering our road upon the right. The fields, as was the Southern fashion at that period of the war, were uncultivated and overgrown with brambles. A large white house stood at some little distance from the road; we saw women and children and a few negroes there. On our left ran the thin forest, pervious to cavalry.

Directly ahead an ascent in the road formed a crest beyond which we could see nothing.

On this crest suddenly appeared two horsemen in gray, sharply outlined against the sky — men and animals looking gigantic. At the same instant a jingling and tramping were audible behind us, and turning in that direction I saw a score of mounted men moving forward at a trot. In the meantime the giants on the crest had multiplied surprisingly. Our invasion of the Gulf States had apparently failed.

There was lively work in the next few seconds. The shots were thick and fast — and uncommonly loud; none, I think, from our side. Cobb was on the extreme left of our advance, I on the right — about two paces apart. He instantly dived into the wood. The three men and I climbed across the fence somehow and struck out across the field — actuated, doubtless, by an intelligent forethought: men on horseback could not immediately follow. Passing near the house, now swarming like a hive of bees, we made for a swamp two or three hundred yards away, where I concealed myself in a jungle, the others continuing — as a defeated commander would put it — to fall back. In my cover, where I lay panting like a hare, I could hear a deal of shouting and hard riding and an occasional shot. I heard some one calling dogs, and the thought of bloodhounds added its fine suggestiveness to the other fancies appropriate to the occasion.

Finding myself unpursued after the lapse of what seemed an hour, but was probably a few minutes, I cautiously sought a place where, still concealed, I could obtain a view of the field of glory. The only enemy in sight was a group of horsemen on a hill a quarter of a mile away. Toward this group a woman was running, followed by the eyes of everybody about the house. I thought she had discovered my hiding-place and was going to "give me away." Taking to my hands and knees I crept as rapidly as possible among the clumps of brambles directly back toward the point in the road where we had met the enemy and failed to make him ours. There I dragged myself into a patch of briars within ten feet of the road, where I lay undiscovered during the remainder of the day, listening to a variety of disparaging remarks upon Yankee valor and to dispiriting declarations of intention conditional on my capture, as members of the Opposition passed and repassed and paused in the road to discuss the morning's events. In this way I learned that the three privates had been headed off and caught within ten minutes. Their destination would naturally be Andersonville;[36] what further became of them God knows. Their captors passed the day making a careful canvass of the swamp for me.

When night had fallen I cautiously left my place of concealment, dodged across the road into the woods and made for the river through the mile of corn. Such corn! It towered above me like a forest, shutting out all the starlight except what came from directly overhead. Many of the ears were a yard out of reach. One who has never seen an Alabama river-bottom cornfield has not exhausted nature's surprises; nor will he know what solitude is until he explores one in a moonless night.

I came at last to the river bank with its fringe of trees and willows and canes. My intention was to swim across, but the current was swift, the water forbiddingly dark and cold. A mist obscured the other bank. I could not, indeed, see the water more than a few yards out. It was a hazardous and horrible undertaking, and I gave it up, following cautiously along the bank in search of the spot where we had moored the boat. True, it was hardly likely that the landing was now unguarded, or, if so, that the boat was still there. Cobb had undoubtedly made for it, having an even more urgent need than I; but hope springs eternal in the human breast, and there was a chance that he had been killed before reaching it. I came at last into the road that we had taken and consumed half the night in cautiously approaching the landing, pistol in hand and heart in mouth. The boat was gone! I continued my journey along the stream — in search of another.

My clothing was still damp from my morning bath, my teeth rattled with cold, but I kept on along the stream until I reached the limit of the cornfields and entered a dense wood. Through this I groped my way, inch by inch, when, suddenly emerging from a thicket into a space slightly more open, I came upon a smoldering camp-fire surrounded by prostrate figures of men, upon one of whom I had almost trodden. A sentinel, who ought to have been shot, sat by the embers, his carbine across his lap, his chin upon his breast. Just beyond was a group of unsaddled horses. The men were asleep; the sentinel was asleep; the

36. The prisoner-of-war camp at Andersonville, Georgia, was the most notorious of the war. It opened in February 1864 and nearly 13,000 Northern prisoners died there from malnutrition, disease, and lack of medical care. CONFED.

horses were asleep. There was something indescribably uncanny about it all. For a moment I believed them all lifeless and O'Hara's familiar line, "The bivouac of the dead," quoted itself in my consciousness.[37] The emotion that I felt was that inspired by a sense of the supernatural; of the actual and imminent peril of my position I had no thought. When at last it occurred to me I felt it as a welcome relief, and stepping silently back into the shadow retraced my course without having awakened a soul. The vividness with which I can now recall that scene is to me one of the marvels of memory.

Getting my bearings again with some difficulty, I now made a wide detour to the left, in the hope of passing around this outpost and striking the river beyond. In this mad attempt I ran upon a more vigilant sentinel, posted in the heart of a thicket, who fired at me without challenge. To a soldier an unexpected shot ringing out at dead of night is fraught with an awful significance. In my circumstances — cut off from my comrades, groping about an unknown country, surrounded by invisible perils which such a signal would call into eager activity — the flash and shock of that firearm were unspeakably dreadful! In any case I should and ought to have fled, and did so; but how much or little of conscious prudence there was in the prompting I do not care to discover by analysis of memory. I went back into the corn, found the river, followed it back a long way and mounted into the fork of a low tree. There I perched until the dawn, a most uncomfortable bird.

In the gray light of the morning I discovered that I was opposite an island of considerable length, separated from the mainland by a narrow and shallow channel, which I promptly waded. The island was low and flat, covered with an almost impenetrable cane-brake interlaced with vines. Working my way through these to the other side, I obtained another look at God's country — Shermany, so to speak. There were no visible inhabitants. The forest and the water met. This did not deter me. For the chill of the water I had no further care, and laying off my boots and outer clothing I prepared to swim. A strange thing now occurred — more accurately, a familiar thing occurred at a strange moment. A

37. Theodore O'Hara (1820–1867) wrote the sentimental poem "A Bivouac of the Dead" (1847) about soldiers killed in the battle of Buena Vista in the Mexican-American War. Bierce borrowed the title for one of his last essays about the Civil War. See Chapter Five.

black cloud seemed to pass before my eyes — the water, the trees, the sky, all vanished in a profound darkness. I heard the roaring of a great cataract, felt the earth sinking from beneath my feet. Then I heard and felt no more.

At the battle of Kennesaw Mountain in the previous June I had been badly wounded in the head, and for three months was incapacitated for service. In truth, I had done no actual duty since, being then, as for many years afterward, subject to fits of fainting, sometimes without assignable immediate cause, but mostly when suffering from exposure, excitement or excessive fatigue. This combination of them all had broken me down — most opportunely, it would seem.

When I regained my consciousness the sun was high. I was still giddy and half blind. To have taken to the water would have been madness; I must have a raft. Exploring my island, I found a pen of slender logs: an old structure without roof or rafters, built for what purpose I do not know. Several of these logs I managed with patient toil to detach and convey to the water, where I floated them, lashing them together with vines. Just before sunset my raft was complete and freighted with my outer clothing, boots and pistol. Having shipped the last article, I returned into the brake, seeking something from which to improvise a paddle. While peering about I heard a sharp metallic click — the cocking of a rifle! I was a prisoner.

The history of this great disaster to the Union arms is brief and simple. A Confederate "home guard," hearing something going on upon the island, rode across, concealed his horse and still-hunted me. And, reader, when you are "held up" in the same way may it be by as fine a fellow. He not only spared my life, but even overlooked a feeble and ungrateful after-attempt upon his own (the particulars of which I shall not relate), merely exacting my word of honor that I would not again try to escape while in his custody. Escape! I could not have escaped a newborn babe.

At my captor's house that evening there was a reception, attended by the elite of the whole vicinity, A Yankee officer in full fig — minus only the boots, which could not be got on to his swollen feet — was something worth seeing, and those who came to scoff remained to stare. What most interested them, I think, was my eating — an entertainment that was prolonged to a late hour. They were a trifle disappointed by the absence of horns, hoof and tail, but bore their chagrin with good-natured fortitude. Among my visitors was a charming young woman from the plantation where we had met the foe the day before — the same lady whom I had suspected of an intention to reveal my hiding-place. She had had no such design; she had run over to the group of horsemen to learn if her father had been hurt — by whom, I should like to know. No restraint was put upon me; my captor even left me with the women and children and went off for instructions as to what disposition he should make of me. Altogether the reception was "a pronounced success," though it is to be regretted that the guest of the evening had the incivility to fall dead asleep in the midst of the festivities, and was put to bed by sympathetic and, he has reason to believe, fair hands.

The next morning I was started off to the rear in custody of two mounted men, heavily armed. They had another prisoner, picked up in some raid beyond the river. He was a most offensive brute — a foreigner of some mongrel sort, with just sufficient command of our tongue to show that he could not control his own. We traveled all day, meeting occasional small bodies of cavalrymen, by whom, with one exception — a Texan officer — I was civilly treated. My guards said, however, that if we should chance to meet Jeff Gatewood he would probably take me from them and hang me to the nearest tree; and once or twice, hearing horsemen approach, they directed me to stand aside, concealed in the brush, one of them remaining near by to keep an eye on me, the other going forward with my fellow-prisoner, for whose neck they seemed to have less tenderness, and whom I heartily wished well hanged.

Jeff Gatewood was a "guerrilla" chief of local notoriety, who was a greater terror to his friends than to his other foes. My guards related almost incredible tales of his cruelties and infamies. By their account it was into his camp that I had blundered on Sunday night.

We put up for the night at a farmhouse, having gone not more than fifteen miles, owing to the condition of my feet. Here we got a bite of supper and were permitted to lie before the fire. My fellow-prisoner took off his boots and was soon sound asleep. I took off nothing and, despite exhaustion, remained equally sound awake. One of the guards also removed his footgear and outer clothing, placed his weapons under his neck and slept the sleep of innocence; the other sat in the chimney corner on watch. The house was a double log cabin, with an open space between the two parts, roofed over — a common type of habitation in that region. The room we were in had its entrance in this open space, the fireplace opposite, at the end. Beside the door was a bed, occupied by the old man of the house and his wife. It was partly curtained off from the room.

In an hour or two the chap on watch began to yawn, then to nod. Pretty soon he stretched himself on the floor, facing us, pistol in hand. For a while he supported himself on his elbow, then laid his head on his arm, blinking like an owl. I performed an occasional snore, watching him narrowly between my eyelashes from the shadow of my arm. The inevitable occurred — he slept audibly.

A half-hour later I rose quietly to my feet, particularly careful not to disturb the blackguard at my side, and moved as silently as possible to the door. Despite my care the latch clicked. The old lady sat bolt upright in bed and stared at me. She was too late. I sprang through the door and struck out for the nearest point of woods, in a direction previously selected, vaulting fences like an accomplished gymnast and followed by a multitude of dogs. It is said that the State of Alabama has more dogs than school-children, and that they cost more for their keep. The estimate of cost is probably too high.

Looking backward as I ran, I saw and heard the place in a turmoil and uproar; and to my joy the old man, evidently oblivious to the facts of the situation, was lifting up his voice and calling his dogs. They were good dogs: they went back; otherwise the malicious old rascal would have had my skeleton. Again the traditional bloodhound did not materialize. Other pursuit there was no reason to fear; my foreign gentleman would occupy the attention of one of the soldiers, and in the darkness of the forest I could easily elude the other, or, if need be, get him at a disadvantage. In point of fact there was no pursuit.

I now took my course by the north star (which I can never sufficiently bless), avoiding all roads and open places about houses, laboriously boring my way through forests, driving myself like a wedge into brush and bramble, swimming every stream I came to (some of them more than once, probably), and pulling myself out of the water by boughs and briars — whatever could be grasped. Let any one try to go a little way across even the most familiar country on a moonless night, and he will have an experience to remember. By dawn I had probably not made three miles. My clothing and skin were alike in rags.

During the day I was compelled to make wide detours to avoid even the fields, unless they were of corn; but in other respects the going was distinctly better. A light breakfast of raw sweet potatoes and persimmons cheered the inner man; a good part of the outer was decorating the several thorns, boughs and sharp rocks along my sylvan wake.

Late in the afternoon I found the river, at what point it was impossible to say. After a half-hour's rest, concluding with a fervent prayer that I might go to the bottom, I swam across. Creeping up the bank and holding my course still northward through a dense undergrowth, I suddenly reeled into a dusty highway and saw a more heavenly vision than ever the eyes of a dying saint were blessed withal — two patriots in blue carrying a stolen pig slung upon a pole!

Late that evening Colonel McConnell and his staff were chatting by a campfire in front of his headquarters. They were in a pleasant humor: some one had just finished a funny story about a man cut in two by a cannon-shot. Suddenly something staggered in among them from the outer darkness and fell into the fire. Somebody dragged it out by what seemed to be a leg. They turned the animal on its back and examined it — they were no cowards.

"What is it, Cobb?" said the chief, who had not taken the trouble to rise.

"I don't know, Colonel, but thank God it is dead!"

It was not.

[1906; CWAB, I]

WHAT OCCURRED AT FRANKLIN

For several days, in snow and rain, General Schofield's little army had crouched in its hastily constructed defenses at Columbia, Tennessee. It had retreated in hot haste from Pulaski, thirty miles to the south, arriving just in time to foil Hood, who, marching from Florence, Alabama, by another road, with a force of more than double our strength, had hoped to intercept us. Had he succeeded, he would indubitably have bagged the whole bunch of us. As it was, he simply took position in front of us and gave us plenty of employment, but did not attack; he knew a trick worth two of that.

Duck River was directly in our rear; I suppose both our flanks rested on it. The town was between them. One night — that of November 27, 1864 — we pulled up stakes and crossed to the north bank to continue our retreat to Nashville, where Thomas and safety lay — such safety as is known in war. It was high time too, for before noon of the next day Forrest's[38] cavalry forded the river a few miles above us and began pushing back our own horse toward Spring Hill, ten miles in our rear, on our only road. Why our infantry was not immediately put in motion toward the threatened point, so vital to our safety, General Schofield could have told better than I. Howbeit, we lay there inactive all day.

The next morning — a bright and beautiful one — the brigade of Colonel P. Sidney Post[39] was thrown out, up the river four or five miles, to see what it could see. What it saw was Hood's head-of-column coming over on a pontoon bridge, and a right pretty spectacle it would have been to one whom it did not concern. It concerned us rather keenly.

As a member of Colonel Post's staff, I was naturally favored with a good view of the performance. We formed in line of battle at a distance

38. Major-General Nathan Bedford Forrest (1821–1877) is recognized by most authorities as the best cavalryman of the Civil War. He was a successful leader who became infamous for his slaughter of African American prisoners of war after the battle of Fort Pillow and for his role in founding the Ku Klux Klan after the war. CONFED.

39. Colonel Philip Sidney Post (1833–1895) won the Medal of Honor for his actions at the Battle of Nashville. BOATNER.

of perhaps a half-mile from the bridge-head, but that unending column of gray and steel gave us no more attention than if we had been a crowd of farmer-folk. Why should it? It had only to face to the left to be itself a line of battle. Meantime it had more urgent business on hand than brushing away a small brigade whose only offense was curiosity; it was making for Spring Hill with all its legs and wheels. Hour after hour we watched that unceasing flow of infantry and artillery toward the rear of our army. It was an unnerving spectacle, yet we never for a moment doubted that, acting on the intelligence supplied by our succession of couriers, our entire force was moving rapidly to the point of contact. The battle of Spring Hill[40] was obviously decreed. Obviously, too, our brigade of observation would be among the last to have a hand in it. The thought annoyed us, made us restless and resentful. Our mounted men rode forward and back behind the line, nervous and distressed; the men in the ranks sought relief in frequent changes of posture, in shifting their weight from one leg to the other, in needless inspection of their weapons and in that unfailing resource of the discontented soldier, audible damning of those in the saddles of authority. But never for more than a moment at a time did any one remove his eyes from that fascinating and portentous pageant.

Toward evening we were recalled, to learn that of our five divisions of infantry, with their batteries, numbering twenty-three thousand men, only one — Stanley's,[41] four thousand weak — had been sent to Spring Hill to meet that formidable movement of Hood's[42] three veteran corps! Why Stanley was not immediately effaced is still a matter of controversy. Hood, who was early on the ground, declared that he gave the needful orders and tried vainly to enforce them; Cheatham,[43] in command of his leading corps, that he did not. Doubtless the dispute is still being carried on between these chieftains from their beds of as-

40. November 29, 1864.

41. See note 7.

42. After his failure to defend Atlanta, Hood and his demoralized army smashed itself apart at Franklin and Nashville in the face of superior Union positions. He was relieved of command after Nashville. CONFED.

43. Major-General Benjamin Franklin Cheatham (1820–1886) fought at Shiloh, Stone's River, Chickamauga, Missionary Ridge, and the Atlanta and Nashville campaigns.

phodel and moly in Elysium. So much is certain: Stanley drove away Forrest and successfully held the junction of the roads against Cleburne's division, the only infantry that attacked him.

That night the entire Confederate army lay within a half mile of our road, while we all sneaked by, infantry, artillery, and trains. The enemy's camp-fires shone redly—miles of them—seemingly only a stone's throw from our hurrying column. His men were plainly visible about them, cooking their suppers—a sight so incredible that many of our own, thinking them friends, strayed over to them and did not return. At intervals of a few hundred yards we passed dim figures on horseback by the roadside, enjoining silence. Needless precaution; we could not have spoken if we had tried, for our hearts were in our throats. But fools are God's peculiar care, and one of his protective methods is the stupidity of other fools. By daybreak our last man and last wagon had passed the fateful spot unchallenged, and our first were entering Franklin, ten miles away. Despite spirited cavalry attacks on trains and rear-guard, all were in Franklin by noon and such of the men as could be kept awake were throwing up a slight line of defense, inclosing the town.

Franklin lies—or at that time did lie; I know not what exploration might now disclose—on the south bank of a small river, the Harpeth by name. For two miles southward was a nearly flat, open plain, extending to a range of low hills through which passed the turnpike by which we had come. From some bluffs on the precipitous north bank of the river was a commanding overlook of all this open ground, which, although more than a mile away, seemed almost at one's feet. On this elevated ground the wagon-train had been parked and General Schofield[44] had stationed himself—the former for security, the latter for outlook. Both were guarded by General Wood's infantry division, of which my brigade was a part. "We are in beautiful luck," said a member of the division staff. With some prevision of what was to come and a lively recollection of the nervous strain of helpless observation, I did not think it luck. In the activity of battle one does not feel one's hair going gray with vicissitudes of emotion.

For some reason to the writer unknown General Schofield had brought along with him General D. S. Stanley, who commanded two of

44. See note 5.

his divisions — ours and another, which was not "in luck." In the ensuing battle, when this excellent officer could stand the strain no longer,
he bolted across the bridge like a shot and found relief in the hell
below, where he was promptly tumbled out of the saddle by a bullet.

Our line, with its reserve brigades, was about a mile and a half long,
both flanks on the river, above and below the town — a mere bridge-
head. It did not look a very formidable obstacle to the march of an
army of more than forty thousand men. In a more tranquil temper
than his failure at Spring Hill had put him into Hood would probably
have passed around our left and turned us out with ease — which would
justly have entitled him to the Humane Society's great gold medal.
Apparently that was not his day for saving life.

About the middle of the afternoon our field-glasses picked up the
Confederate head-of-column emerging from the range of hills previously mentioned, where it is cut by the Columbia road. But — ominous
circumstance! — it did not come on. It turned to its left, at a right angle,
moving along the base of the hills, parallel to our line. Other heads-of-
column came through other gaps and over the crests farther along,
impudently deploying on the level ground with a spectacular display of
flags and glitter of arms. I do not remember that they were molested,
even by the guns of General Wagner,[45] who had been foolishly posted
with two small brigades across the turnpike, a half-mile in our front,
where he was needless for apprisal and powerless for resistance. My
recollection is that our fellows down there in their shallow trenches
noted these portentous dispositions without the least manifestation of
incivility. As a matter of fact, many of them were permitted by their
compassionate officers to sleep. And truly it was good weather for that:
sleep was in the very atmosphere. The sun burned crimson in a gray-
blue sky through a delicate Indian-summer haze, as beautiful as a day-
dream in paradise. If one had been given to moralizing one might have
found material a-plenty for homilies in the contrast between that peaceful autumn afternoon and the bloody business that it had in hand. If
any good chaplain failed to "improve the occasion" let us hope that he
lived to lament in sackcloth-of-gold and ashes-of-roses his intellectual
unthrift.

The putting of that army into battle shape — its change from col-

45. Brigadier-General George Day Wagner (1829–1869). FAUST.

umns into lines — could not have occupied more than an hour or two, yet it seemed an eternity. Its leisurely evolutions were irritating, but at last it moved forward with atoning rapidity and the fight was on. First, the storm struck Wagner's isolated brigades, which, vanishing in fire and smoke, instantly reappeared as a confused mass of fugitives inextricably intermingled with their pursuers. They had not stayed the advance a moment, and as might have been foreseen were now a peril to the main line, which could protect itself only by the slaughter of its friends. To the right and left, however, our guns got into play, and simultaneously a furious infantry fire broke out along the entire front, the paralyzed center excepted. But nothing could stay those gallant rebels from a hand-to-hand encounter with bayonet and butt, and it was accorded to them with hearty good-will.

Meantime Wagner's conquerors were pouring across the breastwork like water over a dam. The guns that had spared the fugitives had now no time to fire; their infantry supports gave way and for a space of more than two hundred yards in the very center of our line the assailants, mad with exultation, had everything their own way. From the right and the left their gray masses converged into the gap, pushed through, and then, spreading, turned our men out of the works so hardly held against the attack in their front. From our viewpoint on the bluff we could mark the constant widening of the gap, the steady encroachment of that blazing and smoking mass against its disordered opposition.

"It is all up with us," said Captain Dawson, of Wood's staff; "I am going to have a quiet smoke."

I do not doubt that he supposed himself to have borne the heat and burden of the strife. In the midst of his preparations for a smoke he paused and looked again — a new tumult of musketry had broken loose. Colonel Emerson Opdycke[46] had rushed his reserve brigade into the *mêlée* and was bitterly disputing the Confederate advantage. Other fresh regiments joined in the countercharge, commanderless groups of retreating men returned to their work, and there ensued a hand-to-hand contest of incredible fury. Two long, irregular, mutable, and tu-

46. Colonel Emerson Opdycke (1830–1884) had long been a hero in Hazen's brigade. At Shiloh he picked up the fallen colors and led a countercharge, at Chickamauga his regiment stood firm, and at Missionary Ridge his men were among the first to reach the summit. FAUST.

multuous blurs of color were consuming each other's edge along the line of contact. Such devil's work does not last long, and we had the great joy to see it ending, not as it began, but "more nearly to the heart's desire." Slowly the mobile blur moved away from the town, and presently the gray half of it dissolved into its elemental units, all in slow recession. The retaken guns in the embrasures pushed up towering clouds of white smoke; to east and to west along the reoccupied parapet ran a line of misty red till the spitfire crest was without a break from flank to flank. Probably there was some Yankee cheering, as doubt-less there had been the "rebel yell,"[47] but my memory recalls neither. There are many battles in a war, and many incidents in a battle: one does not recollect everything. Possibly I have not a retentive ear.

While this lively work had been doing in the center, there had been no lack of diligence elsewhere, and now all were as busy as bees. I have read of many "successive attacks" — "charge after charge" — but I think the only assaults after the first were those of the second Confederate lines and possibly some of the reserves; certainly there were no visible abatement and renewal of effort anywhere except where the men who had been pushed out of the works backward tried to reenter. And all the time there was fighting.

After resetting their line the victors could not clear their front, for the baffled assailants would not desist. All over the open country in their rear, clear back to the base of the hills, drifted the wreck of battle, the wounded that were able to walk; and through the receding throng pushed forward, here and there, horsemen with orders and footmen whom we knew to be bearing ammunition. There were no wagons, no caissons: the enemy was not using, and could not use, his artillery. Along the line of fire we could see, dimly in the smoke, mounted officers, singly and in small groups, attempting to force their horses across the slight parapet, but all went down. Of this devoted band was the gallant General Adams, whose body was found upon the slope, and whose animal's forefeet were actually inside the crest. General Cle-

---

47. A high-pitched scream or shout designed to fortify the man doing the yelling and scare the enemy into thinking the attackers are wild men. Perhaps a mixture between a Scottish battle whoop and an American Indian war cry. For the best explanation of this scream, see Grady McWhiney and Perry Jamieson, *Attack and Die: Civil War Military Tactics and the Southern Heritage* (Tuscaloosa: University of Alabama Press, 1982).

burne lay a few paces farther out, and five or six other general officers sprawled elsewhere. It was a great day for Confederates in the line of promotion.

For many minutes at a time broad spaces of battle were veiled in smoke. Of what might be occurring there conjecture gave a terrifying report. In a visible peril observation is a kind of defense; against the unseen we lift a trembling hand. Always from these regions of obscurity we expected the worst, but always the lifted cloud revealed an unaltered situation.

The assailants began to give way. There was no general retreat; at many points the fight continued, with lessening ferocity and lengthening range, well into the night. It became an affair of twinkling musketry and broad flares of artillery; then it sank to silence in the dark.

Under orders to continue his retreat, Schofield could now do so unmolested: Hood had suffered so terrible a loss in life and morale that he was in no condition for effective pursuit. As at Spring Hill, daybreak found us on the road with all our impedimenta except some of our wounded, and that night we encamped under the protecting guns of Thomas, at Nashville. Our gallant enemy audaciously followed, and fortified himself within rifle-reach, where he remained for two weeks without firing a gun and was then destroyed.

[1888; SOLE]

ON GENERAL SCHOFIELD[48]

An editorial writer in this paper said in last Wednesday's issue: "There were not many famous Generals who went with Sherman to the sea, but of the few Schofield was one." This is an error which my collaborator will not mind having corrected. While Sherman was moving on Savannah from Atlanta, Schofield was moving on Nashville from Pulaski. Schofield was moving faster than Sherman, for Hood was hard after him. I happen to have some knowledge of this movement, for I was a part of it, and it is one of the proudest recollections of my life that although the movement was one of the most rapid and persistent that occurred during the war, I was strong, hardy and resolute enough to keep up with the procession. At Franklin, where we stopped long enough to have a bit of a debate with Hood, I was perched on a bluff on the safe side of a river, overlooking the "forum," and acted as one of the judges. My notion was that Hood failed to maintain the affirmative of the proposition that we were "his'n." That was Schofield's decision too; and he had good opportunities to judge, for he was right with me through the thickest of it. We were guarding the wagons, he and I, and the only property we lost was a mule, which straggled off across the bridge toward the field of glory and we couldn't call it back. The loss of that mule is the only stain upon General Schofield's military escutcheon: he, as Commander-in-Chief, ought to have followed it a little way, and if he couldn't persuade it to return he would have been justified in using violence.

48. "Prattle," *San Francisco Examiner*, August 19, 1888. SOLE, 59–60.

[1888; SOLE]

THE BODY COUNT AT FRANKLIN[49]

One of the cleverest writers that we have in the Golden Out Here is Mr. E. H. Clough, who has recently set up in Oakland a weekly paper named the *Paragraph*, which is as clever as he. But Mr. Clough is a man of peace, and if ever his paper becomes a great military authority, such as the *Century* was before it got a pension and retired to civil life, it is more likely to be through fits in the office than facts in the paper. It has occurred to Mr. Clough that a certain Mr. J. G. Edwards would be a good man for the Pension Agency — or, possibly, that the Pension Agency would be a good office for Mr. Edwards; and the *Paragraph* gives him "a good send-off" by publishing his military "record." According to the paper's account, it was an honorable one, and I do not doubt that it was; but I do doubt that the brigade to which he was attached was detailed at Jonesboro, Georgia, "to accompany Hood to Franklin, where the hardest battle of the war was fought, and where over 10,000 brave men were killed in four hours." My recollection of this matter is that none of our fellows "accompanied" General Hood on that expedition: we went a few miles ahead of him, to show him the way. The distance between him and us was always as great as we could make it and as little as he could make it. Hood was a sociable sort of chap on that march, but we did not encourage his advances; in fact, we felled trees in his way to impede them. If Mr. Edwards ever "accompanied" him it must have been after the war, on the piano.

Franklin was a stubborn little fight, but by no means "the hardest battle of the war." There were no 10,000 men killed in it, nor a quarter of that number.[50] Ten thousand men have not been killed in any modern battle. There were that many killed in some of the ancient ones, but the mortality of battles decreases with the precision and destructiveness of weapons. There have been no improvements in the sword, however, since the siege of Troy, and General Dimond would kill as

---

49. "Prattle," *San Francisco Examiner*, December 23, 1888. SOLE, 60–62.

50. The Union reported 189 killed, 1,033 wounded, and 1,104 missing and the Confederacy reported 1,750 killed, 3,800 wounded, and 702 missing as the official casualties at the Battle of Franklin. LONG, 1864.

many men to-day as he did twenty-five years ago. General Barnes[51] was no more fatal at Gettysburg than he would be at Temescal Creek. But see how it is with other weapons. General Turnbull, whose cheap three-inch field piece mowed down the enemy at Chickamauga faster than they could get up, would probably do so little execution with the Lick telescope[52] that invalids would storm the slopes of Mt. Hamilton in search of longevity.

But modern warfare is not altogether sanitary. Mr. Clough's Mr. Edwards, for example, was in an engagement in which his detachment of 124 Federals was ambushed by 3,500 Confederates, "and in fifteen minutes 117 corpses were stretched upon the field" — all Federals, apparently — at least that is the implication and the way it would naturally be in case of ambush. As the proportion of wounded to dead is commonly about five to one, it is clear that the Federal detachment must have lost all its men and owed the enemy a balance of about 572.

Mr. Clough is truthful and sincere, but, as I said, a man of peace, and he was not there. Evidently enough, he got all this stuff from the Edwards, and had the misfortune to believe it; I was born lucky and do not. It is noticed here as a fair sample of the things that men are willing to say when relating their military experiences. As a rule, they are not to be believed. One would think war horrible enough without the monstrous exaggerations that seem inseparable from the story of it. Nothing is more common than to hear and read about "mowing down" the enemy or being mown down by them, projectiles cutting "wide gaps" through charging columns, "heaps of slain" that clog the cannon wheels, "rivers of blood" and the rest of it. All this is absurd: nothing of the kind occurs — nothing, rather, of the degree. These are phenomena of the camp-fire, the hearthstone, the "rostrum" and the writing-desk. They are subjective — deeds of memory in a frame of mind. They have a fine literary effect when skillfully employed, and in purely literary work are allowable in landscape painting to aggrandize the moun-

51. Major-General Joseph K. Barnes (1817–1883) was a surgeon, medical inspector, and Surgeon General of the United States, beginning in August 1864. He was the attending physician for presidents Lincoln and Garfield in the hours after they were shot. SIFIKAS.

52. In 1874–75, James Lick funded the Hamilton Observatory near San Jose, California, which at one time had the second largest telescope in the world. *The New Columbia Encyclopedia* (New York: Columbia University Press, 1975), 1577.

tains. Outside of literature their use is to humbug the civilian, frighten the children and grapple the women's hearts with hooks of steel tending to the magnification of the narrator. The women, by the way, are worth a word of caution: let them remember how Othello got Desdemona—and what Desdemona got.[53]

Nothing more frightful (and fascinating) than a great battle can be conceived, but it is not frightful in just the way that its historians love to describe it. Men do not fight as heroically as they are said to fight: they are not as brave as they are said to be. If they were, two hostile lines would fight until all of one were down. As long as a man is not disabled he can go forward or stand his ground. When two lines of battle are fighting face to face on even terms and one is "forced back" (which always occurs unless it is ordered back) it is fear that forces it: the men could have stood if they had wanted to. In our civil war I saw scores of such instances. Sometimes the Federals fled, sometimes the Confederates. As a rule the Confederates fought better than our men. On even terms they commonly defeated us; nearly all our victories were won by superior numbers, better arms and advantages of position.

53. Desdemona was strangled. See William Shakespeare, *Othello*.

[1893; CWAB, VII]

THE MAJOR'S TALE

In the days of the Civil War practical joking had not, I think, fallen into that disrepute which characterizes it now. That, doubtless, was owing to our extreme youth — men were much younger than now, and evermore your very young man has a boisterous spirit, running easily to horse-play. You cannot think how young the men were in the early sixties! Why, the average age of the entire Federal Army was not more than twenty-five; I doubt if it was more than twenty-three, but not having the statistics on that point (if there are any) I want to be moderate: we will say twenty-five.[54] It is true a man of twenty-five was in that heroic time a good deal more of a man than one of that age is now; you could see that by looking at him. His face had nothing of that unripeness so conspicuous in his successor. I never see a young fellow now without observing how disagreeably young he really is; but during the war we did not think of a man's age at all unless he happened to be pretty well along in life. In that case one could not help it, for the unloveliness of age assailed the human countenance then much earlier than now; the result, I suppose, of hard service — perhaps, to some extent, of hard drink, for, bless my soul! we did shed the blood of the grape and the grain abundantly during the war. I remember thinking General Grant, who could not have been more than forty, a pretty well preserved old chap, considering his habits.[55] As to men of middle age — say from fifty to sixty — why, they all looked fit to personate the Last of the Hittites, or the Madagascarene Methuselah, in a museum. Depend upon it, my friends, men of that time were greatly younger than men are to-day, but looked much older. The change is quite remarkable.

I said that practical joking had not then gone out of fashion. It had not, at least, in the army; though possibly in the more serious life of the civilian it had no place except in the form of tarring and feathering an

---

54. The average age of the Civil War soldier upon enlistment into the army was 25.8 years old. LONG, 707.

55. Ulysses S. Grant was forty-two years old in 1864.

occasional "copperhead."[56] You all know, I suppose, what a "copperhead" was, so I will go directly at my story without introductory remark, as is my way.

It was a few days before the battle of Nashville. The enemy had driven us up out of northern Georgia and Alabama. At Nashville we had turned at bay and fortified, while old Pap Thomas, our commander, hurried down reinforcements and supplies from Louisville. Meantime Hood, the Confederate commander, had partly invested us and lay close enough to have tossed shells into the heart of the town. As a rule he abstained — he was afraid of killing the families of his own soldiers, I suppose, a great many of whom had lived there. I sometimes wondered what were the feelings of those fellows, gazing over our heads at their own dwellings, where their wives and children or their aged parents were perhaps suffering for the necessaries of life, and certainly (so their reasoning would run) cowering under the tyranny and power of the barbarous Yankees.

To begin, then, at the beginning. I was serving at that time on the staff of a division commander whose name I shall not disclose, for I am relating facts, and the person upon whom they bear hardest may have surviving relatives who would not care to have him traced. Our headquarters were in a large dwelling which stood just behind our line of works. This had been hastily abandoned by the civilian occupants, who had left everything pretty much as it was — had no place to store it, probably, and trusted that Heaven would preserve it from Federal cupidity and Confederate artillery. With regard to the latter we were as solicitous as they.

Rummaging about in some of the chambers and closets one evening, some of us found an abundant supply of lady-gear — gowns, shawls, bonnets, hats, petticoats and the Lord knows what; I could not at that time have named the half of it. The sight of all this pretty plunder inspired one of us with what he was pleased to call an "Idea," which, when submitted to the other scamps and scapegraces of the

56. Officially called "Peace Democrats," a copperhead was a member of the Democratic Party in the North who supported the Union but wanted to make peace with the South. They felt the Republican Party was using the war for its own purposes.

staff, met with instant and enthusiastic approval. We proceeded at once to act upon it for the undoing of one of our comrades.

Our selected victim was an aide, Lieutenant Haberton, so to call him. He was a good soldier — as gallant a chap as ever wore spurs; but he had an intolerable weakness: he was a lady-killer, and like most of his class, even in those days, eager that all should know it. He never tired of relating his amatory exploits, and I need not say how dismal that kind of narrative is to all but the narrator. It would be dismal even if sprightly and vivacious, for all men are rivals in woman's favor, and to relate your successes to another man is to rouse in him a dumb resentment, tempered by disbelief. You will not convince him that you tell the tale for his entertainment; he will hear nothing in it but an expression of your own vanity. Moreover, as most men, whether rakes or not, are willing to be thought rakes, he is very likely to resent a stupid and unjust inference which he suspects you to have drawn from his reticence in the matter of his own adventures — namely, that he has had none. If, on the other hand, he has had no scruple in the matter and his reticence is due to lack of opportunity to talk, or of nimbleness in taking advantage of it, why, then he will be surly because you "have the floor" when he wants it himself. There are, in short, no circumstances under which a man, even from the best of motives, or no motive at all, can relate his feats of love without distinctly lowering himself in the esteem of his male auditor; and herein lies a just punishment for such as kiss and tell. In my younger days I was myself not entirely out of favor with the ladies, and have a memory stored with much concerning them which doubtless I might put into acceptable narrative had I not undertaken another tale, and if it were not my practice to relate one thing at a time, going straight away to the end, without digression.

Lieutenant Haberton was, it must be confessed, a singularly handsome man with engaging manners. He was, I suppose, judging from the imperfect view-point of my sex, what women call "fascinating." Now, the qualities which make a man attractive to ladies entail a double disadvantage. First, they are of a sort readily discerned by other men, and by none more readily than by those who lack them. Their possessor, being feared by all these, is habitually slandered by them in self-defense. To all the ladies in whose welfare they deem themselves entitled to a voice and interest they hint at the vices and general unworth of the "ladies' man" in no uncertain terms, and to their wives relate without shame the most monstrous falsehoods about him. Nor are they restrained by the consideration that he is their friend; the qualities which have engaged their own admiration make it necessary to warn away those to whom the allurement would be a peril. So the man of charming personality, while loved by all the ladies who know him well, yet not too well, must endure with such fortitude as he may the consciousness that those others who know him only "by reputation" consider him a shameless reprobate, a vicious and unworthy man — a type and example of moral depravity. To name the second disadvantage entailed by his charms: he commonly is.

In order to get forward with our busy story (and in my judgment a story once begun should not suffer impedition) it is necessary to explain that a young fellow attached to our headquarters as an orderly was notably effeminate in face and figure. He was not more than seventeen and had a perfectly smooth face and large lustrous eyes, which must have been the envy of many a beautiful woman in those days. And how beautiful the women of those days were! and how gracious! Those of the South showed in their demeanor toward us Yankees something of *hauteur*, but, for my part, I found it less insupportable than the studious indifference with which one's attentions are received by the ladies of this new generation, whom I certainly think destitute of sentiment and sensibility.

This young orderly, whose name was Arman, we persuaded — by what arguments I am not bound to say — to clothe himself in female attire and personate a lady. When we had him arrayed to our satisfaction — and a charming girl he looked — he was conducted to a sofa in the office of the adjutant-general. That officer was in the secret, as indeed were all excepting Haberton and the general; within the awful dignity hedging the latter lay possibilities of disapproval which we were unwilling to confront.

When all was ready I went to Haberton and said: "Lieutenant, there is a young woman in the adjutant-general's office. She is the daughter of the insurgent gentleman who owns this house, and has, I think, called to see about its present occupancy. We none of us know just how to talk to her, but we think perhaps you would say about the right thing — at least you will say things in the right way. Would you mind coming down?"

The lieutenant would not mind; he made a hasty toilet and joined me. As we were going along a passage toward the Presence we encountered a formidable obstacle — the general.

"I say, Broadwood," he said, addressing me in the familiar manner which meant that he was in excellent humor, "there's a lady in Lawson's office. Looks like a devilish fine girl — came on some errand of mercy or justice, no doubt. Have the goodness to conduct her to my quarters. I won't saddle you youngsters with *all* the business of this division," he added facetiously.

This was awkward; something had to be done.

"General," I said, "I did not think the lady's business of sufficient importance to bother you with it. She is one of the Sanitary Commission's nurses, and merely wants to see about some supplies for the smallpox hospital where she is on duty. I'll send her in at once."

"You need not mind," said the general, moving on; "I dare say Lawson will attend to the matter."

Ah, the gallant general! how little I thought, as I looked after his retreating figure and laughed at the success of my ruse, that within the week he would be "dead on the field of honor!" Nor was he the only one of our little military household above whom loomed the shadow of the death angel, and who might almost have heard "the beating of his wings." On that bleak December morning a few days later, when from an hour before dawn until ten o'clock we sat on horseback on those icy hills, waiting for General Smith to open the battle miles away to the right, there were eight of us. At the close of the fighting there were three. There is now one. Bear with him yet a little while, oh, thrifty generation; he is but one of the horrors of war strayed from his era into yours. He is only the harmless skeleton at your feast and peace-dance, responding to your laughter and your footing it featly, with rattling fingers and bobbing skull — albeit upon suitable occasion, with a partner of his choosing, he might do his little dance with the best of you.

As we entered the adjutant-general's office we observed that the entire staff was there. The adjutant-general himself was exceedingly busy at his desk. The commissary of subsistence played cards with the surgeon in a bay window. The rest were in several parts of the room, reading or conversing in low tones. On a sofa in a half lighted nook of the room, at some distance from any of the groups, sat the "lady," closely veiled, her eyes modestly fixed upon her toes.

"Madam," I said, advancing with Haberton, "this officer will be pleased to serve you if it is in his power. I trust that it is."

With a bow I retired to the farther corner of the room and took part in a conversation going on there, though I had not the faintest notion what it was about, and my remarks had no relevancy to anything under the heavens. A close observer would have noticed that we were all intently watching Haberton and only "making believe" to do anything else.

He was worth watching, too; the follow was simply an *édition de luxe* of "Turveydrop on Deportment." As the "lady" slowly unfolded her tale of grievances against our lawless soldiery and mentioned certain instances of wanton disregard of property rights — among them, as to the imminent peril of bursting our sides we partly overheard, the looting of her own wardrobe — the look of sympathetic agony in Haberton's handsome face was the very flower and fruit of histrionic art. His deferential and assenting nods at her several statements were so exquisitely performed that one could not help regretting their unsubstantial nature and the impossibility of preserving them under glass for instruction and delight of posterity. And all the time the wretch was drawing his chair nearer and nearer. Once or twice he looked about to see if we were observing, but we were in appearance blankly oblivious to all but one another and our several diversions. The low hum of our conversation, the gentle tap-tap of the cards as they fell in play and the furious scratching of the adjutant-general's pen as he turned off countless pages of words without sense were the only sounds heard. No — there was another: at long intervals the distant boom of a heavy gun, followed by the approaching rush of the shot. The enemy was amusing himself.

On these occasions the lady was perhaps not the only member of that company who was startled, but she was startled more than the others, sometimes rising from the sofa and standing with clasped hands, the authentic portrait of terror and irresolution. It was no more than natural that Haberton should at these times reseat her with infinite tenderness, assuring her of her safety and regretting her peril in the same breath. It was perhaps right that be should finally possess himself of her gloved hand and a seat beside her on the sofa; but it certainly was highly improper for him to be in the very act of possessing himself of *both* hands when — boom, *whiz*, BANG!

We all sprang to our feet. A shell had crashed into the house and exploded in the room above us. Bushels of plaster fell among us. That modest and murmurous young lady sprang erect.

"Jumping Jee-rusalem!" she cried.

Haberton, who had also risen, stood as one petrified — as a statue of himself erected on the site of his assassination. He neither spoke, nor moved, nor once took his eyes off the face of Orderly Arman, who was now flinging his girl-gear right and left, exposing his charms in the most shameless way; while out upon the night and away over the lighted camps into the black spaces between the hostile lines rolled the billows of our inexhaustible laughter! Ah, what a merry life it was in the old heroic days when men had not forgotten how to laugh!

Haberton slowly came to himself. He looked about the room less blankly; then by degrees fashioned his visage into the sickliest grin that ever libeled all smiling. He shook his head and looked knowing.

"You can't fool *me*!" he said.

[1883; SOLE]

THE BATTLE OF NASHVILLE:
AN ATTACK OF GENERAL DEBILITY[57]

A line in last Tuesday's dispatches, to the effect that a French colony in Senegal has been attacked by typhus fever, recalls an incident of the civil war. After the battle of Nashville I happened to be serving on the staff of the illustrious General Sam Beatty, of Ohio.[58] His command was at one time greatly scattered in pursuit of the enemy, who retired sullenly, and one brigade of it held a peculiarly exposed position some ten miles from General Sam's headquarters. There was a telegraph, however, and one day the commander of this brigade sent the general a dispatch which read thus: "Please relieve me; I am suffering from an attack of General Debility." "The ablest cavalry officer in the Confederate army," said my honored chief, showing me the telegram. "I served under him in Mexico." And he promptly prescribed three regiments of infantry and a battery of Rodman guns.[59]

I was directed to pilot that expedition to the scene of the disaster to our arms. I never felt so brave in all my life. I rode a hundred yards in advance, prepared to expostulate single-handed with the victorious enemy at whatever point I might encounter him. I dashed forward through every open space into every suspicious looking wood and spurred to the crest of every hill, exposing myself recklessly to draw the Confederates' fire and disclose their position. I told the commander of the relief column that he need not throw out any advance guard as a precaution against an ambuscade — I would myself act in that perilous capacity, and by driving in the rebel skirmishers gain time for him to form his line of battle in case I should not be numerically strong

---

57. "Prattle," *Wasp* 363 (July 14, 1883): 5. SOLE, 62.

58. Major-General Samuel Beatty (1820–1885) was a competent and well-loved general who fought at nearly every major battle in the western theater. BOATNER.

59. Giant smoothbore cannon invented by Thomas J. Rodman and used primarily for coastal defenses. Artillerymen commonly referred to the smaller light artillery of the armies as "Rodmans" because their shape resembled the real thing. FAUST.

enough to scoop up the entire opposition at one wild dash. I begged him, however, to recover my body if I fell.

There was no fighting: the forces of General Debility had conquered nobody but the brigade commander — his troops were holding their ground nobly, reading dime novels and playing draw poker pending the arrival of our succoring command. The official reports of this affair explained, a little obscurely, that there had been a misunderstanding; but my unusual gallantry elicited the highest commendation in general orders, and will never, I trust, be forgotten by a grateful country.

[1898; SOLE]

ON BLACK SOLDIERING[60]

A skeptical correspondent asks me for an opinion of the fighting qualities of our colored regiments. Really I had thought the question settled long ago. The Negro will fight and fight well. From the time when we began to use him in civil war, through all his service against Indians on the frontier, to this day he has not failed to acquit himself acceptably to his White officers.[61] I the more cheerfully testify to this because I was at one time a doubter. Under a general order from the headquarters of the Army, or possibly from the War Department, I once in a burst of ambition applied for rank as a field officer of colored troops, being then a line officer of white troops. Before my application was acted on I had repented and persuaded myself that the darkies would not fight; so when ordered to report to the proper board of officers, with a view to gratification of my wish, I "backed out" and secured "influence" which enabled me to remain in my humbler station. But at the battle of Nashville it was borne in upon me that I had made a fool of myself. During the two days of that memorable engagement the only reverse sustained by our arms was in an assault upon Overton Hill, a fortified salient of the Confederate line on the second day. The troops repulsed were a brigade of Beatty's division and a colored brigade of raw troops which had been brought up from a camp of instruction at Chattanooga. I was serving on Gen. Beatty's staff, but was not doing duty that day, being disabled by a wound — just sitting in the saddle and looking on. Seeing the darkies going in on our left I was naturally interested and observed them closely. Better fighting was never done. The front of the enemy's earthworks was protected by an intricate abatis of felled trees denuded of their foliage and twigs. Through this obstacle a cat would have made slow progress; its passage by troops under fire was hopeless from the first — even the inexperienced black chaps must have known that. They did not hesitate a moment: their long lines swept into that fatal obstruction in perfect order

60. "War Topics," *San Francisco Examiner,* June 5, 1898. SOLE, 63.

61. By war's end, nearly 180,000 African Americans served in 166 regiments in the Federal Army; 38,000 died in uniform.

and remained there as long as those of the white veterans on their right. And as many of them in proportion remained until borne away and buried after the action. It was as pretty an example of courage and discipline as one could wish to see. In order that my discomfiture and humiliation might lack nothing of completeness I was told afterward that one of their field officers succeeded in forcing his horse through a break in the abatis and was shot to rags on the slope on the parapet. But for my abjuration of faith in the Negroes' fighting qualities I might perhaps have been so fortunate as to be that man!

CHAPTER FIVE

1865

Phantoms of a Blood-Stained Period,

and Later

His long participation in the active war was over. Perhaps the "Crime at Pickett's Mill," the war of attrition, and the fear of death finally caught up with Ambrose Bierce. He knew that he had deserved to be killed, for that is a soldier's business—getting "what they enlisted for"—but he would be content with an honorable wound and life. Forever afterward, Bierce suffered from dizziness and fainting spells. We cannot be sure of the motivation that led him to resign; whatever the reason, Lt. Bierce showed the courage to accept the recommendation of a physician that he be discharged from active duty. General George Thomas signed the order on January 25, 1865. Certainly, Bierce had done more than his share of fighting.

On April 9, less than three months after Bierce left the army, the war officially concluded at Appomattox Courthouse, Virginia, when Robert E. Lee surrendered to Ulysses S. Grant. Sporadic fighting continued for another two months before everyone got word that it was all over. A grand parade in Washington honored the victorious Union troops as legion upon legion of blue-clad men marched down Pennsylvania Avenue in the time-honored tradition of saluting returning heroes. Confederates had to be content with individual welcomes after their army dissolved and soldiers made their way home alone or in small groups through a landscape changed by war. Mass cheers and parades would be theirs only after the United Confederate Veterans organized and monuments, with accompanying ceremonies and musters, were placed in town squares and on battlefields.

As the country moved from what Bierce called "the period of honorable strife" to the "brazen" age, the old soldiers wondered what they had fought for. Private recollections gave way to a public memory of the war that made some sense of the broader conflict. The Reconstruction era — that period from 1863 to 1877 when the country sought to install central power and to give freed slaves a chance to raise themselves to be whatever they could become under equal law — failed. Corruption and greed swirled together in the days after the war when Bierce worked as a treasury agent in Alabama, watching the rich try to hold on to what was left of lost fortunes, seeing entrepreneurs taking any and every advantage possible to make a quick buck, and looking at race issues that had not been solved by freeing slaves. The broken bodies, smashed homes, and ruined families stood as counterpoint to show what war had been about, a challenge to those seeking ideals and morals stretching from the American Revolution forward.

As time went by, veterans continued to reconcile their traumatic personal experiences with the national memory. Ironically, as the old soldiers died, poignant moments of sacrifice and honor made their way into the national understanding. The deaths of Robert E. Lee on October 12, 1870, Ulysses Grant on July 23, 1885, Tecumseh Sherman on February 14, 1891, and the wide-ranging galaxy of specific community and state champions only punctuated the noble war and revived memories of American manhood fighting nobly for causes they believed in. When the race problems continued to confound resolution, veterans could take refuge in knowing that they had made a good fight. Bierce and others knew that "the brave respect the brave" even if the reasons for the war and the expectations for Reconstruction did not measure up to the realities of the new century. The glorified history, "national encampments" where Confederate veterans reached across old battle lines to shake hands with Union veterans, the surge of monument building, and the dwindling numbers of Civil War soldiers in the face of increasing numbers of buried veterans only served to increase what Bierce called "the deification of the eminent."

The Civil War became Bierce's most important memory. He often retraced, rethought, or rewalked the battlefields. He cherished the innocent times of youth when "just plain, ordinary American, volunteer soldiers, who loved their country, and fought for it" had walked as giants upon the earth. In 1903, Bierce spent a summer in the West Virginia countryside where his first Civil War battles occurred. Ten years later, just before he disappeared into the Mexican Revolution, he made one final tour of "all my old battlefields — Chickamauga, Chattanooga, Stone's River, Franklin, Nashville and Shiloh."

Men on both sides of those battles fought — all other causes aside — because their country called them to do so. Telling their stories became Ambrose Bierce's most significant life's work and a major contribution to American literature.

From *The Devil's Dictionary*

PEACE, *n.* In international affairs, a period of cheating between two periods of fighting.

RECONCILIATION, *n.* A suspension of hostilities. An armed truce for the purpose of digging up the dead.

GHOST, *n.* The outward and visible sign of an inward fear.

EMANCIPATION, *n.* A bondman's change from the tyranny of another to the despotism of himself.

NEGRO, *n.* The *pièce de résistance* in the American political problem. Representing him by the letter *n*, the Republicans begin to build their equation thus: "Let n = the white man."
This, however, appears to give an unsatisfactory solution.

FREEDMAN, *n.* A person whose manacles have sunk so deeply into his flesh that they are no longer visible.

VOTE, *n.* The instrument and symbol of a freeman's power to make a fool of himself and a wreck of his country.

MONUMENT, *n.* A structure intended to commemorate something which either needs no commemoration or cannot be commemorated.

HISTORIAN, *n.* A broad-gauge gossip.

HISTORY, *n.* An account mostly false, of events mostly unimportant, which are brought about by rulers mostly knaves, and soldiers mostly fools.

'WAY DOWN IN ALABAM'

At the break-up of the great Rebellion I found myself at Selma, Alabama, still in the service of the United States, and although my duties were now purely civil my treatment was not uniformly so, and I am not surprised that it was not. I was a minor official in the Treasury Department, engaged in performance of duties exceedingly disagreeable not only to the people of the vicinity, but to myself as well. They consisted in the collection and custody of "captured and abandoned property." The Treasury had covered pretty nearly the entire area of "the States lately in rebellion" with a hierarchy of officials, consisting, as nearly as memory serves, of one supervising agent and a multitude of special agents. Each special agent held dominion over a collection district and was allowed an "agency aide" to assist him in his purposeful activity, besides such clerks, laborers and so forth as he could persuade himself to need. My humble position was that of agency aide. When the special agent was present for duty I was his chief executive officer; in his absence I represented him (with greater or less fidelity to the original and to my conscience) and was invested with his powers. In the Selma agency the property that we were expected to seize and defend as best we might was mostly plantations (whose owners had disappeared; some were dead, others in hiding) and cotton. The country was full of cotton which had been sold to the Confederate Government, but not removed from the plantations to take its chance of export through the blockade. It had been decided that it now belonged to the United States. It was worth about five hundred dollars a bale — say one dollar a pound. The world agreed that that was a pretty good price for cotton.

Naturally the original owners, having received nothing for their product but Confederate money which the result of the war had made worthless, manifested an unamiable reluctance to give it up, for if they could market it for themselves it would more than recoup them for all their losses in the war. They had therefore exercised a considerable ingenuity in effacing all record of its transfer to the Confederate Government, obliterating the marks on the bales, and hiding these away in swamps and other inconspicuous places, fortifying their claims to private ownership with appalling affidavits and "covering their tracks" in an infinite variety of ways generally.

In effecting their purpose they encountered many difficulties. Cotton in bales is not very portable property; it requires for movement and concealment a good deal of cooperation by persons having no interest in keeping the secret and easily accessible to the blandishments of those interested in tracing it. The negroes, by whom the work was necessarily done, were zealous to pay for emancipation by fidelity to the new regime, and many poor devils among them forfeited their lives by services performed with more loyalty than discretion. Railways — even those having a more than nominal equipment of rails and rolling stock — were unavailable for secret conveyance of the cotton. Navigating the Alabama and Tombigbee rivers were a few small steamboats, the half-dozen pilots familiar with these streams exacting one hundred dollars a day for their services; but our agents, backed by military authority, were at all the principal shipping points and no boat could leave without their consent. The port of Mobile was in our hands and the lower waters were patrolled by gunboats. Cotton might, indeed, be dumped down a "slide" by night at some private landing and fall upon the deck of a steamer idling innocently below. It might even arrive at Mobile, but secretly to transfer it to a deep-water vessel and get it out of the country — that was a dream.

On the movement of private cotton we put no restrictions; and such were the freight rates that it was possible to purchase a steamboat at Mobile, go up the river in ballast, bring down a cargo of cotton and make a handsome profit, after deducting the cost of the boat and all expenses of the venture, including the wage of the pilot. With no great knowledge of "business" I venture to think that in Alabama in the latter part of the year of grace 1865 commercial conditions were hardly normal.

Nor were social conditions what I trust they have now become. There was no law in the country except of the unsatisfactory sort known as "martial," and that was effective only within areas covered by the guns of isolated forts and the physical activities of their small garrisons. True, there were the immemorial laws of self-preservation and retaliation, both of which were liberally interpreted. The latter was faithfully administered, mostly against straggling Federal soldiers and too zealous government officials. When my chief had been ordered to Selma he had arrived just in time to act as sole mourner at the funeral of his predecessor—who had had the bad luck to interpret his instructions in a sense that was disagreeable to a gentleman whose interests were affected by the interpretation. Early one pleasant morning shortly afterward two United States marshals were observed by the roadside in a suburb of the town. They looked comfortable enough there in the sunshine, but each

> had that across his throat
> Which you had hardly cared to see.

When dispatched on business of a delicate nature men in the service of the agency had a significant trick of disappearing—they were of "the unreturning brave." Really the mortality among the unacclimated in the Selma district at that time was excessive. When my chief and I parted at dinner time (our palates were not in harmony) we commonly shook hands and tried to say something memorable that was worthy to serve as "last words." We had been in the army together and had many a time gone into battle without having taken that precaution in the interest of history.

Of course the better class of the people were not accountable for this state of affairs, and I do not remember that I greatly blamed the others. The country was full of the "elements of combustion." The people were impoverished and smarting with a sense of defeat. Organized resistance was no longer possible, but many men trained to the use of arms did not consider themselves included in the surrender and conscientiously believed it both right and expedient to prolong the struggle by private enterprise. Many, no doubt, made the easy and natural transition from soldiering to assassination by insensible degrees, unconscious of the moral difference, such as it is. Selma was little better than a ruin; in the concluding period of the war General Wilson's cavalry had raided it and nearly destroyed it, and the work begun by the battery had been completed by the torch. The conflagration was generally attributed to the negroes, who certainly augmented it, for a number of those suspected of the crime were flung into the flames by the maddened populace. None the less were the Yankee invaders held responsible.

Every Northern man represented some form or phase of an author-

ity which these luckless people horribly hated, and to which they submitted only because, and in so far as, they had to. Fancy such a community, utterly without the restraints of law and with no means of
ascertaining public opinion — for newspapers were not — denied even
the moral advantage of the pulpit! Considering what human nature has
the misfortune to be, it is wonderful that there was so little of violence
and crime.

As the carcass invites the vulture, this prostrate land drew adven-
turers from all points of the compass. Many, I am sorry to say, were in
the service of the United States Government. Truth to tell, the special
agents of the Treasury were themselves, as a body, not altogether spotless. I could name some of them, and some of their assistants, who
made large fortunes by their opportunities. The special agents were
allowed one-fourth of the value of the confiscated cotton for expenses
of collection — none too much, considering the arduous and perilous
character of the service; but the plan opened up such possibilities of
fraud as have seldom been accorded by any system of conducting the
public business, and never without disastrous results to official morality. Against bribery no provision could have provided an adequate safe-
guard; the magnitude of the interests involved was too great, the administration of the trust too loose and irresponsible. The system as it
was, hastily devised in the storm and stress of a closing war, broke down
in the end, and it is doubtful if the Government might not more profit-
ably have let the "captured and abandoned property" alone.

As an instance of the temptations to which we were exposed, and of
our tactical dispositions in resistance, I venture to relate a single experience of my own. During an absence of my chief I got upon the trail of a
lot of cotton — seven hundred bales, as nearly as I now recollect —
which had been hidden with so exceptional ingenuity that I was unable
to trace it. One day there came to my office two well-dressed and man-
nerly fellows who suffered me to infer that they knew all about this
cotton and controlled it. When our conference on the subject ended it
was past dinner time and they civilly invited me to dine with them,
which, in hope of eliciting information over the wine, I did. I knew well
enough that they indulged a similar selfish hope, so I had no scruples
about using their hospitality to their disadvantage if I could. The subject, however, was not mentioned at table, and we were all singularly
abstemious in the matter of champagne — so much so that as we rose

from a rather long session at the board we disclosed our sense of the ludicrousness of the situation by laughing outright. Nevertheless, neither party would accept defeat, and for the next few weeks the war of hospitality was fast and furious. We dined together nearly every day, sometimes at my expense, sometimes at theirs. We drove, rode, walked, played at billiards and made many a night of it; but youth and temperance (in drink) pulled me through without serious inroads on my health. We had early come to an understanding and a deadlock. Failing to get the slenderest clew to the location of the cotton I offered them one-fourth if they would surrender it or disclose its hiding-place; they offered me one-fourth if I would sign a permit for its shipment as private property.

All things have an end, and this amusing contest finally closed. Over the remains of a farewell dinner, unusually luxurious, as befitted the occasion, we parted with expressions of mutual esteem — not, I hope, altogether insincere, and the ultimate fate of the cotton is to me unknown. Up to the date of my departure from the agency not a bale of it had either come into possession of the Government or found an outlet. I am sometimes disloyal enough to indulge myself in the hope that they baffled my successors as skilfully as they did me. One cannot help feeling a certain tenderness for men who know and value a good dinner.

Another corrupt proposal that I had the good fortune to be afraid to entertain came, as it were, from within. There was a dare-devil fellow whom, as I know him to be dead, I feel justified in naming Jack Harris. He was engaged in all manner of speculative ventures on his own account, but the special agent had so frequently employed him in "enterprises of great pith and moment" that he was in a certain sense and to a certain extent one of us. He seemed to me at the time unique, but shortly afterward I had learned to classify him as a type of the Californian adventurer with whose peculiarities of manner, speech and disposition most of us are to-day familiar enough. He never spoke of his past, having doubtless good reasons for reticence, but any one learned in Western slang — a knowledge then denied me — would have catalogued him with infallible accuracy. He was a rather large, strong fellow, swarthy, blackbearded, black-eyed, black-hearted and entertaining, no end; ignorant with an ignorance whose frankness redeemed it from offensiveness, vulgar with a vulgarity that expressed itself in such metaphors and similes as would have made its peace with the most implacable refinement. He drank hard, gambled high, swore like a parrot, scoffed at everything, was openly and proudly a rascal, did not know the meaning of fear, borrowed money abundantly, and squandered it with royal disregard. Desiring one day to go to Mobile, but reluctant to leave Montgomery and its pleasures — unwilling to quit certainty for hope — he persuaded the captain of a loaded steamboat to wait four days for him at an expense of $400 a day; and lest time should hang too heavy on the obliging skipper's hands, Jack permitted him to share the orgies gratis. But that is not my story.

One day Jack came to me with a rather more sinful proposal than he had heretofore done me the honor to submit. He knew of about a thousand bales of cotton, some of it private property, some of it confiscable, stored at various points on the banks of the Alabama. He had a steamboat in readiness, "with a gallant, gallant crew," and he proposed to drop quietly down to the various landings by night, seize the cotton, load it on his boat and make off down the river. What he wanted from me, and was willing to pay for, was only my official signature to some blank shipping permits; or if I would accompany the expedition and share its fortunes no papers would be necessary. In declining this truly generous offer I felt that I owed it to Jack to give him a reason that he was capable of understanding, so I explained to him the arrangements at Mobile, which would prevent him from transferring his cargo to a ship and getting the necessary papers permitting her to sail. He was astonished and, I think, pained by my simplicity. Did I think him a fool? He did not purpose — not he — to tranship at all: the perfected plan was to dispense with all hampering formality by slipping through Mobile Bay in the black of the night and navigating his laden river craft across the Gulf to Havana! The rascal was in dead earnest, and that natural timidity of disposition which compelled me to withhold my cooperation greatly lowered me in his esteem, I fear.

It was in Cuba, by the way, that Jack came to grief some years later. He was one of the crew of the filibustering vessel *Virginius*, and was captured and shot along with the others. Something in his demeanor as he knelt in the line to receive the fatal fusillade prompted a priest to inquire his religion. "I am an atheist, by God!" said Jack, and with this quiet profession of faith that gentle spirit winged its way to other tropics.

Having expounded with some particularity the precarious tenure by which I held my office and my life in those "thrilling regions" where my duties lay, I ought to explain by what unhappy chance I am still able to afflict the reader. There lived in Selma a certain once wealthy and still influential citizen, whose two sons, of about my own age, had served as officers in the Confederate Army. I will designate them simply as Charles and Frank. They were types of a class now, I fear, almost extinct. Born and bred in luxury and knowing nothing of the seamy side of life — except, indeed, what they had learned in the war — well educated, brave, generous, sensitive to points of honor, and of engaging manners, these brother's were by all respected, by many loved and by some feared. For they had quick fingers upon the pistol-trigger withal, and would rather fight a duel than eat — nay, drink. Nor were they over-particular about the combat taking the form of a duel — almost any form was good enough. I made their acquaintance by chance and cultivated it for the pleasure it gave me. It was long afterward that I gave a thought to its advantages; but from the time that I became generally, known as their friend my safety was assured through all that region; an army with banners could not have given me the same immunity from danger, obstruction or even insult in the performance of my disagreeable duties. What glorious fellows they were, to be sure — these my late antagonists of the dark days when, God forgive us, we were trying to cut one another's throat. To this day I feel a sense of regret when I think of my instrumentality, however small, in depriving the world of many such men in the criminal insanity that we call battle.

Life in Selma became worth living even as the chance of living it augmented. With my new friends and a friend of theirs, whose name — the more shame to me — I cannot now recall, but should not write here if I could, I passed most of my leisure hours. At the houses of themselves and their friends I did most of my dining; and, heaven be praised! there was no necessity for moderation in wine. In their society I committed my sins, and together beneath that noble orb unknown to colder skies, the Southern moon, we atoned for them by acts of devotion performed with song and lute beneath the shrine window of many a local divinity.

One night we had an adventure. We were out late — so late that it was night only astronomically. The streets were "deserted and drear," and, of course, unlighted — the late Confederacy had no gas and no oil. Nevertheless, we saw that we were followed. A man keeping at a fixed distance behind turned as we turned, paused as we paused, and pursued as we moved on. We stopped, went back and remonstrated; asked his intentions in, I dare say, no gentle words. He gave us no reply, but as we left him he followed. Again we stopped, and I felt my pistol plucked out of my pocket. Frank had unceremoniously possessed himself of it and was advancing on the enemy. I do not remember if I had any wish to interpose a protest—anyhow there was no time. Frank fired and the man fell. In a moment all the chamber-windows in the street were thrown open with a head visible (and audible) in each. We told Frank to go home, which to our surprise he did; the rest of us, assisted by somebody's private policeman—who afterward apprised us that we were in arrest—carried the man to a hotel. It was found that his leg was broken above the knee, and the next day it was amputated. We paid his surgeon and his hotel bill, and when he had sufficiently recovered sent him to an address which he gave us in Mobile; but not a word could anybody get out of him as to who he had the misfortune to be, or why he had persisted, against the light, in following a quartet of stray revelers.

On the morning of the shooting, when everything possible had been done for the comfort of the victim, we three accomplices were released on our own recognizance by an old gentleman of severe aspect, who had resumed his function of justice of the peace where he had laid it down during the war. I did not then know that he had no more legal authority than I had myself, and I was somewhat disturbed in mind as I reflected on the possibilities of the situation. The opportunity to get rid of an offensive Federal official must of course be very tempting, and after all the shooting was a trifle hasty and not altogether justifiable.

On the day appointed for our preliminary examination, all of us except Frank were released and put on the witness-stand. We gave a true and congruent history of the affair. The holdover justice listened to it all very patiently and then, with commendable brevity and directness of action, fined Frank five dollars and costs for disorderly conduct. There was no appeal.

There were queer characters in Alabama in those days, as you shall see. Once upon a time the special agent and I started down the Tombigbee River with a steamboat load of government cotton—some six hundred bales. At one of the military stations we took on a guard of a dozen or fifteen soldiers under command of a non-commissioned officer. One evening, just before dusk, as we were rounding a bend where the current set strongly against the left bank of the stream and the channel lay close to that shore, we were suddenly saluted with a volley of bullets and buckshot from that direction. The din of the firing, the rattle and crash of the missiles splintering the woodwork and the jingle of broken glass made a very rude arousing from the tranquil indolence of a warm afternoon on the sluggish Tombigbee. The left bank, which at this point was a trifle higher than the hurricane deck of a steamer, was now swarming with men who, almost near enough to jump aboard, looked unreasonably large and active as they sprang about from cover to cover, pouring in their fire. At the first volley the pilot had deserted his wheel, as well he might, and the boat, drifting in to the bank under the boughs of a tree, was helpless. Her jackstaff and yawl were carried away, her guards broken in, and her deck-load of cotton was tumbling into the stream a dozen bales at once. The captain was nowhere to be seen, the engineer had evidently abandoned his post and the special agent had gone to hunt up the soldiers. I happened to be on the hurricane deck, armed with a revolver, which I fired as rapidly as I could, listening all the time for the fire of the soldiers — and listening in vain. It transpired later that they had not a cartridge among them; and of all helpless mortals a soldier without a cartridge is the most imbecile. But all this time the continuous rattle of the enemy's guns and the petulant pop of my own pocket firearm were punctuated, as it were, by pretty regularly recurring loud explosions, as of a small cannon. They came from somewhere forward — I supposed, from the opposition, as I knew we had no artillery on board.

The failure of our military guard made the situation somewhat grave. For two of us, at least, capture meant hanging out of hand. I had never been hanged in all my life and was not enamored of the prospect. Fortunately for us the bandits had selected their point of attack without military foresight. Immediately below them a bayou, impassable to them, let into the river. The moment we had drifted below it we were safe from boarding and capture. The captain was found in hiding and an empty pistol at his ear persuaded him to resume command of his vessel; the engineer and pilot were encouraged to go back to their posts and after some remarkably long minutes, during which we were under an increasingly long-range fire, we got under way. A few cotton bales piled about the pilot-house made us tolerably safe from that sort of thing in the future and then we took account of our damages. Nobody had been killed and only a few were wounded. This gratifying result was attributable to the fact that, being unarmed, nearly everybody had dived below at the first fire and taken cover among the cotton bales. While issuing a multitude of needless commands from the front of the hurricane-deck I looked below, and there, stretched out at full length on his stomach, lay a long, ungainly person, clad in faded butternut, bareheaded, his long, lank hair falling down each side of his neck, his coat-tails similarly parted, and his enormous feet spreading their soles to the blue sky. He had an old-fashioned horsepistol, some two feet long, which he was in the act of sighting across his left palm for a parting shot at the now distant assailants. A more ludicrous figure I never saw; I laughed outright; but when his weapon went off it was matter for gratitude to be above it instead of before it. It was the "cannon" whose note I had marked all through the unequal fray.

The fellow was a returned Confederate whom we had taken on at one of the upper landings as our only passenger; we were deadheading him to Mobile. He was undoubtedly in hearty sympathy with the enemy, and I at first suspected him of collusion, but circumstances not necessary to detail here rendered this impossible. Moreover, I had distinctly seen one of the "guerrillas" fall and remain down after my own weapon was empty, and no man else on board except the passenger had fired a shot or had a shot to fire. When everything had been made snug again, and we were gliding along under the stars, without apprehension; when I had counted fifty-odd bullet holes through the pilot-house (which had not received the attention that by its prominence and importance it was justly entitled to) and everybody was variously boasting his prowess, I approached my butternut comrade-in-arms and thanked him for his kindly aid. "But," said I, "how the devil does it happen that *you* fight *that* crowd?"

"Wal, Cap," he drawled, as he rubbed the powder grime from his antique artillery, — "I allowed it was mouty clever in you-all to take me on, seein' I hadn't ary cent, so thought I'd jist kinder work my passage."

[1907; CWAB, III]

THE OTHER LODGERS

"In order to take that train," said Colonel Levering, sitting in the Waldorf-Astoria hotel, "you will have to remain nearly all night in Atlanta. That is a fine city, but I advise you not to put up at the Breathitt House, one of the principal hotels. It is an old wooden building in urgent need of repairs. There are breaches in the walls that you could throw a cat through. The bedrooms have no locks on the doors, no furniture but a single chair in each, and a bedstead without bedding — just a mattress. Even these meager accommodations you cannot be sure that you will have in monopoly; you must take your chance of being stowed in with a lot of others. Sir, it is a most abominable hotel.

"The night that I passed in it was an uncomfortable night. I got in late and was shown to my room on the ground floor by an apologetic night-clerk with a tallow candle, which he considerately left with me. I was worn out by two days and a night of hard railway travel and had not entirely recovered from a gunshot wound in the head, received in an altercation. Rather than look for better quarters I lay down on the mattress without removing my clothing and fell asleep.

"Along toward morning I awoke. The moon had risen and was shining in at the uncurtained window, illuminating the room with a soft, bluish light which seemed, somehow, a bit spooky, though I dare say it had no uncommon quality; all moonlight is that way if you will observe it. Imagine my surprise and indignation when I saw the floor occupied by at least a dozen other lodgers! I sat up, earnestly damning the management of that unthinkable hotel, and was about to spring from the bed to go and make trouble for the night-clerk — him of the apologetic manner and the tallow candle — when something in the situation affected me with a strange indisposition to move. I suppose I was what a story-writer might call 'frozen with terror.' For those men were obviously all dead!

"They lay on their backs, disposed orderly along three sides of the room, their feet to the walls — against the other wall, farthest from the door, stood my bed and the chair. All the faces were covered, but under their white cloths the features of the two bodies that lay in the square patch of moonlight near the window showed in sharp profile as to nose and chin.

"I thought this is a bad dream and tried to cry out, as one does in a nightmare, but could make no sound. At last, with a desperate effort I threw my feet to the floor and passing between the two rows of clouted faces and the two bodies that lay nearest the door, I escaped from the infernal place and ran to the office. The night-clerk was there, behind the desk, sitting in the dim light of another tallow candle — just sitting and staring. He did not rise: my abrupt entrance produced no effect upon him, though I must have looked a veritable corpse myself. It occurred to me then that I had not before really observed the fellow. He was a little chap, with a colorless face and the whitest, blankest eyes I ever saw. He had no more expression than the back of my hand. His clothing was a dirty gray.

" 'Damn you!' I said; 'what do you mean?'

"Just the same, I was shaking like a leaf in the wind and did not recognize my own voice.

"The night-clerk rose, bowed (apologetically) and — well, he was no longer there, and at that moment I felt a hand laid upon my shoulder from behind. Just fancy that if you can! Unspeakably frightened, I turned and saw a portly, kind-faced gentleman, who asked:

" 'What is the matter, my friend?'

"I was not long in telling him, but before I made an end of it he went pale himself. 'See here,' he said, 'are you telling the truth?'

"I had now got myself in hand and terror had given place to indignation. 'If you dare to doubt it,' I said, 'I'll hammer the life out of you!'

" 'No,' he replied, 'don't do that; just sit down till I tell you. This is not a hotel. It used to be; afterward it was a hospital. Now it is unoccupied, awaiting a tenant. The room that you mention was the dead-room — there were always plenty of dead. The fellow that you call the night-clerk used to be that, but later he booked the patients as they were brought in. I don't understand his being here. He has been dead a few weeks.'

" 'And who are you?' I blurted out.

" 'Oh, I look after the premises. I happened to be passing just now, and seeing a light in here came in to investigate. Let us have a look into that room,' he added, lifting the sputtering candle from the desk.

" 'I'll see you at the devil first!' said I, bolting out of the door into the street.

"Sir, that Breathitt House, in Atlanta, is a beastly place! Don't you stop there."

"God forbid! Your account of it certainly does not suggest comfort. By the way, Colonel, when did all that occur?"

"In September, 1864 — shortly after the seige."

[1903; CWAB, III]

A RESUMED IDENTITY

I

THE REVIEW AS A FORM OF WELCOME

One summer night a man stood on a low hill overlooking a wide expanse of forest and field. By the full moon hanging low in the west he knew what he might not have known otherwise: that it was near the hour of dawn. A light mist lay along the earth, partly veiling the lower features of the landscape, but above it the taller trees showed in well-defined masses against a clear sky. Two or three farmhouses were visible through the haze, but in none of them, naturally, was a light. Nowhere, indeed, was any sign or suggestion of life except the barking of a distant dog, which, repeated with mechanical iteration, served rather to accentuate than dispel the loneliness of the scene.

The man looked curiously about him on all sides, as one who among familiar surroundings is unable to determine his exact place and part in the scheme of things. It is so, perhaps, that we shall act when, risen from the dead, we await the call to judgment.

A hundred yards away was a straight road, showing white in the moonlight. Endeavoring to orient himself, as a surveyor or navigator might say, the man moved his eyes slowly along its visible length and at a distance of a quarter-mile to the south of his station saw, dim and gray in the haze, a group of horsemen riding to the north. Behind them were men afoot, marching in column, with dimly gleaming rifles aslant above their shoulders. They moved slowly and in silence. Another group of horsemen, another regiment of infantry, another and another — all in unceasing motion toward the man's point of view, past it, and beyond. A battery of artillery followed, the cannoneers riding with folded arms on limber and caisson. And still the interminable procession came out of the obscurity to south and passed into the obscurity to north, with never a sound of voice, nor hoof, nor wheel.

The man could not rightly understand: he thought himself deaf; said so, and heard his own voice, although it had an unfamiliar quality that almost alarmed him; it disappointed his ears' expectancy in the matter of *timbre* and resonance. But he was not deaf, and that for the moment sufficed.

Then he remembered that there are natural phenomena to which some one has given the name "acoustic shadows." If you stand in an acoustic shadow there is one direction from which you will hear nothing. At the battle of Gaines's Mill,[1] one of the fiercest conflicts of the Civil War, with a hundred guns in play, spectators a mile and a half away on the opposite side of the Chickahominy valley heard nothing of what they clearly saw. The bombardment of Port Royal,[2] heard and felt at St. Augustine, a hundred and fifty miles to the south, was inaudible two miles to the north in a still atmosphere. A few days before the surrender at Appomattox[3] a thunderous engagement between the commands of Sheridan[4] and Pickett[5] was unknown to the latter commander, a mile in the rear of his own line.

These instances were not known to the man of whom we write, but less striking ones of the same character had not escaped his observation. He was profoundly disquieted, but for another reason than the uncanny silence of that moonlight march.

"Good Lord!" he said to himself — and again it was as if another had spoken his thought — "if those people are what I take them to be we have lost the battle and they are moving on Nashville!"

1. Part of McClellan's 1862 campaign against Richmond, the battle of Gaine's Mill was fought on June 27, 1862.

2. On November 7, 1861, the Northern fleet under Admiral Samuel DuPont led a successful naval bombardment of the forts protecting the best natural harbor on the South's Atlantic coast, a port the Union navy used throughout the war to raid and blockade Southern ports.

3. Appomattox Courthouse, Virginia, was site of Lee's capitulation to Grant on April 9, 1865, and is recognized as the end of the war, even if fighting continued for sometime thereafter.

4. Sheridan's "scorch and burn" policy fit squarely into Sherman and Grant's strategy to make the South surrender. He defeated George Pickett's army near Appomattox in the battle of Five Forks on April 1, 1865. Also see Chapter Four, note 10.

5. Major-General George Edward Pickett (1825–1875) is best known for "Pickett's Charge," the failed assault by 13,000 Confederate soldiers on the Union position behind a stone wall at Cemetery Ridge, Gettysburg, July 3, 1863. The charge and failure is often called the "high tide of the Confederacy" as a way to mark the point when the Union took command of the war.

Then came a thought of self — an apprehension — a strong sense of personal peril, such as in another we call fear. He stepped quickly into the shadow of a tree. And still the silent battalions moved slowly forward in the haze.

The chill of a sudden breeze upon the back of his neck drew his attention to the quarter whence it came, and turning to the east he saw a faint gray light along the horizon — the first sign of returning day. This increased his apprehension.

"I must get away from here," he thought, "or I shall be discovered and taken."

He moved out of the shadow, walking rapidly toward the graying east. From the safer seclusion of a clump of cedars he looked back. The entire column had passed out of sight: the straight white road lay bare and desolate in the moonlight!

Puzzled before, he was now inexpressibly astonished. So swift a passing of so slow an army! — he could not comprehend it. Minute after minute passed unnoted; he had lost his sense of time. He sought with a terrible earnestness a solution of the mystery, but sought in vain. When at last he roused himself from his abstraction the sun's rim was visible above the hills, but in the new conditions he found no other light than that of day; his understanding was involved as darkly in doubt as before.

On every side lay cultivated fields showing no sign of war and war's ravages. From the chimneys of the farmhouses thin ascensions of blue smoke signaled preparations for a day's peaceful toil. Having stilled its immemorial allocution to the moon, the watchdog was assisting a Negro who, prefixing a team of mules to the plow, was flatting and sharping contentedly at his task. The hero of this tale stared stupidly at the pastoral picture as if he had never seen such a thing in all his life; then he put his hand to his head, passed it through his hair and, withdrawing it, attentively considered the palm — a singular thing to do. Apparently reassured by the act, he walked confidently toward the road.

II

WHEN YOU HAVE LOST YOUR LIFE
CONSULT A PHYSICIAN

Dr. Stilling Malson, of Murfreesboro, having visited a patient six or seven miles away, on the Nashville road, had remained with him all night. At daybreak he set out for home on horseback, as was the custom of doctors of the time and region. He had passed into the neighborhood of Stone's River battlefield when a man approached him from the roadside and saluted in the military fashion, with a movement of the right hand to the hat-brim. But the hat was not a military hat, the man was not in uniform and had not a martial bearing. The doctor nodded civilly, half thinking that the stranger's uncommon greeting was perhaps in deference to the historic surroundings. As the stranger evidently desired speech with him he courteously reined in his horse and waited.

"Sir," said the stranger, "although a civilian, you are perhaps an enemy."

"I am a physician," was the non-committal reply.

"Thank you," said the other. "I am a lieutenant, of the staff of General Hazen." He paused a moment and looked sharply at the person whom he was addressing, then added, "of the Federal army."

The physician merely nodded.

"Kindly tell me," continued the other, "what has happened here. Where are the armies? Which has won the battle?"

The physician regarded his questioner curiously with half shut eyes. After a professional scrutiny, prolonged to the limit of politeness, "Pardon me," he said; "one asking information should be willing to impart it. Are you wounded?" he added, smiling.

"Not seriously — it seems."

The man removed the unmilitary hat, put his hand to his head, passed it through his hair and, withdrawing it, attentively considered the palm.

"I was struck by a bullet and have been unconscious. It must have been a light, glancing blow: I find no blood and feel no pain. I will not trouble you for treatment, but will you kindly direct me to my command — to any part of the Federal army — if you know?"

Again the doctor did not immediately reply: he was recalling much that is recorded in the books of his profession — something about lost identity and the effect of familiar scenes in restoring it. At length he looked the man in the face, smiled and said:

"Lieutenant, you are not wearing the uniform of your rank and service."

At this the man glanced down at his civilian attire, lifted his eyes, and said with hesitation:

"That is true. I—I don't quite understand."

Still regarding him sharply but not unsympathetically the man of science bluntly inquired:

"How old are you?"

"Twenty-three—if that has anything to do with it."

"You don't look it; I should hardly have guessed you to be just that."

The man was growing impatient. "We need not discuss that," he said; "I want to know about the army. Not two hours ago I saw a column of troops moving northward on this road. You must have met them. Be good enough to tell me the color of their clothing, which I was unable to make out, and I'll trouble you no more."

"You are quite sure that you saw them?"

"Sure? My God, sir, I could have counted them!"

"Why, really," said the physician, with an amusing consciousness of his own resemblance to the loquacious barber of the Arabian Nights, "this is very interesting. I met no troops."

The man looked at him coldly, as if he had himself observed the likeness to the barber. "It is plain," he said, "that you do not care to assist me. Sir, you may go to the devil!"

He turned and strode away, very much at random, across the dewy fields, his half-penitent tormentor quietly watching him from his point of vantage in the saddle till he disappeared beyond an array of trees.

III

THE DANGER OF LOOKING
INTO A POOL OF WATER

After leaving the road the man slackened his pace, and now went forward, rather deviously, with a distinct feeling of fatigue. He could not account for this, though truly the interminable loquacity of that country doctor offered itself in explanation. Seating himself upon a rock, he laid one hand upon his knee, back upward, and casually looked at it. It was lean and withered. He lifted both hands to his face. It was seamed and furrowed; he could trace the lines with the tips of his fingers. How strange! — a mere bullet-stroke and a brief unconsciousness should not make one a physical wreck.

"I must have been a long time in hospital," he said aloud. "Why what a fool I am! The battle was in December, and it is now summer!" He laughed. "No wonder that fellow thought me an escaped lunatic. He was wrong: I am only an escaped patient."

At a little distance a small plot of ground enclosed by a stone wall caught his attention. With no very definite intent he rose and went to it. In the center was a square, solid monument of hewn stone.[6] It was brown with age, weather-worn at the angles, spotted with moss and lichen. Between the massive blocks were strips of grass the leverage of whose roots had pushed them apart. In answer to the challenge of this ambitious structure Time had laid his destroying hand upon it, and it would soon be "one with Nineveh and Tyre." In an inscription on one side his eye caught a familiar name. Shaking with excitement, he craned his body across the wall and read:

HAZEN'S BRIGADE
to
The Memory of Its Soldiers
who fell at
Stone River, Dec. 31, 1862.

The man fell back from the wall, faint and sick. Almost within an arm's length was a little depression in the earth; it had been filled by a recent rain-a pool of clear water. He crept to it to revive himself, lifted the upper part of his body on his trembling arms, thrust forward his head and saw the reflection of his face, as in a mirror. He uttered a terrible cry. His arms gave way; he fell, face downward, into the pool and yielded up the life that had spanned another life.

6. See G. C. Kniffin, "The Battle of Stone's River," *Battles and Leaders of the Civil War*, 3:617, for an illustration of the Hazen monument.

[N.D.; CWAB, X]

THE NATURE OF WAR

The Bald Campaigner was looking over the tops of his spectacle lenses, silent, obviously wise, a thing of beauty. . . .

"As to devastation — did you mention devastation? — [said the Bald Campaigner] that is the purpose of war. War is made, not against the bodies of adult males, but against the means of subsistence of a people. The fighting is incident to the devastation: we kill soldiers because they protect their material resources — get between us and the fields that feed them, the factories that clothe them, the arsenals that arm them. We cannot hope to kill a great proportion of them at best; the humane thing is to overcome them by means of hunger and nakedness. The earlier we can do so, the less effusion of blood. Leave the enemy his resources and he will fight forever. He will beget soldiers faster than you can destroy them.

"Do you cherish the delusion that in our great civil war, for example, the South was subdued by killing her able-bodied males who could bear arms? Look at the statistics and learn, to your astonishment, how small a proportion of them we really did kill, even before I lost my arm.

"The killing was an incident. I speak of the latter part of the conflict, when we had learned how to conduct military operations. As long as our main purpose was bloodshed we made little progress. Our armies actually guarded the homes and property of the men they were sent to conquer — the very men that were fighting them, and who, therefore, assured of the comfort and safety of their families, continued fighting with cheerful alacrity. If we had continued that rosewater policy they might have fought us to this day."

The reporter involuntarily glanced at a calender on the wall, and the war oracle continued:

"Wisdom came of experience: we adopted the more effective and more humane policy of devastation. With Sherman desolating the country from Atlanta to Goldsborough and Sheridan so wasting the Shenandoah Valley that he boasted the impossibility of a crow passing over it without carrying rations, the hopes of Confederate success went up in smoke.

"And," concluded the hairless veteran, rising and opening the door as a delicate intimation that there was nothing more to say, "I beg leave to think that the essential character of the *Ultima Ratio* is not permanently obscurable by the sentimental vaguries of blithering civilians such as you have the lack of distinction to be."

The Timorous Reporter retired to his base of operations and the war-drum throbbed no longer in his ear.

[1899; CWAB, IX]

MODERN WARFARE

The dream of a time when the nation shall war no more is a pleasant dream and an ancient. Countless generations have indulged in it, and to countless others, doubtless, it will prove a solace and a benefaction. . . .

"War," these excellent persons reason, "will at last become so dreadful that men will no longer engage in it" — happily unconscious of the fact that men's sense of their power to make it dreadful is precisely the thing that most encourages them to wage it. Another popular promise of peace is seen in the enormous cost of modern armaments and military methods. The cost of shot and cartridge of a heavy gun to-day cost hundreds of dollars, the gun itself tens of thousands. It is at an expense of thousands that a torpedo is discharged, which may or may not wreck a ship worth millions. To secure its safety from the machinations of its wicked neighbors while itself engaged in the arts of peace, a nation of to-day must have an immense sum of money invested in the military plant alone. It is not in the nature of man to impoverish himself by investments from which he hopes for no return except security in the condition entailed in the outlay. Men do not construct expensive machinery, taxing themselves poor to keep it in working order, without ultimately setting it going. The more of its income a nation has to spend in preparation for war, the more certainly it will go to war. Its means of defense are means of aggression, and the stronger it feels itself to strike for its altars and its fires, the more spirited becomes its desire to go across the border to upset the altars and extinguish the fires of its neighbors.

But the notion that improved weapons give modern armies and navies an increased killing ability — that the warfare of the future will be a bloodier business than that which we have the happiness to know — is an error which the observant lover of peace is denied the satisfaction of entertaining. Compare, for example, a naval engagement of to-day with Salamis, Lepanto or Trafalgar. Compare the famous duel between the *Monitor* and the *Merrimac* with almost any encounter between the old wooden line-of-battle ships, continued, as was the reprehensible custom, until one or both, with hundreds of dead and wounded, incarnadined the seas by going to the bottom.

As long ago as 1861 a terrific engagement occurred in the harbor of Charleston, South Carolina. It lasted forty hours, and was fought with hundreds of the biggest and best guns of the period. Not a man was killed nor wounded.

In the spring of 1862, below New Orleans, Porter's mortar boats bombarded Fort Jackson for nearly five days and nights, throwing about 16,800 shells, mostly thirteen inches in diameter. "Nearly every shell," says the commandant of the fort, "lodged inside the works." Even in those days, it will be observed, there were "arms of precision"; and an exploding 13-inch shell is still highly esteemed and respected. As nearly as I can learn, the slaughter amounted to two men.

A year later Admiral Dupont attacked Fort Sumter, then in the hands of the Confederates, with the *New Ironsides*, the double-turret monitor *Keokuk*, and seven single-turret monitors. The big guns of the fort were too much for him. One of his vessels was struck 90 times, and afterward sank. Another was struck 53 times; another, 35 times; another, 14; another, 47; another, 20; another, 47; another, 95; another 36, and disabled. But they threw 151 shots from their own "destructive" weapons, and these, being "arms of precision," killed a whole man by cutting down a flag-staff, which fell upon him. The total number of shots fired by the enemy was 2,209, and if more than two men were killed by them I am unable to find any account of it. But it was a splendid battle, as every Quaker will allow!

In the stubbornest land engagements of our great rebellion, and of the later and more scientific Franco-German and Turko-Russian wars, the proportionate mortality was not nearly so great as in those where "Greek met Greek" hand to hand, or where the Roman with his short sword, the most destructive weapon ever invented, played at give and take with the naked barbarian or the Roman of another political faith. . . .

It has been said that to kill a man in battle a man's weight in lead is required. But if the battle happens to be fought by modern warships or forts, or both, about a hundred tons of iron would seem to be a reasonable allowance for the making of a military corpse. In fighting in the open the figures are more cheering. What it cost in our civil war to kill a Confederate soldier is not accurately computable; we don't know exactly how many we had the good luck to kill. But the "best estimates" are easily accessible.

II

In the *Century* magazine several years ago was a paper on machine guns and dynamite guns. As might have been expected, it opened with a prediction by a distinguished general of the Union armies that, so murderous have warlike weapons become, "the next war will be marked by terrific and fearful slaughter." This is naturally followed by the writer's smug and comfortable assurance that "in the extreme mortality of modern war will be found the only hope that man can have of even a partial cessation of war." If this were so, let us see how it would work. The chronological sequence of events would necessarily (obviously, one would think) be something like this:

1. Murderous perfection of warlike weapons.
2. War marked by "terrific and fearful slaughter."
3. Consequent cessation of war and disarmament of nations.
4. Stoppage of the manufacture of military weapons, with resulting decay of dependent industries, that is to say, decay of the ability to produce the weapons. Diversion of intellectual activity to the arts of peace.
5. War no longer capable of being marked by "terrific and fearful slaughter." *Ergo,*
6. Revival of war. . . .

In our civil war — and that is very ancient history to the long-range tactician of to-day — it was my fortune to assist at a sufficing number of assaults with bayonet and assaults with sabre, but I have never had the gratification to see a half-dozen men, friends or enemies, who had fallen by either the one weapon or the other. Whenever the opposing lines actually met it was the rifle, the carbine, or the revolver that did the work. . . .

All mechanical devices tend to make cowards of those whom they protect. Men long accustomed to the security of even such slight earthworks as are thrown up by armies operating against each other in the open country lose something out of their general efficiency. The particular thing that they lose is courage. In long sieges the sallies and assaults are commonly feeble, spiritless affairs, easily repelled. So manifestly does a soldier's comparative safety indispose him to incure even such perils as beset him in it that during the last years of our civil war, when it was customary for armies in the field to cover their fronts with breastworks, any intelligent officer, conceding the need of some protection, yet made their works much slighter than was easily possible. Except when the firing was heavy, close and continuous, "head-logs" (for example) for the men to fire under were distinctly demoralizing. The soldier who has least security is least reluctant to forego what security he has. That is to say, he is the bravest. . . .

When the patriot's heart is duly fired by his newspaper and his politician he will probably enlist henceforth, as he has done heretofore, and be as ready to assist in covering the enemy's half of the landscape with a rain of bullets, falling where it shall please Heaven, as his bellicose ancestor was to meet the foeman in the flesh and engage him in personal combat; but it will be a stupid business, despite all that the special correspondent can do for its celebration by verbal fireworks. Tales of the "firing line" emanating from the chimney corner of the future will urge the young male afield with a weaker suasion. By the way, I do not remember to have heard the term "firing line" during our civil war. We had the thing, of course, but it did not last long enough (except in siege operations, when it was called something else) to get a name. Troops on the "firing line" either held their fire until the enemy signified a desire for it by coming to get it, or they themselves advanced and served him with it where he stood.

I should not like to say that this is an age of human cowardice; I say only that the men of all civilized nations are taking a deal of pains to invent offensive weapons that will wield themselves and defenses that can take the place of the human breast. A modern battle is a quarrel of skulkers trying to have all the killing done a long way from their persons.

They will attack at a distance, they will defend if inaccessible. As much of the fighting as possible is done by machinery, preferably automatic. When we shall so have perfected our arms of precision and other destructive weapons that they will need no human agency to start and keep them going, war will be foremost among the arts of peace.

Meantime it is still a trifle perilous, sometimes fatal; those who practice it must expect bloody noses and cracked crowns. It may be to the advantage of our countrymen to know that if they have no forethought but thrift they can have no safety but peace; that in the school of emergency nothing is taught but how to weep; that there are no effective substitutes for courage and devotion. America's best defenses are the breasts of American soldiers and the brains of American commanders. Confidence in any "revolutionizing" device is fatal faith.

[May 9, 1897; *San Francisco Examiner*]

A'SOLDIERING FOR FREEDOM

. . . "Liberty!" is a stirring word, hallowed by noble associations, but if I were asked if I believe in Liberty I should reply: "Liberty of whom to do what?" A good deal depends.

I once made a similar "reply." The question being put to me — indignantly, as to one capable of affirming the whiteness of black — whether I thought slavery right. I asked in turn: "Slavery of whom by whom? It is not always that a soft answer turneth away wrath, and I am pained to remember that my interlocutor who was a most holy man and a pillar of the church, afterward thought it his duty to spread abroad in the land a statement affecting unfavorably my reputation for morality — an act which I thought irrelevant.

At one time in my green and salad days I was sufficiently zealous for universal and unqualified Freedom to engage in a four years' battle for its promotion. There were other issues involved, but they did not count for much with me. I am now glad that they were involved, for their presence as threads to the Fate-woven fabric of events spares me the disquieting consciousness of misguided zeal.

———

Time was, in that far fair world of youth when I went a'soldiering for Freedom, when the moral character of every thought and word and deed was determined by reference to a set of infinitely precious "principles" — infallible criteria — moral solvents mordant to all base metals, and warranted by manufacturers and vendors to disclose the gold in every proposition submitted to the test. Alas, I have no longer the advantage of their service, but must judge everything on its own merits, each case as it comes up. I have learned that slavery is not always unrighteous, nor liberty always desirable, except for oneself, that tyranny and despotism are sometimes beneficent, that patriotism is but a broader selfishness, a narrower philanthropy, and that falsehood may be the highest and most imperative duty. I shudder to think that further examination may disclose a moral element in murder. In brief, I unload a "principle" every little while, and shall soon by flying light. . . .

[1901; CWAB, IV]

THE HESITATING VETERAN

When I was young and full of faith
    And other fads that youngsters cherish
A cry rose as of one that saith
    With emphasis: "Help or I perish!"
'Twas heard in all the land, and men
    The sound were each to each repeating.
It made my heart beat faster then
    Than any heart can now be beating.

For the world is old and the world is gray —
    Grown prudent and, I think, more witty.
She's cut her wisdom teeth, they say,
    And doesn't now go in for Pity.
Besides, the melancholy cry
    Was that of one, 'tis now conceded,
Whose plight no one beneath the sky
    Felt half so poignantly as he did.

Moreover, he was black. And yet
    That sentimental generation
With an austere compassion set
    Its face and faith to the occasion.
Then there were hate and strife to spare,
    And various hard knocks a-plenty;
And I ('twas more than my true share,
    I must confess) took five-and-twenty.

That all is over now — the reign
    Of love and trade stills all dissensions,
And the clear heavens arch again
    Above a land of peace and pensions.
The black chap — at the last we gave
    Him everything that he had cried for,
Though many white chaps in the grave
    'Twould puzzle to say what they died for.

I hope he's better off — I trust
    That his society and his master's
Are worth the price we paid, and must
    Continue paying, in disasters;
But sometimes doubts press thronging round
    ('Tis mostly when my hurts are aching)
If war for Union was a sound
    And profitable undertaking.

'Tis said they mean to take away
    The Negro's vote for he's unlettered.
'Tis true he sits in darkness day
    And night, as formerly, when fettered;
But pray observe — howe'er he vote
    To whatsoever party turning,
He'll be with gentlemen of note
    And wealth and consequence and learning.

With saints and sages on each side,
    How could a fool through lack of knowledge,
Vote wrong? If learning is no guide
    Why ought one to have been in college?
O Son of Day, O Son of Night!
    What are your preferences made of?
I know not which of you is right,
    Nor which to be the more afraid of.

The world is old and the world is bad,
    And creaks and grinds upon its axis;
And man's an ape and the gods are mad! —
    There's nothing sure, not even our taxes.
No mortal man can Truth restore,
    Or say where she is to be sought for.
I know what uniform I wore —
    O, that I knew which side I fought for!

[1888; CWAB, IV]

INVOCATION

Read at the Celebration of Independence in San Francisco, in 1888.

Goddess of Liberty! O thou
    Whose tearless eyes behold the chain,
    And look unmoved upon the slain,
Eternal peace upon thy brow, —

Before thy shrine the races press,
    Thy perfect favor to implore —
    The proudest tyrant asks no more,
The ironed anarchist no less.

Thine altar-coals that touch the lips
    Of prophets kindle, too, the brand
    By Discord flung with wanton hand
Among the houses and the ships.

Upon thy tranquil front the star
    Burns bleak and passionless and white,
    Its cold inclemency of light
More dreadful than the shadows are.

Thy name we do not here invoke
    Our civic rites to sanctify:
    Enthroned in thy remoter sky,
Thou heedest not our broken yoke.

Thou carest not for such as we:
    Our millions die to serve thee still
    And secret purpose of thy will.
They perish — what is that to thee?

The light that fills the patriot's tomb
    Is not of thee. The shining crown
    Compassionately offered down
To those who falter in the gloom,

And fall, and call upon thy name,
    And die desiring — 'tis the sign
    Of a diviner love than thine,
Rewarding with a richer fame.

To him alone let freemen cry
    Who hears alike the victor's shout,
    The song of faith, the moan of doubt,
And bends him from his nearer sky.

God of my country and my race!
    So greater than the gods of old —
    So fairer than the prophets told
Who dimly saw and feared thy face, —

Who didst but half reveal thy will
    And gracious ends to their desire,
    Behind the dawn's advancing fire
Thy tender day-beam veiling still, —

To whom the unceasing suns belong,
    And cause is one with consequence, —
    To whose divine, inclusive sense
The moan is blended with the song, —

Whose laws, imperfect and unjust,
    Thy just and perfect purpose serve:
    The needle, howsoe'er it swerve,
Still warranting the sailor's trust, —

God, lift thy hand and make us free
    To crown the work thou hast designed.
    O, strike away the chains that bind
Our souls to one idolatry!

The liberty thy love hath given
    We thank thee for. We thank thee for
    Our great dead fathers' holy war
Wherein our manacles were riven.

We thank thee for the stronger stroke
 Ourselves delivered and incurred
 When — thine incitement half unheard —
The chains we riveted we broke.

We thank thee that beyond the sea
 Thy people, growing ever wise,
 Turn to the west their serious eyes
And dumbly strive to be as we.

As when the sun's returning flame
 Upon the Nileside statue shone,
 And struck from the enchanted stone
The music of a mighty fame,

Let Man salute the rising day
 Of Liberty, but not adore.
 'Tis Opportunity — no more —
A useful, not a sacred, ray.

It bringeth good, it bringeth ill,
 As he possessing shall elect.
 He maketh it of none effect
Who walketh not within thy will.

Give thou more or less, as we
 Shall serve the right or serve the wrong.
 Confirm our freedom but so long
As we are worthy to be free.

But when (O, distant be the time!)
 Majorities in passion draw
 Insurgent swords to murder Law,
And all the land is red with crime;

Or — nearer menace! — when the band
 Of feeble spirits cringe and plead
 To the gigantic strength of Greed,
And fawn upon his iron hand; —

Nay, when the steps to state are worn
    In hollows by the feet of thieves,
    And Mammon sits among the sheaves
And chuckles while the reapers mourn:

Then stay thy miracle! — replace
    The broken throne, repair the chain,
    Restore the interrupted reign
And veil again thy patient face.

Lo! here upon the world's extreme
    We stand with lifted arms and dare
    By thine eternal name to swear
Our country, which so fair we deem —

Upon whose hills, a bannered throng,
    The spirits of the sun display
    Their flashing lances day by day
And hear the sea's pacific song —

Shall be so ruled in right and grace
    That men shall say: "O, drive afield
    The lawless eagle from the shield,
And call an angel to the place!"

[1885; CWAB, IV]

THE DEATH OF GRANT[7]

Father! whose hard and cruel law
 Is part of thy compassion's plan,
 Thy works presumptuously we scan
For what the prophets say they saw.

Unbidden still the awful slope
 Walling us in we climb to gain
 Assurance of the shining plain
That faith has certified to hope.

In vain! — beyond the circling hill
 The shadow and the cloud abide.
 Subdue the doubt, our spirits guide
To trust the record and be still.

To trust it loyally as he
 Who, heedful of his high design,
 Ne'er raised a seeking eye to thine,
But wrought thy will unconsciously,

Disputing not of chance or fate,
 Nor questioning of cause or creed;
 For anything but duty's deed
Too simply wise, too humbly great.

The cannon syllabled his name;
 His shadow shifted o'er the land,
 Portentous, as at his demand
Successive bastions sprang to flame!

He flared the continent with fire,
 The rivers ran in lines of light!
 Thy will be done on earth — if right
Or wrong he cared not to inquire.

7. Ulysses Simpson Grant died of throat cancer on July 23, 1885, at his home at Mount McGregor, New York. He had rushed to write his memoirs, beginning them in August 1884 and completing the two volumes on July 19, 1885.

His was the heavy hand, and his
  The service of the despot blade;
  His the soft answer that allayed
War's giant animosities.

Let us have peace: our clouded eyes,
  Fill, Father, with another light,
  That we may see with clearer sight
Thy servant's soul in Paradise.

[1885; CWAB, IV]

CONTENTMENT

Sleep fell upon my senses and I dreamed
    Long years had circled since my life had fled.
The world was different, and all things seemed
    Remote and strange, like noises to the dead.
    And one great Voice there was; and some one said:
"Posterity is speaking — rightly deemed
Infallible"; and so I gave attention,
Hoping Posterity my name would mention.

"Illustrious Spirit," said the Voice, "appear!
    While we confirm eternally thy fame,
Before our dread tribunal answer, here,
    Why do no statues celebrate thy name,
    No monuments thy services proclaim?
Why did not thy contemporaries rear
To thee some schoolhouse or memorial college?
It looks almighty queer, you must acknowledge."

Up spake I hotly: "That is where you err!"
    But some one thundered in my ear: "You shan't
Be interrupting these proceedings, sir;
    The question was addressed to General Grant."
    Some other things were spoken which I can't
Distinctly now recall, but I infer,
By certain flushings of my cheek and forehead,
Posterity's environment is torrid.

Then heard I (this was in a dream, remark)
    Another Voice, clear, comfortable, strong,
As Grant's great shade, replying from the dark,
    Said in a tone that rang the earth along,
    And thrilled the senses of the judges' throng:
"I'd rather you would question why, in park
And street, my monuments were not erected
Than why they were." Then, waking, I reflected.

[1885; SOLE]

THE DEATH OF GENERAL GRANT[8]

There are signs that the brainless *claque* of *laudatores hominum* who have been proning their unwholesome carcasses to slaver the dead feet of grand old Grant, and doing their little best to affect all healthy souls with a wasting indisposition of his name and fame, have had their day. Already the brazen serpent of truth has been elevated (somewhat hesitatingly) in the midst of the multitude, and many a sufferer, doubtless, lifting to its luster the despairing regard of a great disgust has felt the reptilian errors relax their constriction and fall away from his understanding like cut cords. In the current number of the Century magazine[9] General James H. Wilson,[10] a splendid soldier with a gentleman's head on his neck and a gentleman's eyes in his head, ("the better to see with, my dear") has a paper of reminiscences of Grant, conceived in a spirit of honest and sane admiration. General Wilson, however, points out what every man having knowledge of the matter and brains to digest the knowledge with has all along known: namely, that the great strategist was a poor tactician — which is to say that he did not skillfully move his troops in actual battle. Doubtless General Wilson, for his temerity, will have the entire pack of hero-worshipers yappeting and snatching at his heels — the superpatriotic person, "hell-bent" (as Carlyle[11] would say) on having an American Napoleon but imperfectly informed as to the Corsican Napoleon; the simple soul with an iron faith that "the hour brings the man"; the chap from Galena, who

8. "Prattle," *Wasp* 481 (October 17, 1885): 5. SOLE, 188–89.

9. *Century Magazine* was the first to recognize the potential of printing the Civil War reminiscences of famous generals. In a series of articles from 1884 to 1887, the magazine led the way for thousands of subsequent reminiscences and books. The *Century* articles are reproduced entirely in the four volumes of *Battles and Leaders of the Civil War* (1887–88), from which this note is taken, 1:ix–xi.

10. Major-General James Harrison Wilson (1837–1925) seems to have served everywhere during the war, from Yazoo Pass to Antietam to Wilderness to Nashville. He was first chief of the U.S. Cavalry Bureau. Wilson, "Reminiscences of General Grant," *Century Magazine* 8 (October 1885): 947–54. See also his *Life of Ulysses S. Grant* (1868).

11. Probably refers to the Scottish historian and critic Thomas Carlyle (1795–1881).

"knew him personally, sir"; the self-made man who is proud of him as "a man of the people"; the moral monster for whom the truth as an ingredient of history isn't good enough and the unclassible savage whose raw sympathies and unsalted sentiments reek an audible incense round every kind of distinction, mistaking it all for perfection of character and a flawless life. This rabble, destitute alike of discernment and moderation, in whose mental perspective the fame which is nearest looks biggest, would be very unhappy if it could return to earth some centuries hence and entering its Pantheon behold the ravages of time and truth.

It is pleasant, too, to know from General Wilson that Grant cherished personal resentments and "lay for" his private enemies till he got opportunity to pay them off, and that Lincoln, had he not been assured immediately after the fall of Vicksburg that Grant did not aspire to the Presidency, was none too good to have broken the back of him. Really the unnatural and impulsive whitewash of these grand figures in our history begins to be tenderly tempered with a suffusion of warm rosy light. In an age of manlier thought and freer judgment, it may happen that they will escape the awful fate of Washington — that able person of amusing infirmities and surprising vices, who, as paragoned by sycophantic historians and biographers, affects the world, which otherwise might have loved him, with sentiments of reverence and aversion.

What a miserable business it is, this deification of the eminent. And to what a measureless length it is urged. Not a famous character but it has distorted out of all semblance to nature. The sycophants have added terrors to renown; their hateful existence bars the way to public service. The animosities, intrigues, envy, obloquy and falsehoods alurk along the paths of renown like rattlesnakes infesting a mountain trail may be lightly and gayly encountered; none but the maddest ambitionist, the hardiest philanthroper or the most insensible blockhead will incur public admiration and surrender himself naked to his eulogists. I would rather be a dead dog among buzzards than a dead hero among admirers.

[1886; CWAB, V]

AT A "NATIONAL ENCAMPMENT"

You're grayer than one would have thought you:
     The climate you have over there
In the East has apparently brought you
     Disorders affecting the hair,
     Which — pardon me — seems a bit spare.

You'll not take offence at my giving
     Expression to notions like these.
You might have been stronger if living
     Out here in our sanative breeze.
     It's unhealthy here for disease.

No, I'm not so plump as a pullet,
     But that's the old wound, you see.
Remember my paunching a bullet? —
     And how that it didn't agree
     With? — well, honest hardtack for me.

Just pass me the wine — I've a helly
     And horrible kind of drouth!
When a fellow has that in his belly
     Which didn't go in at his mouth
     He's hotter than all Down South?

Great Scott! what a nasty day *that* was —
     When every galoot in our crack
Division who didn't lie flat was
     Dissuaded from further attack
     By the bullet's felicitous whack.

'Twas there that our major slept under
     Some cannon of ours on the crest,
Till they woke him by stilling their thunder,
     And he cursed them for breaking his rest,
     And died in the midst of his jest.

That night — it was late in November
    The dead seemed uncommonly chill
To the touch; and a chap I remember
    Who took it exceedingly ill
    When I dragged myself over his bill.

Well, comrades, I'm off now — good morning.
    Your talk is as pleasant as pie,
But, pardon me, one word of warning:
    Speak little and seldom, say I.
    That's my way. God bless you. Good-bye.

[1889; SOLE]

ON JEFFERSON DAVIS'S DEATH[12]

Faith in the authenticity of distinguished men's "last words" is an amiable infirmity; but if those of Jefferson Davis[13] were "Pray excuse me," they were exceedingly appropriate, not especially upon his lips, but upon those of any one engaged in dying. To leave life with a courteous apology to those remaining, as one leaves a drawing-room to go to bed, evinces thoughtfulness and good breeding. The finest "last words" (and they are pretty well authenticated) were those of Stonewall Jackson: "Let us pass over the river and rest in the shade of the trees." It is not creditable to American poets that these beautiful words have not been embalmed in immortal verse. Given the poet, the pen and such a theme, and one would think the great poem would write itself.

Jefferson Davis died impenitent, a political outlaw, but there are some who feel that loyalty does not require his execration. When beaten it is best to submit, and this he did; but it is not always well that all should fraternize with the victors. In this world are as good things as goodwill, and constancy may be, under certain circumstances, one of them. It is not always, and in the large way, a practicable virtue. An individual may rightly enough practice political devotion as an example — to keep alive the sentiment of devotion in general; but a community can hardly afford the luxury of a needless and unprofitable heroism, sacrificing its material interest to its moral. Davis's attitude toward the Government was less ignoble than we of the North are disposed to admit; and many a Southern leader, brave, able and wise, must have felt in his presence that life had something higher if not better than expediency — a loftier spiritual plane than is attained by the smooth and easy gradients of common sense. Davis stood upon his height alone, as it was fitting that he should stand. He asked none of his vanquished

12. "Prattle," *San Francisco Examiner*, December 8, 1898. SOLE, 64–65.

13. Jefferson Finis Davis (1808–1889) was a U.S. senator from Mississippi, Secretary of War in the administration of Franklin Pierce, and the first and only president of the Confederate States of America. He supported the "Lost Cause" in his book, *The Rise and Fall of the Confederate Government* (1881), but he never issued such apologetic "last words," and remained unrepentant. CONFED.

people to share his chill and comfortless eminence; and with an intuitive sense of his Great Obligation, they abstained from affection's importunities, nor besought him to be as they. His isolation was no doubt distasteful to loyalty's hot-gospellers, who see in their fad the supreme good and goal; but no generous antagonist to the lost, and justly lost, cause could have wished to mitigate, even by gentle means, the stony immobility of that sole human monument, which death alone could overthrow.

[1891; CWAB, IV]

THE CONFEDERATE FLAGS

Tut-tut! give back the flags — how can you care,
    You veterans and heroes?
Why should you at a kind intention swear
    Like twenty Neros?

Suppose the act was not so overwise —
    Suppose it was illegal;
Is't well on such a question to arise
    And pinch the Eagle?

Nay, let's economize his breath to scold
    And terrify the alien
Who tackles him, as Hercules of old
    The bird Stymphalian.

Among the rebels when we made a breach
    Was it to get their banners?
That was but incidental — 'twas to teach
    Them better manners.

They know the lesson well enough to-day;
    Now, let us try to show them
That we're not only stronger far than they,
    (How we did mow them!)

But more magnanimous. My lads, 'tis plain
    'Twas an uncommon riot;
The warlike tribes of Europe fight for gain;
    We fought for quiet.

If we were victors, then we all must live
    With the same flag above us:
'Twas all in vain unless we now forgive
    And make them love us.

Let kings keep trophies to display above
    Their doors like any savage;
The freeman's trophy is the foeman's love,
    Despite war's ravage.

"Make treason odious?" My friends, you'll find
    You can't, in right and reason,
While "Washington" and "treason" are combined—
    "Hugo" and "treason."

All human governments must take the chance
    And hazard of sedition.
O wretch! to pledge your manhood in advance
    To blind submission.

It may be wrong, it may be right, to rise
    In warlike insurrection:
The loyalty that fools so dearly prize
    May mean subjection.

Be loyal to your country, yes—but how
    If tyrants hold dominion?
The South believed they did; can't you allow
    For that opinion?

He who will never rise though rulers plot,
    His liberties despising—
How is he manlier than the *sans-culottes*
    Who's always rising?

Give back the foolish flags whose bearers fell,
    Too valiant to forsake them.
Is it presumptuous, this counsel? Well,
    I helped to take them.

[1903; CWAB, V]

TO E. S. SALOMON,

Who in a Memorial Day oration protested bitterly against
decorating the graves of Confederate dead.

What! Salomon! such words from you,
    Who call yourself a soldier? Well,
    The Southern brother where he fell
Slept all your base oration through.

Alike to him — he cannot know
    Your praise or blame: as little harm
    Your tongue can do him as your arm
A quarter-century ago.

The brave respect the brave. The brave
    Respect the dead; but *you* — you draw
    That ancient blade, the ass's jaw,
And shake it o'er a hero's grave.

Are you not he who makes to-day
    A merchandise of old renown
    Which he persuades this easy town
He won in battle far away?

Nay, those the fallen who revile
    Have ne'er before the living stood
    And stoutly made their battle good
And greeted danger with a smile.

What if the dead whom still you hate
    Were wrong? Are you so surely right?
    We know the issues of the fight —
The sword is but an advocate.

Men live and die, and other men
    Arise with knowledges diverse:
    What seemed a blessing seems a curse,
And Now is still at odds with Then.

The years go on, the old comes back
　　To mock the new — beneath the sun
　　Is *nothing* new; ideas run
Recurrent in an endless track.

What most we censure, men as wise
　　Have reverently practised; nor
　　Will future wisdom fail to war
On principles we dearly prize.

We do not know — we can but deem,
　　And he is loyalest and best
　　Who takes the light full on his breast
And follows it throughout the dream.

The broken light, the shadows wide —
　　Behold the battle-field displayed!
　　God save the vanquished from the blade,
The victor from the victor's pride!

If, Salomon, the blessed dew
　　That falls upon the Blue and Gray
　　Is powerless to wash away
The sin of differing from you,

Remember how the flood of years
　　Has rolled across the erring slain;
　　Remember, too, the cleansing rain
Of widows' and of orphans' tears.

The dead are dead — let that atone:
　　And though with equal hand we strew
　　The blooms on saint and sinner too,
Yet God will know to choose his own.

The wretch, whate'er his life and lot,
　　Who does not love the harmless dead
　　With all his heart and all his head —
May God forgive him, *I* shall not.

When, Salomon, you come to quaff
    The Darker Cup with meeker face,
    I, loving you at last, shall trace
Upon your tomb this epitaph:

"Draw near, ye generous and brave —
    Kneel round this monument and weep
    For one who tried in vain to keep
A flower from a soldier's grave."

[1903; ABPO]

A TRAVEL LETTER TO GEORGE[14]

Aurora, W. Virginia

September 12, 1903

Dear Sterling,[15]

. . . My friends have returned to Washington, and I'm having great times climbing peaks (they are knobs) and exploring gulches and canyons — for which these people have no names — poor things. My dreamland is still unrevisited.

They found a Confederate soldier over there the other day, with his rifle alongside. I'm going over to beg his pardon.

Ever yours,

Ambrose Bierce

14. ABPO, 75.

15. George Sterling (1869–1926). At one time a Bierce friend and protégé, who submitted poems to Bierce for criticism, and who loaned Bierce money to publish *Shapes of Clay* (1903). He wrote poems filled with exotic romanticism and regular verse. He committed suicide in 1926. James D. Hart, *The Oxford Companion to American Literature* (New York: Oxford University Press, 1950), 724.

[1903; CWAB, IV]

A YEAR'S "CASUALTIES"

Slain as they lay by the secret, slow,
Pitiless hand of an unseen foe,
Two score thousand old soldiers have crossed
The river to join the loved and lost.
In the space of a year their spirits fled,
Silent and white, to the camp of the dead.

One after one they fall asleep
And the pension agents awake to weep,
And orphaned statesmen are loud in their wail
As the souls flit by on the evening gale.
O Father of Battles, pray give us release
From the horrors of peace, the horrors of peace!

[1903; CWAB, IX]

A BIVOUAC OF THE DEAD

Away up in the heart of the Allegheny mountains, in Pocahontas county, West Virginia, is a beautiful little valley through which flows the east fork of the Greenbrier river. At a point where the valley road intersects the old Staunton and Parkersburg turnpike, a famous thoroughfare in its day, is a postoffice in a farm house. The name of the place is Travelers' Repose, for it was once a tavern. Crowning some low hills within a stone's throw of the house are long lines of old Confederate fortifications, skilfully designed and so well "preserved" that an hour's work by a brigade would put them into serviceable shape for the next civil war. This place had its battle — what was called a battle in the "green and salad days" of the great rebellion. A brigade of Federal troops, the writer's regiment among them, came over Cheat mountain, fifteen miles to the westward, and, stringing its lines across the little valley, felt the enemy all day; and the enemy did a little feeling, too. There was a great cannonading, which killed about a dozen on each side; then, finding the place too strong for assault, the Federals called the affair a reconnaissance in force, and burying their dead withdrew to the more comfortable place whence they had come. Those dead now lie in a beautiful national cemetery at Grafton, duly registered, so far as identified, and companioned by other Federal dead gathered from the several camps and battlefields of West Virginia. The fallen soldier (the word "hero" appears to be a later invention) has such humble honors as it is possible to give.

> His part in all the pomp that fills
> The circuit of the Summer hills
> Is that his grave is green.

True, more than a half of the green graves in the Grafton cemetery are marked "Unknown," and sometimes it occurs that one thinks of the contradiction involved in "honoring the memory" of him of whom no memory remains to honor; but the attempt seems to do no great harm to the living, even to the logical.

A few hundred yards to the rear of the old Confederate earthworks is a wooded hill. Years ago it was not wooded. Here, among the trees and in the undergrowth, are rows of shallow depressions, discoverable by removing the accumulated forest leaves. From some of them may be taken (and reverently replaced), small thin slabs of the split stone of the country, with rude and reticent inscriptions by comrades. I found only one with a date, only one with full names of man and regiment. The entire number found was eight.

In these forgotten graves rest the Confederate dead—between eighty and one hundred, as nearly as can be made out. Some fell in the "battle;" the majority died of disease. Two, only two, have apparently been disinterred for reburial at their homes. So neglected and obscure in this *campo santo* that only he upon whose farm it is—the aged postmaster of Travelers' Repose—appears to know about it. Men living within a mile have never heard of it. Yet other men must be still living who assisted to lay these Southern soldiers where they are, and could identify some of the graves. Is there a man, North or South, who would begrudge the expense of giving to these fallen brothers the tribute of green graves? One would rather not think so. True, there are several hundreds of such places still discoverable in the track of the great war. All the stronger is the dumb demand—the silent plea of these fallen brothers to what is "likest God within the soul."

They were honest and courageous foemen, having little in common with the political madmen who persuaded them to their doom and the literary bearers of false witness in the aftertime. They did not live through the period of honorable strife into the period of vilification — did not pass from the iron age to the brazen—from the era of the sword to that of the tongue and pen. Among them is no member of the Southern Historical Society.[16] Their valor was not the fury of the non-combatant; they have no voice in the thunder of the civilians and the shouting. Not by them are impaired the dignity and infinite pathos of the Lost Cause. Give them, these blameless gentlemen, their rightful part in all the pomp that fills the circuit of the summer hills.

16. Founded in 1869 by Confederate veterans to venerate and protect the South's interpretation of the Civil War and to promote the myth of the "Lost Cause."

[1911; ABPO]

A LETTER FROM D.C.[17]

Washington, D.C.

February 15, 1911

Dear George [Sterling],

. . . If I had my way nobody should remain in the civil service[18] more than five years — at the end of that period all are disloyal. Not one of them cares a rap for the good of the service or the country — as we soldiers used to do on thirteen dollars a month (with starvation, disease and death thrown in). Their grievance is that the Government does not undertake to maintain them in the style to which they choose to accustom themselves. They fix their standard of living just a little higher than they can afford, and would do so no matter what salary they got, as all salary-persons invariably do. Then they damn their employer for not enabling them to live up to it.

If they can do better "outside" why don't they go outside and do so; if they can't (which means that they are getting more than they are worth) what are they complaining about?

What this country needs — what every country needs occasionally — is a good hard bloody war to revive the vice of patriotism on which its existence as a nation depends. Meantime, you socialers, anarchists and other sentimentaliters and futilitarians will find the civil-service your best recruiting ground, for it is the Land of Reasonless Discontent. . . .

Yours sincerely,

Ambrose Bierce

17. ABPO, 170.

18. Civil service, or government employment outside the military, had depended upon a "spoils system" whereby elected politicians named their supporters to government jobs and offices. That began to change in 1883 with the Pendleton Act, which made positions "lifetime" and initial employment based upon competitive examinations.

FRAGMENTS FROM LAST LETTERS

[1911; LOVEMAN]

Dear Mr. Loveman,[19]

I'm sorry you could not "go home by way of Washington." But you saw Chattanooga and Chickamauga — as I did four or five years ago, many, many years after I fought on those historic fields. That region is good to see — even to one not having my interest in it. It beats Cleveland. . . .

Sincerely yours,
Ambrose Bierce.

September 18, 1911

[1913; LOVEMAN]

Dear Mr. Loveman,

This is only to say good-bye. I am going away to South America in a few weeks, and have not the faintest notion when I shall return.

May you prosper and be happy.

Sincerely,
Ambrose Bierce.

September 10, 1913

[1913; SOLE]

Sept. 29, 1913
Dear Helen,[20]

. . . I am about to leave here — shall go on Wednesday, or Thursday, so you'd better not write. In about two weeks I shall probably be in San

19. Samuel Loveman (1887–1976), a minor poet from Cleveland, Ohio, tried to enlist Bierce's help in publishing his poems. His *Twenty-one Letters of Ambrose Bierce,* edited by Samuel Loveman (Cleveland: George Kirk, 1922), contains all of Bierce's letters to him, tracing the series of attempts and rejections in publishing Loveman's poem "Pierrot." Loveman used the occasion of the collection of Bierce letters finally to publish the poem himself as an appendix to the volume.

20. Bierce to Helen Cowden, September 29, 1913, Yale Collection of American Literature, Beinecke Rare Book and Manuscript Library, Yale University; SOLE, 296. Bierce's daughter Helen (1875–?).

Antonio, Texas; I want to visit five or six of my old civil war battlefields first. *Then* if I can get into Mexico in a way to suit me I shall do so. It is probably easier to get in than out, but I mean to try to pass through the country (mostly on horseback, doubtless) to some Pacific port; thence to South America.

It is a fool plan, of course, — that is why I like it. I want to see (and *be*) "something going on."

[1913; ABPO]

Oct. 1, 1913
Dear Lora,[21]

. . . Good-bye — if you hear of my being stood up against a Mexican stone wall and shot to rags please know that I think that a pretty good way to depart this life. It beats old age, disease, or falling down the cellar stairs. To be a Gringo in Mexico — ah, that is euthanasia![22]

[1913; SOLE]

Oct. 30, 1913
Dear Helen,[23]

. . . I visited all my old battlefields — Chickamauga, Chattanooga, Stone's River, Franklin, Nashville and Shiloh — arriving here on Monday last pretty well worn out. Shall stay a few days longer. After that I shall be out of reach of letters, so can not hear from you.

21. Bierce to Lora Bierce, October 1, 1913; ABPO, 196–97. Lora Bierce was a niece who somehow remained close to her difficult, aging uncle. MORRIS, 248.

22. See Carlos Fuentes, *The Old Gringo,* translated by Margaret Sayers Peden (New York: Farrar Straus Giroux, 1985), for the best fictional account of Bierce in Mexico.

23. Bierce to Helen Cowden, October 30, 1913, Ella Strong Library, Scripps College, Claremont, California, quoted in SOLE, 296.

Alternate Table of Contents

(BY PUBLICATION DATE)

Basic Military Organization

UNIT	COMPOSITION	COMMANDED BY
Squadron	a small group of men	Sergeant
Company	100 men	Captain, Lieutenant
Battalion	3 or 4 companies	Lieutenant-colonel, Major
Regiment	10 companies	Colonel
Brigade	2 to 6 regiments	Brigadier-general
Division	3 or 4 brigades	Major-general
Corps	2 or more divisions	Major-general
Army	2 or more corps	Lieutenant-general

Glossary of Military Terms

Abatis. Obstructions, usually felled trees with branches turned to face the enemy. Sharpened sticks facing outward from a fortification to impede infantry attacks by slowing advances and giving defenders more shots at each attacker. In *The Devil's Dictionary*, Bierce defined "abatis" as the "rubbish in front of a fort, to prevent the rubbish outside from molesting the rubbish inside."

Absent-without-leave (AWOL). Being unaccounted for at roll call. Can be upgraded to **deserter** as necessary.

Acoustic shadow. Atmospheric phenomenon creating a pocket of silence whereby people only a short distance from a battle — perhaps even observing the battle — cannot hear it, while miles away, people who can't see the fighting can hear it clearly.

Adjutant. A staff officer responsible to a commanding officer for all official written correspondence, orders, and records.

Aide-de-camp. An officer appointed by the **general** commanding a **corps**, **division**, or **brigade**, to serve as the general's right hand, writing orders, keeping track of the various components of the general's **army**, and having the trust and proxy of the general in directing manuevers.

Army. The largest organizational **division** of the military, composed of two or more **corps**, and headed by a **lieutenant-general**. The North named its armies after rivers, as the Army of the Potomac, Army of the Ohio, etc., while the South used geographical regions, Army of Northern Virginia, Army of Tennessee, etc. Over the course of the Civil War, there were 39 distinct armies.

Artillery. Either smoothbore or rifled cannon designed to fire a variety of ordnance adapted to long range or close combat. Designed to demolish forts with solid shot, stop infantry attacks with **cannister** or **grape shot**, and create terror with a variety of fuses and explosions.

Battalion. A tactical unit of three or four **companies**.

Battery. A set of six matched guns with separate horseteams and ammunition chests, and served by a complement of 150 men, officered by a **captain** and four **lieutenants**.

Bivouac. An overnight camp in the open or with the barest cover.

Brigade. Two or more **regiments**; usually four to six regiments.

Brigadier-general. Officer rank of those commanding **brigades**, though small brigades sometimes had **colonels** in charge.

Buck and gag. Common military punishment for minor offenses, such as failing to keep up with the march ("straggling"). The offender was made to sit with his ankles and wrists tied together. To increase the discomfort and embarrassment, a stick was forced under his knees and over the bend in his arms and another stick was tightly bound between his teeth.

Butternut. A synonym for a "rebel" or Confederate soldier derived from the color of homemade uniforms.

Cannister. An **artillery** load of a can filled with iron balls — usually 48 — designed for use against infantry attacks. Grape shot consisted of bigger balls, 9 to 21 usually.

Captain. Ranking officer of a **company**.

Colonel. Ranking offier of a **regiment**.

Color-bearer. A position of honor given to a soldier who will carry the nation's flag into battle. During the Civil War, protection or capture of the **colors** was so important that the Medal of Honor could be won only for saving or taking colors.

Colors. One of the flags of a **company**, including the American or Confederate flag, a state flag, a regimental flag, and a company flag. Most often the term denotes the national flag.

Colt army revolver. Most common handgun used in the Civil War. Fired six .44-caliber rounds.

Column. Formation made up of two to ten lines of men in single file; used primarily for marching men from here to there.

Commissioned officer. Officers of the rank of second **lieutenant** or above are called "commissioned." Commissioned oficers serve by government appointment, and although commissioned officers in peace time are usually graduates of a military academy, such as West Point or Annapolis, during the Civil War the government commissioned many officers who had little or no formal preparation for their work.

Company. Military unit of one hundred men.

Corps. Military unit composed of two or more **divisions** and headed by a **major-general**.

Court-martial. Military trial to ascertain guilt or innocence and to set the punishment, which includes dishonorable discharges, prison, and the death penalty.

Division. Military unit composed of three or four **brigades**.

Deserter. A soldier intentionally absent from his unit without leave. More serious and often of longer duration than being **AWOL**. Because desertion implies more permanent shirking of duty, punishments are severe or capital.

Dragoon. Mounted infantry. Soldiers who used horses for transportation to and from a battle, but who dismounted to fight.

Embrasure. An opening in a defensive wall from which a weapon can be fired.

Enlisted man. An individual who voluntarily joins or is drafted into the army; often called an "enlistee."

Envelopment. An attack on the flank of the opponent in a effort to concentrate firepower and dislodge the enemy's line, usually rolling it back.

Fatigue duty. Non-military work done by soldiers, such as washing dishes, cleaning latrines, doing laundry, etc.

File. Formation with one man behind another, all facing the same direction and used for marching from here to there.

Flank. As a noun, the end of a line of battle; as a verb, a movement to get around an enemy's defensive line.

Furlough. Official permission granted for a soldier to leave his unit for a certain period of time.

Fusillade. A coordinated, simultaneous firing of arms, as in "Ready. Aim. Fire!"

Garrison. Soldiers stationed to protect a fort, or the stationing of troops to protect a fort.

General. A rank first created for Ulysses S. Grant to denote his status over all the **armies** of the North.

Grape Shot. See **Cannister**.

Home Guard. A state militia unit.

Leave of Absence. See **Furlough**.

Lieutenant. Lowest-ranking officer in the military. Subordinate to **cap-**

tain at the **company** level and divided into second and first lieutenants, the former being the lesser rank.

Lieutenant-colonel. The second-ranking officer in a **regiment**.

Lieutenant-general. Highest officer rank until U. S. Grant became the
nation's first "four-star" general in 1865. Lieutenant-generals commanded **armies**.

Line. A formation of soldiers on defense or offense, usually abreast of
one another.

Line of sight. A line of vision between the eye and the enemy.

Loopholes. Openings in walls designed to allow defensive **rifle** fire.

Loyalty oath. A pledge of allegiance to the government.

Major. Regimental-level officer below a **lieutenant-colonel.**

Major-general. Ranking officer of a **corps**.

Musket. A designation indicating inferior firepower to the more advanced weaponry, the **rifle**. Muskets shot a round ball and were not
effective beyond a hundred yards. Often, the term is a synonym for
smoothbore.

Orderly. A soldier who serves as attendant to an officer, carrying out his
orders to "do this" or "do that."

Parapet. A pile of dirt or other materials thrown up in front of a trench
to protect soldiers, or a wall or other device on a fort to protect the
defenders' persons or equipment.

Picket. An outpost or guard at a distance around a large force of
infantry or cavalry with the job of giving warning if the enemy
approached.

Private. The common soldier of lowest rank during the Civil War.

Provost marshall. An officer assigned to oversee and inspect matters of
discipline, security, and prisoners.

Quartermaster. Officer in charge of military supplies and equipment.

Reconnaissance in force. Moving forward to scout the terrain or locate
the enemy with the main body of troops. Usually, reconnaissance
was done by the cavalry or small numbers of soldiers operating as a
unit.

Regiment. Ten **companies** under command of a **colonel**.

Rifle. A musket with an interior barrel having metal ridges that force a
cone-shaped bullet into a tight spin resulting in greater accurancy
and killing distance.

Scout. A soldier in uniform seeking reconnaissance or information concerning the enemy and not concealing his identity as a spy would do.

Sergeant. A non-**commissioned officer** of a **squadron**.

Sergeant-major. The highest-ranking enlisted soldier in a **regiment**.

Skirmish. A battle of the smallest sort.

Skirmish line. A line of soldiers or "skirmishers" in advance of a marching army, with the job of engaging the enemy for enough time to allow the army to get into battle formation.

Springfield Rifle. Main infantry weapon of the war, manufactured in Springfield, Massachusetts. The primary rifle of the Union army, even though both sides often carried the Enfield Rifle, manufactured and supplied from England. Both fired a similar load of approximately .58 caliber and weighed nine pounds.

Spy. A person engaged in sabotage or the transfer of military information to a soldier and wearing civilian clothes or the uniform of the enemy.

Squad or squadron. A small group of soldiers assembled for or assigned to a specific duty.

Staff officer. An officer working directly for a commanding officer and acting as contact with regular combat officers. Staff officers usually observed and helped plan but did not engage directly in combat.

Three-months volunteer. A soldier who enlisted in support of Lincoln's call for volunteers to serve for ninety days, by which time, they thought, the rebellion would be over.

Three-year volunteer regiment. The primary military unit of the Civil War, composed of one thousand men in ten **companies** volunteering for a three-year tour of duty. Volunteer regiments are differentiated from regular **regiments** in that the latter units are made up of professional career soldiers and officers.

Vidette. A **picket** mounted on a horse.